SLCCEE

Studies on Language and Culture
in Central and Eastern Europe

Herausgegeben von
Christian Voß

Band 20

Verlag Otto Sagner

München – Berlin – Washington D.C.

Doing Gender – Doing the Balkans

Dynamics and Persistence of Gender Relations
in Yugoslavia and the Yugoslav successor states

Herausgegeben von

Roswitha Kersten-Pejanić, Simone Rajilić, Christian Voß

Verlag Otto Sagner · München – Berlin – Washington D.C.

2012

Bibliografische Information der Deutschen Bibliothek
Die Deutsche Bibliothek verzeichnet diese Publikation in der Deutschen
Nationalbibliografie; detaillierte bibliografische Informationen sind im Internet
über http://dnb.ddb.de abrufbar.

© 2012 bei Kubon & Sagner GmbH
Heßstraße 39/41   Friedrichstraße 200
80798 München   10117 Berlin

Telefon +49 (0)89 54 218-107
Telefax +49 (0)89 54 218-226
verlag@kubon-sagner.de
www.vos-digital.de

Die Auslieferung für die USA übernimmt die Kubon & Sagner Inc., Washington D.C.

«**Verlag Otto Sagner**» ist ein Imprint der Kubon & Sagner GmbH

Anschrift des Herausgebers:

Prof. Dr. Christian Voß
Humboldt-Universität zu Berlin
Institut für Slawistik
Dorotheenstraße 65
10117 Berlin

Telefon +49 (0)30 2093-5185
christian.voss@staff.hu-berlin.de

Umschlaggestaltung: Christopher Triplett, Marburg
Druck und Bindung: Difo-Druck, Bamberg
Printed in Germany

Alle Rechte vorbehalten

ISSN 1868-2936
ISBN: 978-3-86688-326-0
ISBN (eBook): 978-3-86688-327-7

Table of Contents

Roswitha Kersten-Pejanić, Simone Rajilić and Christian Voß
Introduction ... 7

1. Setting the Agenda: Politics and Society

Marina Blagojević Hughson
Undoing Gender, Undoing the Balkans:
Towards Ethnic and Gender Reconciliation ... 17

Marina Katnić-Bakaršić
Gender Relations in Bosnia and Herzegovina
between Theory and Practice ... 43

Andrea Spehar
European Union and Western Balkans:
What Prospect for Gender Equality? ... 53

Mario Vinković
Prostitution as a Profession –
Searching for Answers between the Headlines ... 65

Petra Bläss-Rafajlovski
Gendering Politics. The Impact of Women Politicians
and NGOs in the Western Balkans ... 83

2. Constructions of Gender in Language and the Media

Zorica Mršević
Women experts – Public Disbelief in Women Professionals in Serbia ... 91

Delina Binaj
Gender and Language in Albania ... 101

Ljiljana Marković
Language and Gender in Tertiary-Level Education ... 109

Renata Šribar
"Performing – Women" and the Socio-Political Regime:
Addressing in Socialist Slovenia Compared to Today 127

Zrinjka Glovacki-Bernardi
Job Advertisements in Croatian Newspapers – Gender Perspective 147

Roswitha Kersten-Pejanić
Creating Public Concern about a Woman's Ability
to Govern the Country: The Case of Jadranka Kosor and the Media 161

3. History and Anthropology

Rada Drezgić
Reproduction, Nation, and Masculinity: Serbia in the 1990s 185

Dean Vuletic
Law, Politics and Homosexuality in Croatia, 1941–1952 197

Natalja Herbst
Women in Socialist Yugoslavia in the 1950s. The Example
of Rajka Borojević and the Dragačevo Women's Cooperative 209

Nataša Mišković
Jovanka and Josip Broz Tito:
Gender and Power at the Top of Communist Yugoslavia 221

Notes on contributors 241

Introduction

Roswitha Kersten-Pejanić, Simone Rajilić and Christian Voß

When, in May 2011, a range of specialists working on gender issues took part in the conference "Doing gender – Doing the Balkans. Dynamics and Persistence of Gender Relations in South-Eastern Europe", the expectations of such a meeting were high. We aimed at offering a valuable contribution to the already-existing dialogue on this theme and the ongoing research patterns and networks.

During the conference and the months that followed, it became evident that by insisting on the gender practices and enactments, we, indeed, managed to add a significant perspective to this field. However, the concept of this conference – developed by the editors of this book – must also accept the criticism that this dialogue has left the door wide open for additional essentialisation. For, what is the point of considering gender issues in one region alone, especially at a time when parts of this greater region diverge significantly from one another and are, for example, in various stages of EU integration? The point – or the pointlessness – of area studies in a multi-polar global era continues to be debated vehemently, and it has affected the tone of our conference and these proceedings. Clearly, our conference was not meant to be perceived in such a way and it was not to result in generalizations along the line of "everything is different in the Balkans". The goal is not to identify features unique to the Balkans but to delve into the intersection of two strands of constructivist discourses – those of gender and of so-called *mental maps*[1]. Challenges to biological gender and the refusal to accept primordialist concepts of ethnicity and nationality are quite comparable; as are the cliché-driven mental maps of so-called *Balkanism*[2], regardless whether it is seen as an inner-

---

[1] On the conception of *mental maps* see Schenk, Frithjof Benjamin, Mental Maps. Die Konstruktion von geographischen Räumen in Europa seit der Aufklärung, in: Geschichte und Gesellschaft 28/2002, 493-514 and Wolff, Larry, Inventing Eastern Europe. The Map of Civilization on the Mind of Enlightment, Stanford 1994.

[2] See Said, Edward, Orientalism, New York 1978; Todorova, Maria, The Balkans. From Discovery to Invention, in: Slavic Review 53/2, 1994, 453-482; Todorova, Maria, Imagining the Balkans, Oxford and New York 1997; Bakić-Hayden, Milica and Robert M. Hayden, Orientalist Variations on the Theme "Balkans": Symbolic Geography in Recent Yugoslav Cultural Politics, in: Slavic Review 51/1, 1992, 1-15 and Bakić-Hayden, Milica, Nesting Orientalism: The Case of Former Yugoslavia, in: Slavic Review 54/4, 1995, 917-931.

European variant of Said's *orientalism*[3] or a different discourse with its own idiosyncratic logic.

Gender and the Balkans, two categories present in the title of our conference and this book, for a long time have been defined by hegemonic groups. During the conference and with this volume, we insist that they need to be understood and examined especially in their communicative performativity. As with the term gender, the exclusivist dichotomy of Europe vs. the Balkans is gradually devolving into a question of degree, allowing for hybrid forms and osmosis.

The fruitful discussions that took place in Berlin certainly produced an expected benefit of an interdisciplinary approach to questions of gender and South Eastern Europe. The following articles are a compilation of the many contributions to the conference, structured in three different sections dealing with different parts of societal settings in which gender can be traced convincingly.

Gender relations in their political and societal reality constitute an important framework for examining the effects and proving the consequences that the ongoing prevalent gender contract has on individuals and on societies. Arguably, this has always been at the core of gender studies and the scientific discussion of the impact of the leading gender order on people's lives. This leading gender order, however, is constructed, manifested and maintained through its perpetual recreation in public as well as in private on a daily basis. Especially through persisting conducts that may seem neutral (and "natural") at first sight, which nonetheless reveal their deeply-rooted and constantly enshrined reflection and ensuing materialization of unequal treatment of certain groups of people, the constructed and continual image-building of gender becomes obvious. Language use as well as the media altogether are such conduct patterns where the manifestation of habits in handling and in "doing" gender[4] can vividly be traced. The relevance of these constructs and the impacts on groups of people and individuals, on their lives and on the (im)possibilities we are given in living our life, gain even more substance when put into specific contemporary and historical contexts and when proven to be a decisive factor for people in different parts of society and in different times and periods.

---

[3] For more on the interrelation between orientalist and essentialist ways of thinking regarding gender see Lykke, Nina, Feminist. Studies. A Guide to Intersectional Theory, Methodology and Writing, New York and Abingdon 2010, 24.

[4] See West, Candace and Don H. Zimmermann, Doing Gender, in: Gender and Society 1:1987, 125-151 for the concept of "Doing Gender".

The following contributions provide novel aspects and gripping examples of gender studies in South Eastern Europe by offering a profound and vivid insight in the current scientific discussion and the state of art of the international study of gender questions in South Eastern Europe.

Content of this book

The first section, *Setting the Agenda: Politics and Society*, assembles five studies from very different fields of interest and guides us straight into the theoretical discussions as well as into the practical impacts of gender issues in South Eastern Europe.

Marina Blagojević Hughson introduces the concept of *pozistorija* (meaning positive history) as an innovative way of living together in the Balkans (and elsewhere) while stressing the need of emerged focusing on gender as well as on ethnic reconciliation. With her focus on arguments for the deconstruction and de-essentialization of, on the one hand, gender and nation, and on the other hand, of the Balkans, she leads us right into the overall discussion behind this book and shows us the necessity of further work to be done in this domain.

Marina Katnić-Bakaršić provides an overview of gender studies at Universities and other institutions in Bosnia and Herzegovina, which she states are relatively well developed in the country, despite the fact that gender as an identity concept is perpetually overruled by the main concern of the country, namely ethnic and ethnic identity questions. In addition to the theoretical work, she points to the need for further *practical* input to improve people's, and especially women's, lives in a range of different aspects of life and society, and to actively promote the decrease of constraints set upon people due to their gender identity.

Andrea Spehar examines the influence of the EU's *gender acquis* on Croatia and Macedonia and asks whether the EU candidacy and accession process really contributes to a positive development in gender politics as well as in people's lives. She states that both at the EU as well as at the national countries' level, the tendency to limit the efforts to enhance gender equality to declarations and law-making without narrowly watching the subsequent implementation of these laws and declarations, has clearly constricted the outcomes of the often well-intentioned efforts of promoting gender equality.

Mario Vinković gives us a profound comparative overview of the legal handling of prostitution in different countries in Western, Northern and South Eastern Europe. He examines if prostitution can be regarded as a "normal" profession and and as a form of providing services, as it has been stated by the European Court of Justice for instance, to the neglect of the human rights factor. He argues against such an approach where prostitutes simply fulfill an "economic activity", and points to the fact that "legal" prostitution is often hardly separable from forced prostitution, while at the same time the aspect of prostitution as *sex slavery* should not be neglected.

Petra Bläss-Rafajlovski provides the reader with a thorough insight into the work done by women's grassroots movements in actively involving women's voices in different fields of political happenings. She draws a range of conclusions from these initiatives for the general improvement of women's part-taking in politics and decision-making as she stresses the point that party lines should be neglected by women who want to tackle the existing male-dominated political structures.

The second part of this book entitled *Constructions of gender in language and the media*, addresses the enormous impact of linguistic practices on gender (un)equality as argued by the following six articles.

Zorica Mršević analyses Serbian public disbelief in women professionals. On the basis of five examples, the author shows that women in public or leading positions are exposed to significantly more media attacks than men professionals in similar positions. Serbian media hereby mirrors a wider lack of gender equality in society as Mršević concludes.

Delina Binaj delivers insight into the field of language and gender in Albania. Even though standard Albanian uses gender-specific forms when naming concrete female persons, the author finds that masculine generic nouns are still used for both male and female persons – a fact known from many other languages that are considered to be sexist by making women less linguistic visible than men. Up to now there has been little research on gender and the Albanian language while guidelines to avoid sexist language practices still do not exist.

Ljiljana Marković presents the results of a small-scale quantitative and qualitative study conducted among Serbian university students, examining the usage of, attitude to and knowledge of gender-sensitive language. When asked to write the candidacy of a female student for president of the students' organization, she finds that only few students consistently use feminine forms of nomina agentis, however more than 80% of the participants convey the gender information throughout the text by different devices. Marković concludes that one can trace a gender-sensitive language reform taking roots in Serbia.

Renata Šribar compares modes of addressing men and women in socialist and present day Slovenia. Her indirectly obtained data on socialist Slovenia via questionnaires, depended on the recollection of the participants. She observes that the addressing modes are different for the two periods, which corresponds to changed ways in which inequalities appear in different areas of life. She investigates formal addressing modes in a professional and educational sphere, informal addressing modes with house-maids or house-aids, as well as name calling among minors and adult expressions of friendship and attraction.

Zrinjka Glovacki-Bernardi presents the results of a job advertisement analysis that focuses on the gender perspective. The author's study is a complement to an analysis conducted by the Gender Equality Ombudsperson on a Croatian newspaper corpus, which found that between 2006 and 2010 the percentage of advertisements violateing the Gender Equality Act has decreased tenfold. Glovacki-Bernardi investigates an entirely different corpus of advertisements for mostly less qualified jobs and finds still dominant male-female stereotypes.

Roswitha Kersten-Pejanić's article deals with Jadranka Kosor, Croatia's first female Prime Minister since independence. The author analyses the public perception and media coverage of Kosor as a "public woman", especially in summer 2009, the days around her assumption of office. Kersten-Pejanić also considers Kosor's statements on women's rights. Although being a conservative politician and a controversial person, Kosor made a valuable contribution to the discussion about the perception and construction of gender in the Croatian public area.

The third topic of this book is *History and Anthropology* bringing together two very active fields of study in the framework of South Eastern European as well as gender studies by showing the direct impact of gender constructions in people's lives through fieldwork as well as historical analyses.

Rada Drezgić analyses the image of rural masculinity in a non-profit match-making project called *Village Hearth* which was aimed at renewing the Serbian rural family for the sake of a national renewal by bringing together Serbian men with Ukrainian women. The attempts of the neo-traditionalist conceptions the project typifies were thwarted by the unwillingness of the middle-aged Serbian men of the given village who were the target of the whole project to actually join the arranged meeting with the Ukrainian women. After all, the sought-after contribution to the empowerment of nationhood led to an even more marginalizing discourse about rural masculinity.

Dean Vuletic provides us with a multi-layered and source-intensive insight into the regulations concerning the public treatment of same-sex relationships in the years after the Second World War. Yugoslavia, which evolved into one of the most liberal Eastern European countries in the 1950s, had evident struggles in developing a common stance towards homosexuality, as the author shows through an analysis of different types of historical sources. Despite the lack of historical analyses and the long-lasting marginalization of sexual minorities in society as well as in science, the article comprises a range of different approaches to historical sources and shows ways of addressing long concealed issues.

Natalja Herbst portrayal of the life of Rajka Borojević, reveals the importance of the foundation of the Dragačevo Women's Cooperative which made an important contribution to peasant women's empowerment in socialist Yugoslavia. With her commitment in different economic fields, Rajka Borojević was herself an outstanding example of women's emancipation in the times around the Second World War. Furthermore, with her sensible approach and cooperative way of working with the rural women, she was able to not only improve their situation inside their families and in the village, but also to exceedingly contribute to their economic and educational development.

Nataša Mišković outlines the life and the position of the probably most well-known woman of socialist Yugoslavia: Jovanka Broz-Budisavljević. The marriage between Josip Broz Tito and his last wife allows for an analysis of the remaining patriarchal discourses about gender, marriage and power in Yugoslavia in socialist times. Despite the strong start after the Second World War in effort-making to enable women economic as well as political participation, the real implementation of gender equality was insufficient and stopped soon after it started.

Assumptions and images of the assumed Other are mainly thriven on appreciations and stereotype classifications whose validity seldom proves true when contested. Nonetheless, often these constructed dedications seem to be widely accepted in society and constitute strong parts of an elementary judgmental discourse about other groups of people, of other nation states, regions etc. The Balkans – at least since Maria Todorova's elucidations exposed as a projection screen of negative ideas of ("Western") scientists – as much as traditional patterns of gender orders, whose negative consequences for many people worldwide are certainly beyond question, are two such constructed dedications. The examination of gender and South Eastern Europe encompasses two components of our field of interest. By opening up an assorted range of issues and questions, we consider this field to be a platform for scientific networking and interconnectedness of different disciplines working on gender and the Balkans. In addition to the primary focus of our research centered on discourses, debates and assessments of the subject of gender in different countries of the region and within different scientific fields, this aspect of academic networks in the region and beyond deserves to have an equally important role in our current and future research agenda.

We can only hope to be able to organise and take part in future meetings and conferences of this kind again and we will definitely do our best in order to enable comparable events. We wish to thank the *Humboldt-Universität zu Berlin*, the *Südosteuropa-Gesellschaft* as well as the *Otto Sagner* publishing house for the financial support of the conference and its publication. Without the funding of the German Research Foundation (*DFG*) of the project "Language and Gender in South-Eastern Europe. Linguistic Manifestations of Gender Conceptualisations in Albania, Croatia and Serbia", this conference would certainly not have been possible at all.

For the compositional as well as the academic input to the conference it was a great appreciation for us to have Rozita Dimova, Lann Hornscheidt, Petra Bläss-Rafajlovski and Dubravka Žarkov as valuable supporters to a very successful conference in their functioning as Chairs for the different thematic panels. Furthermore we would like to thank our colleague Rumjana Slodička for carefully editing the proceedings.

Berlin, July 2012   The editors

1. Setting the Agenda: Politics and Society

Undoing Gender, Undoing the Balkans: Towards Ethnic and Gender Reconciliation[1]

Marina Blagojević Hughson

Introduction

In order to analyze any contemporary social issue, including gender, there are basically two possible directions which can be taken. One is to look backward, to the history of ideas, and possibly 'real' history, which is often presented as history of wars, hierarchies and antagonisms, and the other is to look forward, to envision the future, and then, from that perspective, to try to encourage and speed up social change in a desirable direction. While certainly there are lessons to be learned from the first, it is actually more challenging to take the second road, since a necessary shift in the dominant interpretation of history is deeply connected to the possibilities of social transformation. Social and economic crises denote periods of time when weakened social structures allow for human agency to be stronger and more effective. Therefore, it is especially important to inspire that agency by restoring trust and hope and by generating visions of constructive solutions. The normative will eventually become real, if more and more people embrace new visions.[2] The question is, though, how to get from 'here' to 'there' and this paper is an attempt to define one possible road.

So, the aim of this paper is twofold: to put the Balkan wars in the wider context of globalization, on one hand, which will enhance deeper understanding of dynamics of war production, and, on the other hand, to promote the idea of inevitability of connection of gender and ethnic reconciliation. However, the main purpose of this paper is to promote the idea of *pozistorija* (positive history), the history of living together which has been largely marginalized in the Balkans and elsewhere. *Pozistorija*, as a method of deconstruction of discourses of hate and exclusions, and as an approach which can disclose marginalized evidence on real and lived multiculturalisms in former Yugoslavia, can feed the hope and encourage reconciliation processes in the Balkans.

In the first part of the paper the author will argue that the wars have been produced 'from the above' and that an essential part of that process was identity

---

[1] This paper is a part of the subproject related to Social Inequalities and Social Exclusion, within the Institute for Criminological and Sociological Research, Belgrade, financed by the Ministry of Education and Science of the Republic of Serbia (No47011).

[2] About the expansion of the idea of human rights, see for example the work of CHARLES TAYLOR (2000).

politics. 'Identity politics' essentialized both gender and nations, but, *to 'de-essentialize' identity politics itself, it is necessary to contextualize it within the semiperiphery*. Therefore, a deeper understanding of the production of the wars in countries in transition, such as Balkan countries, requires theoretical elaboration on the position of the semiperiphery within the wider globalization process.

In the second part of the paper, 'identity politics' is more widely discussed in relation to gender and nation. It is argued that due to 'identity politics' not only the very idea of difference has been brought to the extreme, but the whole world view has been constructed so that it simply promoted competitiveness, exclusion and opposition, in fact values which are highly compatible with the neoliberal agenda applied on the semiperiphery. Ethnic wars had a parallel in 'gender wars' and both were instrumental for building up a competitive, conflictual and antagonistic perspective on social reality. However, ethnification, which was/is closely linked to re-traditionalization and re-patriarchalization of the Balkan societies, was as much produced and constructed within as without. The 'Balkanization' of Balkan societies, as yet another strategy of exclusion and domination was re-/invented in the 90s (TODOROVA 1997).

In the third part of the paper the idea of *pozistorija* will be offered as an approach, grounded on feminist epistemic legacies, which could contribute to the shift of scholarly knowledge and public discourses towards a non-antagonistic, collaborative paradigm of defining social groups and their mutual relations. 'Undoing' gender means to step out from the 'blame circle' by arguing that it is necessary to de-essentialize and de-naturalize gender, as well as nation, by disclosing deeper structural and discursive configurations, globally and locally, at the roots of identity politics. Accordingly, gender reconciliation and ethnic reconciliation are inseparable. Further on, 'undoing gender' in the Balkans is inseparable from 'undoing' the Balkans, since it is the *essentialization and gendering of the Balkans* as a region, which is reproducing the *balkanization of the Balkans,* its semiperipheriality and, consequently, its existing gender and national regimes.

Semiperiphery: contextualizing identity politics in the Balkans

Whatever the definition of globalization, it is obvious that transition is a sort of globalization. The WTO, the IMF and the World Bank have more impact on the development patterns of transition countries than any of their national governments.

With all the influx of cultural studies products from the 90s on, with the explosion of 'cultural shift' in humanities and social sciences, which unfortunately coincided with Yugoslav wars, some basic 'truths' about the wars almost seemed to be forgotten. Wars are being produced because of the redistribution of wealth. As Sonja Lokar[3] is stating "modern wars, like the former ones, have very earthly reasons – ownership and control over economic and natural resources. Actually, the Balkans war was caused by the attempt of the old and new political elite to keep or get the upper hand over the process of privatization on as big a territory as possible." (LOKAR 2003) However, for the analytical purposes of this paper it is necessary to differentiate the issue of 'why' the wars happened from the issue of 'how' they happened. These two aspects are closely connected, although necessarily approached from different disciplinary backgrounds. Gender studies, being interdisciplinary, can contribute to bridging the gap between the two sets of explanations, those that are rooted into the logic of social sciences, and those that are rooted into the logic of cultural studies.

Economic crises – and the former Yugoslavia was deep in crises since the beginning of the 80s – are just 'ideal' settings for wars. Only after the Yugoslav wars, the World Bank made a report with a clear conclusion that civil wars in recent history are strongly connected to economic crisis.[4] In addition to economic crises in the former Yugoslavia, which was very tangible and measurable, and widely discussed in many former Yugoslav and international forums during the 80s, there was a parallel institutional crises characteristic of other former communist societies as well (BLAGOJEVIĆ 1999). It is also often forgotten that the collapse of 'communism' was in fact an institutional collapse that proceeded what was often experienced and interpreted as a sudden change, 'fall of the wall' or set of 'revolutions'. Institutions in the Second World, the former 'communist block', were collapsing; the system was imploding, while at the same time globalization took off. These two processes were closely connected.[5]

Wars in the former Yugoslavia happened in the institutional setting which was seriously weakened, in a transition from one structure to another, from the socialist to the capitalist system, from party state to democracy, from command

---

[3] Sonja Lokar, sociologist and feminist, was a top Slovenian politician at the moment of former Yugoslav dissolution. She was also one of the founders of Gender Task Force of Stability Pact (http://www.stabilitypact.org/gender/default.asp) whose main objective was the promotion of greater women's political participation in South Eastern Europe. Her statments could be regarded as both insightful and objective.

[4] This information is from the women's discussion list "ženskaposla" (May 21, 2003). The information refers to the latest report made by the World Bank, based on the research of Paul Collier, director of the Center for African economies. The news was published by the news agency "Beta" on May 15, 2003.

[5] Here is not the place to discuss how much of the "change" was engineered by the power centers which were governing the process of globalization.

economy to the market economy. It was the lack of structuring, an increasing vacuum that was a background of the wars, rather than some well-defined deterministic system. This makes the question of 'how' the wars were produced equally relevant as the question of 'why' the wars happened, because 'why' presupposes determinism, an explanation based on logical and chronological connection between causes and consequences. 'How', instead, can disclose mechanisms of war production which could be linked to identity politics. Emphasizing 'how' or 'why' leads to a different type of explanation. 'How' corresponds to a self-fulfilling prophecy type of explanation, where intentionality is prioritized, and 'why' relates to causal explanations, where structure is prioritized. To simplify, it could be said that economic crises were a necessary condition, while identity politics provided sufficient condition for wars to happen. Also, a structural vacuum and corresponding institutional insufficiency enormously increased the power of individual and collective social agents, those who actually created identity politics, and therefore bear the major responsibility for choosing war over peace.

While it is not difficult to claim, and empirically document, that there was an increasing institutional and structural vacuum in former Yugoslavia which was preceding the wars, it is not to say that there was no other deterministic system, no other structure, which was effective and influencing the wars. Although prevailing 'explanations' are to be found in the realms of political science and history, the 'real' determinism can be addressed only from the perspective of political economy. There was/is a deterministic set up which was coming from another, higher, global level. That other structure, increasingly influential with growing 'local' structural vacuum, was/is the structure of neo-liberal globalization, which was repositioning global and local power hierarchies, including the relationship and connection between the core and the semi-periphery. *The other side of globalization is actually fragmentation.* Transition was/is very instrumental in fragmentation. So, it is the force of fragmentation which empowered identity politics at the semiperiphery, including former Yugoslavia, in general. Institutional destruction on the federal level which preceded the wars provided the background for sweeping nationalistic discourses which denoted a new era in the Balkans.

To fully grasp the relevance of identity politics in former Yugoslavia it is important to situate it within the wider social context, that one of the semi-periphery. Semiperiphery as a concept which originated in the world-system theory (WALLERSTEIN 1979) is quite a useful tool to be applied to countries 'in transition', and the Balkans in particular. For the purpose of this text only two characteristics of the semiperiphery will be discussed briefly: lagging behind and de-development.[6] The semiperiphery is 'lagging behind' the core, because the core is not only more developed, but it is also setting up the norms, it serves as a model and it has the power to shape the semiperiphery. The semiperiphery is trying to 'catch up', and it is being molded both by the core (i.e. politics of conditionality of the EU) and through its own effort to match the core. But, simultaneously, the semiperiphery is always also in strong resistance to the core, swinging politically from one extreme to another. Since it is reactive in relation to the core, it is also necessarily 'lagging behind', and since it is 'lagging behind', it is never in a position to actually 'reach' the core, although it is constantly reaching out, because the core is always, by definition, a moving target.[7] The relationship with the core, to the 'West' or 'Europe', is having a crucial impact on ideological wars within the semiperipheral countries, and accordingly it infuses enormous energy into identity politics.

Besides lagging behind and catching-up with the core, another crucial structural characteristic of the present day semiperiphery of Europe, the one which was created by the transition from communism to post-communism, is *de-development*. Although de-development is the main feature of many post-communist societies it has been largely ignored, mainly due to political reasons, and it is certainly under-researched.[8] However, the semiperipheral condition of Eastern and Southeastern Europe is profoundly the one of de-development in many dimensions, in terms of socio-economic development and worsening conditions of everyday life. In the economic domain de-development refers to structural change related to *depreciation of human, institutional and infrastructural capital* (MEURS/ RANASINGHE 2003). This depreciation has become a precondition for the exploitation of those resources within the framework of global neoliberal capitalism. In the social domain semi-

---

[6] More on semiperiphery and gender, see in: Knowledge Production at the Semiperiphery: A Gender Perspective (2009a).

[7] This produces quite complex effects on the ground. Semiperiphery is filled with diachronicities.

[8] Complexities of political reasons can not be discussed here, but it is worth noting that 'semiperiphery' is a politically not popular concept because it discloses hierarchy, and it is not accepted, paradoxically, by both those who want to see their respective countries as part of 'Europe' and those who oppose too much of amalgamation within EU and advocate for an authentic, even essentialist, difference of their nations. So, semiperiphery as a concept seems to be contested by both political camps: by liberals and by conservatives. Specific aspects of de-development have been researched, but the connection between them, which would enable deeper understanding of a general backward movement, has been ignored. This is why the term 'de-development' is not in a wider use.

peripheriality is related to *increased poverty, increased social insecurity, decreased social protection and stability, institutional destruction, anomie, increased crime and violence, population crises, high inclination to migration, increased mortality and even 'barbarization' through the violent conflicts* (BLAGOJEVIĆ 2009a). The overall framework of depreciation of human capital, together with prioritization of technological development, has led to the phenomena of a "surplus of humans" (BLAGOJEVIĆ 2009b), which affects large numbers of *both* women and men belonging to the semiperiphery who find themselves on the side of the 'losers' of transition. There is a profound difference between poverty and impoverishment, between absence of development (as in some remote areas of the world), slowed down development (as in some European countries faced with economic crises) and regressive trends of development in combination with some aspects of technological modernization (as in many post-communist countries).[9]

'Lagging behind' and consequential 'catching up', throughout the history of the semiperipheral societies and nowadays as well, have important effects on gender regimes which have been shaped in a way to massively use and exhaust women's human resources both in private and in public spheres. This explains the paradoxical quality of East-European patriarchies, in which women often occupy high public positions while at the same time they can be denied much of the real equality or exposed to high-level misogyny in public discourses.[10] To effectively use women's resources countries in Eastern Europe relatively early allowed women's public education and gave voting rights. Throughout Eastern Europe women are seen as 'strong', 'heroic', 'big mothers', and there is a kind of "self/sacrificing micro-matriarchy" (BLAGOJEVIĆ 1995), which means that although having very pronounced private power women were also expected to 'sacrifice' for family members. Therefore, women's human resources are often mobilized and exploited for the gap between the center and the semiperiphery to be bridged. At the same time, conservative patriarchal ideologies are used to pacify women and to counterbalance huge dependencies on women's resources on micro and macro scale. It is important to understand that *aggressive patriarchal ideologies at the semiperiphery correspond to the very real dependency on women's resources both in private and in public*, and that they

---

[9] For example, in rural areas of Azerbaijan, very poor women will still have secondary level education and go to regular checkups if pregnant. Some civilizational gains from former communist regimes simply can not be ignored nor annihilated.

[10] In fact this appears as paradoxical only because there is a model expectation that there should be parallel development in the process of public recognition of women's equality and the improvement of their position in the private sphere, which again is a model expectation based on Western experiences.

are instrumental for 'keeping women in place'. During transition, 'masculinity crises', in fact crises of male identities within the new economic and political framework of 'transition', additionally encouraged the process of re-patriarchalization on the discursive level, and even violence against women (NIKOLIĆ-RISTANOVIĆ 2008). De-development had many negative effects on both women and men, and it is reshaping gender regimes, often in a way, which furthermore destabilizes male gender roles, while additionally exhausting women's resources as well. Because of the worsening conditions of everyday life and increased economic and general insecurity and competition, de-development creates an even deeper gap between genders which can easily be turned into ideological 'gender wars'. At the same time, on the level of everyday reality it strengthens family ties as the most accessible survival strategy, well in accordance to the emergence of 'network society' (CASTELLS 2000).

Engendering identity politics

Identity politics leading to the wars was mainly channeled through media and well supported by 'scholarly' knowledge; in fact intellectual elites were highly mobilized for national projects (POPOV 2000). It has been already established that in the case of the Balkan wars, media wars played an essential role.[11] The importance of media wars could only be adequately understood if they are linked to the weak structural determinants of wars, as discussed above. Media, the main generator of nationalistic public discourses, was compensating for the lack of 'real reasons' and redirecting public discontent generated through the economic crises from dissatisfaction with political elites at the times into the hatred towards Others. In the case of the Balkan wars it is safe to say that 'how' was even more relevant than 'why'. Yugoslav wars were the *wars of states-to-be against society*. The problem was that there were too many 'states-to-be' and only one society which was necessary to be ripped apart so that states could get 'their' territories (BLAGOJEVIĆ 2006). The fact that the wars actually did happen does not imply that they were 'logical', 'determined', 'inevitable' and therefore 'explicable'. It is only the 'scientific' approach to reality that constructs

---

[11] According to the prosecution at the ICTY trial against Slobodan Milošević, for example, propaganda was used as part of the indictment. The Independent Association of Journalists of Serbia, NUNS, filed a criminal charge in 2009 against unnamed journalists for the "criminal act of organising and promoting the implementation of genocide and war crimes on the basis of Article 145 of the Criminal Code of the Republic of Serbia" (http://www.ejc.net/magazine/ article/reactions_from_belgrade_serbian_journalists_indicted_for_promoting_enablin/). However, until the end of 2011 nothing has been done in that regard.

and re-constructs 'the reason', the 'why'. For the vast majority of people living in ex-Yugoslavia, back in the late 1980s and early 1990s, wars were not expected, not logical and not justified. Post factum it became clear that the war promoters were the winners of the process, if not individually (because some of them were punished), then as a political class, and that 'nationalism' is still the major 'game in town', corresponding to conditions of semiperipheriality, and strengthened by the current global economic crises. The winners are, therefore, the states and the political elites. Losers are so called 'ordinary people'.

It would be logical to expect that the real reasons for ethnic wars would be based on religious tensions and/or discrimination. Yet neither of these existed to any substantial degree in former Yugoslavia, certainly not in comparison to any Western democracy (BLAGOJEVIĆ 1996). The population was primarily atheistic (in the 1970s, 80s, and early 90s), and discrimination against minority ethnic groups, in each of the republics/provinces, was extremely weak. In fact, data from the 1981 census demonstrated convincingly that almost nowhere in former Yugoslavia individual upward mobility depended on ethnic origin. For the majority of the population, regardless of ethnic origin, there was a high probability that an individual born after WWII could live the whole of his/her life, till the end of the 1980s, without experiencing or feeling ethnic or religious discrimination. This was especially true in urban settings, of which Sarajevo was a prime example. Before the wars started, the majority of the former Yugoslav population did not even regard separatism as a valid option (GOATI 1991). Until the mid-80s, ethnic distance was at a stable low, and even decreasing further. But at the end of the 1980s, as a consequence of deep economic crises, the Communist party dissolution, the competition between the republics and the open war propaganda, ethnic distance increased throughout the former Yugoslavia (GOLUBOVIĆ/ KUZMANOVIĆ/ VASOVIĆ 1995). However, after the wars, both interethnic relations and the position of all minorities have considerably worsened. Another paradox of the former Yugoslav wars is that they started in the name of the protection of minorities, as minorities have felt 'threatened', but at the end of the process of dissolution the position of all minorities is actually degraded, as predicted by some authors already at the beginning of the 90s. This is yet another evidence that the wars were not 'logical', but more ideological, with the major ideology being nationalism (JANSEN 2005).[12]

---

[12] However, it should be noted that demographic research on ethnic marriages and especially ethnic migrations have proven that there was a process of ethnification of society especially from the 70s on. Nations, as shown in research done by the demographer Ruža Petrović had a tendency to concentrate on the territories of their maximal

Identity politics in former Yugoslavia had a shift from 'unity and brotherhood' and 'equality of sexes' until the 90s to nationalism and sexism from the 90s on. In many ways what was happening in the space of former Yugoslavia was typical for other post-communist societies, which only proves the point about the relevance of the semiperipheral analytical perspective. Classical postulates of the 'scapegoat theory' could easily be connected to the Yugoslav situation in the 90s – economic crisis and search for somebody to blame. 'Somebody' had to be invented, through the process of intense differentiation of 'we-ness' versus 'they-ness', which easily turned into the opposition to Otherness and hate towards the Other. There was a gradual process of distancing, from the 'discovery' of difference within the entity of 'brotherhood and unity' within Yugoslavia, to emphasizing difference and claiming that they are more relevant than the similarities, and that they are almost eternal and essential. At the end of that process of distancing stood the claims about 'non-negotiable differences' and 'unavoidable' war as a necessary 'defense'. The final step in the distancing process was de-humanization of the Other, where the Other was portrayed as an essential threat to survival.

As it has been widely documented in a vast number of feminist publications the very logic of gender and nation construction is the same – differences are interpreted as inequalities and serve as a ground for social hierarchy (IVEKOVIĆ 1993). In the case of ethnic/national differences the issue is not only about hierarchy, as much as it is about exclusion or even annihilation. But in both cases, differences are essentialized, generalized and naturalized (beyond what seems to be 'natural' or obvious in case of sex/gender differences). It is the hypertrophy of difference at the cost of sameness or similarity that is in the base of both sexism and nationalism. Moreover, war violence was prepared by genderization and sexualization of the inter-ethnic relationships, as claimed by Jalušić. Jalušić states that:

> Using violence demands legitimization and quite a high degree of rationalization. Before brutalizing and annihilating the other, the other has to be excluded from the community. This is generally done by bestowing on him or her non-human or pseudo-human characteristics [...] These patterns were present long before the real violence and the war started and facilitated the extreme use of violence finally resulting in 'ethnic cleansing' [...] In a process of ethnic revival, the described genderization and sexualization of the

---

concentration (PETROVIĆ 1987). These tendencies have continued in the 90s due to the wars and after 2000 when the wars are finished. So, it would be possible to speak about a long term process of concentration of nations which corresponded to the ideology of national elites and nation states formation.

inter-ethnic relationships also contributed to (re)creating one's own identity through violence. (JALUŠIĆ 2004: 48)

So, not only that there is a high connection between sexism and nationalism, but in the case of former Yugoslavia war violence itself was introduced by the process of national identity formation grounded in violence. Feminist authors claim that Serbian nationalism was largely constructed and the Serbian nation mobilized for the war through the media campaign related to the cases of rapes of Serbian women by Albanian men in Kosovo (SLAPŠAK 1990; PAPIĆ 2002; JALUŠIĆ 2004). While the factual side of that particular case remains vague, since really reliable data does not exist, it is not to be doubted that media constructs were instrumental for the increased and wide spread feeling of Serbian victimhood and 'necessary' defense, and as such they were highly instrumental for the war and national mobilization.[13]

Although in nationalistic discourses throughout former Yugoslavia gender hierarchy was based on presupposed universality and transhistoricity of gender differences, to serve the purpose of national mobilization it had to be additionally ethnicized. Different national contexts shaped different arguments, which corresponded to national foundational myths, but also to political and historical circumstances.

This interplay between the universal and contextual in interpretation of gender differences could best be seen in the Serbian public discourse of the 90s. Since Serbian nationalism in the 90s was articulated in strong opposition to the West, women were constructed as 'Westernized' Others. The Serbian matrix of gender oppositions was the opposite from these of metaphysical oppositions distinctive for the Western tradition. In Serbian public discourse women were linked to culture, while men to nature (BLAGOJEVIĆ 1995; 2006). However, the relationship to the West was not involved in discursive practices of nation building only in the Serbian case, but in the case of other nations as well. As Jalušić has analyzed: "Even in the eighties, one could see derogatory images of a presumed Balkan and uncivilized enemy throughout Yugoslavia: on the one hand 'Balkan man' was depicted as lazy, indifferent and violent; on the other there were images of a diligent, hard-working, honest, civilized *non-Balkan* man." (JALUŠIĆ 2004: 49) The genderization of the Balkans was both internal

---

[13] Facts about the number of rapes are highly disputable, since already in the late 80s institutions in Kosovo were highly ethnicized and dominated by Albanians and therefore official statistics from that period is misleading (more about the system of discrimination existing on Kosovo against Serbian minority, see in BLAGOJEVIĆ 2000a). However, Milošević manipulated with the 'real problems' to encourage Serbian nationalism and mobilize Serbian nation for the war (see also BLAGOJEVIĆ 2009c).

and external: inside it referred to hierarchization of men and masculinities, along the West–East division, assumed boundaries between the Balkans and the West and outside it referred to genderization of the Balkans as a region of Europe.

It was during the 90s that the former Yugoslav space emerged as 'the Balkans' with the entire negative connotation. (TODOROVA 1997; BJELIĆ 2002) The wars were, especially in the media, often presented as wars between uncivilized, undeveloped and barbarian nations. The very idea of 'lagging behind', in what was understood as the only possible path of modernization, became dominant discourse. The major prescription for 'catching up' developed into the one which promoted formation of nation states as the 'natural' path towards 'democracy' and development. The history of modernization through the Yugoslav socialist and federal project was interpreted as a failure, climaxing in the wars of 'barbarian' nations ones against the others, but in a 'logical' step towards the creation of nation states. Although Bjelić is claiming that "like *Orientalism, Balkanism* has been organized around a sense of binaries (rational/irrational, center/periphery, civilization/barbarism) arranged hierarchically so that the first sign ('Whiteness' or 'Europe'), is always primary and definitional of the second ('Blackness' or 'Balkans')" (BJELIĆ 2002: 3), Balkanism as a discourse is most often defined by its liminality, in-betweeness, something being 'neither-nor'. Balkanism as a discourse is nevertheless possible only because it essentializes the Other, even when it is a bit unclear what the Otherness is about. Similarly to previous examples of how the Otherness in the former Yugoslav context has been invented to serve to identity politics, the Otherness of the Balkans was so pronounced, and still is, in media and political discourses, because the difference is vague and in many ways unconvincing. However, Balkanism, being both a representational mechanism, as well as subjectivational process (BJELIĆ 2002: 4–5), remains relevant for power structures and social hierarchies built on them, internally and externally.

The negative imagery of the Balkans which dominated the Western press and politics during the 90s was not only following the line of West–East divisions and general logic of hierarchy based on the simplified idea of modernization, but it was also founded on very gendered representations of the main social actors: women were presented as powerless victims, and men as macho, wild and cruel soldiers. In visual terms, the most frequent representations were those of rural women with scarves on their heads and crying, and men with beards and savage, barbarian looks. It was the overall 'ruralization' of the imagery which was strengthening the negative stereotyping of the Balkans as 'backward' and prepared the ground for paternalistic interventions from the outside. Todorova claims that the Balkans has an undeniable masculine image, which is well connected to perceptions about medieval knighthood, arms and conspirators. She also emphasizes that, as opposed to the orientalist discourse which uses femininity as a metaphor, Balkanism as a discourse is exclusively masculinist (TODOROVA 1997). That masculinist discourse on the Balkans was well in concordance with the masculinist hegemonic discourse of neo-colonialism through globalization, materialized in different international decision-making bodies. So, even when it appeared as protective to 'women-victims' it was actually strengthening the global masculine hierarchies of power, best documented by military 'solutions' and construction of ethnic boundaries.

Prevailing gender representations during the wars were in sharp contrast to former Yugoslav media representations of women and very different from what many of the former Yugoslavs perceived to be their reality. This imagery created a kind of wave over collective consciousness, both in the West and in the Balkans, which was erasing the memories of urban, middle class, European population, which had been previously embracing values, lifestyles and consumption patterns similar to the ones in the West. Nevertheless, the wars were related to undeniable victimization the way the images were gendered, encouraged re-traditionalization within the Balkans, and pronounced the difference between the Balkans and the 'rest' of Europe. In a way, that representation was part of the self-fulfilling prophecy, a contribution to the negative spiral of a downward trend of distancing from Europe, and in many ways distancing from the Balkans' own historical path of development. De-development as part of the semiperipheral condition is connected to the deepening of that 'difference', to essentialization and naturalization of that difference. In a paradoxical way, similarly to identity politics leading and preparing for the wars, 'balkanization', the imposition of negative perceptions of the Balkans, internally and externally, was preparing for real distancing of the Balkans from Europe. There was also something of a prescribed and pronounced difference of the Balkans which justified 'rational' Western intervention into the wars. However, the paradox of that intervention was the actual reproduction not only of the core-semiperiphery hierarchy, but also the normalization of ethnicized solutions for peace. As claimed by Campbell, many external academic and political analyses of the Bosnian conflict have themselves embodied the hegemony of explanations which were centered on certain understanding of nationhood: "the settled norms of international society – in particular, the idea that the national community requires the nexus of demarcated territory and fixed identity – were not only insufficient to enable a response to the Bosnian war, they were complicit in and necessary for the conduct of the war itself." (CAMPBELL 1998: 13) As it is becoming more and more widely accepted, ethnification of the identities in the former Yugoslav space had very tangible outputs in the 'solutions' which were prescribed:

> Disciplinary power effects a problematization through strategies of normalization. These strategies work on people and places as to compare, differentiate, hierarchies, and homogenize them in ways that map them as manageable problems amenable to solutions that more often than not involve distribution, enclosure, and surveillance. In the case of Bosnia, perhaps the most prevalent problematization involves the ethnification of the political field. With its array of historical, statistical, cartographic, and other procedures, this has helped organize Bosnia into an 'intractable' problem such as apartheid politics of partition could be proposed as the most 'realistic' solution. (CAMPBELL 1998: XI)

Towards reconciliation: *pozistorija* – positive history approach

> This driver's twelve-year-old son had been killed by a shell the year before while playing on the streets outside the family apartment. Yet on more than one occasion during that tour, unprompted by any particular question, he turned to us with genuine puzzlement and asked why the many other foreigners he met always assumed that because he was Muslim, he would naturally hate all Serbs. "I presume a Serb fired the shell that killed my son" he said, "but I do not know which one. So, why would I hate all Serbs? I live with them, I walk with them, I work with them, and many are my friends." (CAMPBELL 1998: 2)

Discursive strategies implied in identity politics and centered on difference, as shown above, were the key element in populist mobilization for the wars. Whether internal, within the Balkans, or external, between the West and the Balkans, national differences were essentialized and naturalized, building on gender hierarchy. It was the gendering of the differences which actually enabled its essentializing, since gender differences serve as a model for all other socially constructed differences. But, it was also shown that discourses on difference were highly contextualized and dependent on conditions of semi-peripheriality within the project of neoliberal globalization. The major lesson which could be learned from discursive strategies employed in the dissolution of the former Yugoslavia is actually the one on *identities being relational, temporal and contextual and under permanent change*. The question is, thus, how to define and promote constructive public policies related to reconciliation building on these assumptions.

As the construction of identities was a key element of the self-fulfilling prophecy in a process of dissolution of the former Yugoslavia, accordingly, it can also be a key element in the process of reconciliation. To empower social agents to act towards reconciliation, it is important, in the first place, to promote the idea of history as a choice, within a set of structural constraints, but still a choice. For that purpose it is necessary to deconstruct discursive strategies of identity formation which emphasized the difference, opposition, and hierarchy. The very same mechanisms that empowered pro-war discursive strategies could actually be used to empower pro-reconciliation discursive strategies. The very same weakness of social structures in a 'transition' could also empower constructive solutions, instead of destructive ones. In fact, the same process of self-fulfilling prophecies could be applied to reconciliation. And powerful lessons for that paradigm shift and that direction of social activism could be drawn from feminist legacies. *As wars were grounded and supported by a certain type of knowledge, the one which was essentializing the difference and emphasizing the opposition and conflict, similarly, reconciliation has to be grounded in a certain type of knowledge, but a kind of counter knowledge, the one which will not only de-essentialize the difference, but also put the emphasis on cooperation, exchange and connectedness.* The potential of this knowledge is grounded on the experiences of 'ordinary people' and so far it has been largely underestimated within the androcentric and most often nationalistic knowledge prevailing in the academic institutions in the Balkans.

Building on feminist legacies to create knowledge which will enhance the reconciliation process means to go far beyond the 'gender and war' perspective, although that is not to deny its relevance. Adding up the gender perspective in issues on reconciliation cannot be reduced to the argument that women were the major victims of the wars, nor that they were the major proponents of peace through their engagement in peace movements. Engendering reconciliation, theoretically and practically, means reshaping dominant discourses on both reconciliation and women's issues connected to the war. Engendering reconciliation is not seen here as 'mainstreaming' gender into peacemaking and reconciliation efforts, but as a *profound change of the epistemic and theoretical perspective*, as well as a discursive shift which is so necessary to encourage a process of reconciliation. What makes a paradigm shift is exactly this '*engendering*', as a first step, meaning adding up a gender dimension, but also, '*de-gendering*', as a second step, only after 'engendering', meaning de-naturalization of gender and moving towards a perspective which will discourage gender power hierarchies (patriarchies, in fact), while encouraging gender differences and/or similarities. In fact, 'de-gendering' means empowering individual varieties and choices, out of the 'boxes', social constructs, which enslave and obstruct expressions and enjoyment of diversities.

However, it is important to state that *de-gendering is possible only after engendering*. The second one happened relatively late, only in the last decade being more accepted internationally that women do represent the major civilian victims and that they do make a majority of peace activists. There is, however, an obvious movement from an essentialized perception of a woman as a 'natural peacemaker' to a more critical examination of the different positioning of women and men in different locations related to the war. Both women and men could be victims, warriors, or peace activists (BIJELIĆ 2004; POPOV 2000). *Numbers or percentages cannot be really indicative of the 'real nature' of women or men.* In fact, they can only be the starting point in an analysis of how society has conditioned and constructed both genders, so that in times of conflict they continue to perform in a manner which has been already defined by society. Feminist based scholarship has contributed to the increase of knowledge related to specific gender-related aspects of conflicts and reconciliation, but here it is argued that engendering is not enough, although necessary.

Reconciliation, as any other social practice, is closely connected to knowledges: legitimate, official, tacit, or subversive knowledges. It is also being discursively shaped accordingly, and spread through media as a set of theoretical ideas, expert recommendations, political formulas, or simple common sense opinions. At present, the territory of discourse on reconciliation has increasingly been 'occupied' by politicians who are faced with EU requests on 'regional cooperation'. It is increasingly becoming 'rationalized', linked to the economic rationalities of creating a common regional market. While structural changes in this direction could certainly be beneficial for the project of regional reconciliation, it is also a threat to the genuine meaning of reconciliation which has an *important spiritual dimension*, and which exists as an issue *beyond economic rationality*, as a necessity for harmonious social life, for a successful social inclusion of minorities, for smooth communication between diversities, for cooperation as a dominant mode of human existence. Re-establishing the true meaning of reconciliation is, thus, a link to the major legacies of feminist theory. If the discourse on reconciliation stays within an 'engendering' paradigm, it ends up in a paradox: that gender differences are more relevant than those related to ethnic/national differences. The only way out is toward 'de-gendering', meaning de-essentialization of gender, ethnic and all other differences based on prescribed social roles and performances. The approach to reconciliation needs to be not only gender sensitive, but also gender integrative.

So, the question remains: what other feminist epistemic legacies can be additionally employed in the creation of knowledges and discourses towards reconciliation? Let's make an overview of some of the key postulates here, to be able to move towards the idea of *pozistorija*. Firstly, the feminist axiom that knowledge is embodied and embedded in fact reaffirms the idea that history is 'wo/man made', in a sense that it is a result of human agency, and consequently, gendered human agency (or ethnicized, genderized, localized etc. agency). Human agency produces the social structures at the first place, human agency changes them, and human agency allows for choice. Mere understanding of the relevance of human agency reinforces that agency, but also the responsibility of social agents. Therefore, reconciliation is a choice, as much as war is a choice.

Also, an immanent feminist knowledge project would need to deal with the mission of 'decolonizing' knowledge, from the theoretical assumptions, often supported by empirical research, which create and maintain social hierarchies, based on whatever criteria (gender, class, ethnicity, religion, citizenship, location, age, ability…), and justify social exclusions. It would seek to abolish simplified black and white oppositions and deconstruct interests which create them. Postcolonialism and feminism are constructing critical discourses by affirming standpoints of the marginalized, outsiders, those who do not have the power to create dominant knowledge paradigms. This approach eventually increases objectivity: "[s]tarting thought from 'marginalized lives' as standpoint epistemologies recommend thus provides more rigorous, more competent standards for maximizing objectivity." (HARDING 1987: 18) So, it is 'stronger objectivity', not weaker, which is the result of standpoint theories.

The feminist approach also aims at deconstructing 'the knower' him/herself. To be able to do that, the knower, the one who produces knowledge, needs to position him/herself in relation to the topic of his/her investigation and to enable this position to be exposed and transparent in the process of knowledge production and knowledge communication. Moreover, the 'knower', one who is authorized to make knowledge, should reflect on his/her own interests and practices in knowledge production. In addition, s/he should be aware of the very influence that knowledge production is exercising upon reality. The ideal position would be one of a "critique in which the authors critically and reflexively engage with both themselves and the topic, within the emancipatory context" (HEARN 2004: 60), but also clear and transparent responsibility towards (global) society. Therefore, especially in social sciences, it is not simply exploring the 'causes' of events, following the tradition of hard sciences, especially physics, as much as it is exploring the connection between the knowledge and reality in a manner of 'self-fulfilling prophecies'. Knowledge is creating preconditions for certain outcomes in social reality. Social reality is shaped by knowledge and its application. The one who produces knowledge needs to reflect on the process of knowledge making, as well as on possible consequences produced by knowledge. In the feminist tradition, discovering 'blind spots', or 'gray areas', is as important as exposing dominant knowledge paradigms to critique. The identification of the invisible, unknown, and unnamed problems experienced by women (and men), especially marginalized women (and men), is in the core of women's and gender studies. But, also exploring and reflecting on men and masculinities in relation to war is essential for the deconstruction of dominant scientific and public discourses on wars. In the feminist epistemic project, ignorance – or better to say, 'systemic ignorance' (HARDING 1998), the absence of knowledge about the things which are relevant for the lives of those who are powerless – is perceived as a result of systematic structural inequalities, not as a fact of coincidence. Without the deconstruction of male hierarchies related to the losses and gains from wars, in the mode of Critical Studies on Men, as suggested by HEARN (2004), it is impossible to deconstruct wars as social phenomena.

Finally, another question is also very important for the issue of reconciliation. That question is: how can we judge between competing interpretations of social reality (CAMBELL 1998: 41)? What criteria do we use? Since feminism is all about the empowerment of the 'weaker side', the interpretation which is empowering that side, and which also brings in the quality of an authentic voice, is usually taken as stronger. However, there is an increasing awareness of the existence of the multiplicity of 'truths' connected to the multiplicity of social locations. Still, the analysis of power relations in structural terms is what produces, at the end, a favorable interpretation from the feminist perspective. An interpretation of the wars would, therefore, become focused on those who neither had the power to produce the wars, nor to interpret the wars. From that point of view, reconciliation would also favor the viewpoint in which those who were lacking the power to produce wars would be connected, to reflect on their position and to make solidarity networks across gender, ethnic, racial, or religious lines. So, the dominant interpretation would be the one which favors *the perspective of the powerless*, those who did not have the power to produce the wars, to oppose them, or to stop them, and especially those who were the major 'losers' of the wars. However, this would also mean that the reconciliation effort should provide the interpretation which would diminish the possibility for creating a hierarchy of victimhood, since that hierarchy would create tensions and endanger solidarity between the powerless, across the lines of conflicting sides.

Feminist epistemological starting points, in other words, allow for a much deeper intervention into knowledge, in comparison to what has been usually done within the efforts of 'adding up women' or 'gender mainstreaming'. They allow – in fact, they call for the creation of a different paradigm, which would deeply *challenge the dominant interpretation of war conflicts*. That paradigm would also reframe the issue of 'gender and reconciliation' and deeply influence reconciliation efforts in practice. It can connect 'objectivity', in fact 'stronger objectivity', to the responsibility of the knowers, and it can also disclose the connection between 'knowledge' and the very process of war making, or peacemaking. It would be critical towards 'objectivity' which constructs sides in conflict as blocks, as supra-identities of 'nations', 'states', or religious or ethnic groups. Instead, it can offer a subtle and disaggregated picture of ethnic or gender 'blocks', demystifying and deconstructing the collectives in conflict, while empowering individuals and their diversities.

To summarize, major lessons for the knowledge project, based on feminist epistemic legacies, which could reframe and de-gender the reconciliation project, are the following:

- deconstructing gender and ethnic essentialism;
- arguing for a gender-sensitive and gender-integrative approach in a manner of "critical studies on men" (HEARN 2004);
- deconstructing and positioning of the 'knowers';
- deconstructing of the practitioners of reconciliation;
- deconstructing structural power relations related to the war making, but also for peacemaking and reconciliation;
- understanding that knowledge is a construct, gendered construct, and empowering the powerless to deconstruct it;
- discovering the 'blind spots' closely connected to powerlessness in relation to war; bringing powerlessness from all sides and social locations into the light;
- reaffirming the perspective 'from below', from everyday life (using personal narratives and qualitative methodologies);
- understanding that individual agency is closely connected to social hierarchies and power;
- connecting guilt, responsibility and accountability with limits of the structural constraints within which that agency is being expressed, whether individual or collective agency;
- integrating different knowledges articulated in different social locations into the body of knowledge about the war and the reconciliation;
- creating inclusive meta-narratives which will integrate different knowledges and micro narratives 'from below', coming from different social locations;
- advocating for knowledge which will have healing and not disruptive and conflictual power.

In a spirit of those feminist legacies and lessons which can be drawn from them the project of *pozistorija*, the positive history approach is offered here. There is a profound need for new research to support that approach, which could eventually lead to the creation of a different body of knowledge, a different set of databases which will change not only our perspectives on the wars, but actually our world view. More than ever human kind is capable of learning lessons fast and creating its own reality exactly because of the crash of the dominant structural order. It is in times of 'transition', as 'we' from the Balkans have already learned, that self-fulfilling prophecies became even more effective than before. The human agency could be empowered by structural weaknesses, both in a constructive and destructive direction. Constructive solutions need the creation of new knowledges. *Pozistorija* is such a knowledge project. It puts emphasis on everyday life and social history, and not on political history. It includes a deconstruction of gendered practices and discourses on the level of everyday life, and it is enabling a perspective from below, coming from those who were/are powerless, or who had/have very limited agency to influence major war events, being either women or men. *Pozistorija* could become a feminist healing knowledge project, where healing knowledge becomes part of the actual healing and reconciliation project.

Pozistorija is here used as a "strategic concept" (HARDING 1998), which means that there is no claim to universality and that it does not mean that this concept could be applied everywhere, in any situation. However, its relevance is obvious in the case of former Yugoslavia where commonalities played an important role before the outbreak of wars. The essence of *pozistorija* is its emphasis on commonalities, shared experiences, common practices and discourses, intercultural exchanges. It is an affirmation of social history as opposed to political history. Positive history explores the realities of everyday life, of actual 'living together'. It starts with the assumption that history has two sides: one of cooperation, communication, adaptation, exchange, building commonalities, and the other, of separation, confrontation, war conflicts. In the case of the Balkan wars, the history of 'living together' lasted longer than the history of conflicts.

Pozistorija includes two different, but interrelated research areas: one related to 'living together', and the other related to opposition to the wars. The first domain deals with practices, everyday life experiences, supranational identities (such as Yugoslav), multiculturalism, inter-group mixing in everyday life, exchange, shared discourses and meta-narratives of 'togetherness' ('brotherhood and unity'), attitudes reflecting small ethnic distance, interethnic marriages; memories on commonalities, Yugo-nostalgia; spatial mobility throughout common territory and emotional appropriation of that territory (emotional maps); cultural hybrids consisting of different cultural traditions; shared cultural space; kinship and friendship networks throughout the common space; professional former Yugoslav communities and business contacts; shared media space etc.

The second research field, related to the opposition to the wars, would include the following: institutional resistance to the dissolution; civilian resistance (mutual help, solidarity with victims, solidarity between the victims); resistance of soldiers and warriors (subversive behavior, help to the other side in the conflict, refusal of mobilization); active resistance to the war in the form of peace movements, solidarity of NGOs across borders, creative resistance (resistance of artists, scientists, prominent public personalities), and media resistance of independent media (BLAGOJEVIĆ 1998; SUŠAK 2000; POPOV 2000).

The important feature of shared commonalities as an essential part of positive history is that they were lived, experienced, memorized. They cannot be reduced to simple 'communist propaganda' since they were exercised daily, they were generally acknowledged, intelligible to the majority of people, practiced on a daily basis, and part of public discourses, and they were generally believed in (GOLUBOVIĆ/ KUZMANOVIĆ/ VASOVIĆ 1995). Wars did not 'prove' the opposite, and they simply could not, logically. The causes of wars belong to a very different deterministic network of social vectors, so those things simply do not relate on the same level.

While the prevailing explanation of the wars deals with the public sphere, the prevailing explanation related to *pozistorija* should deal with the private sphere, everyday life. These two perspectives do not exclude each other, but rather complement each other. Adding *pozistorija* also means introducing the gender perspective, by disclosing the private, the invisible, the individual and the day-to-day. Change of the perspective, to the one from below, from the level of everyday life, is an essentially feminist epistemic strategy which is necessary for 'stronger objectivity'. However, this is not to say that the everyday life perspective is useful only for the positive history approach. On the contrary, to understand increased animosities it is equally relevant to understand how economic crises, media influence, and political constellations were mediated through everyday life to the level of the individual. People experience social reality, collapse of structures, wars and peace on the everyday life level. That experience is so important that the violence in war could best be described as a "violent disruption of everyday life practices" (BLAGOJEVIĆ 2000b).

Contrary to the position of 'the knower', who, embodied as an expert, scholar or politician, inhabited and appropriated the space of interpretation, *pozistorija* is calling for another, feminist, strategy of 'knowing'. Not only the one which deconstructs scholarly or political texts related to the wars in former Yugoslavia, or some other context, but the one which insists on the validity of knowledge produced in the concrete contexts of former Yugoslav society, and again, not solely scholarly knowledge, but everyday life knowledge, common knowledge of 'ordinary' people. 'Stronger objectivity' is created by giving credentials to the knowledge and self-understanding of ordinary people and their often 'floating' narratives, those which are not yet situated into the wider interpretative framework. The issue is not about 'adding' the perspective of *pozistorija* to counterbalance the other one, but to offer a different understanding of the very causality of the wars and the fact that they were produced and reproduced *counter* to, and not according to, the interests of the majority of the populations in former Yugoslavia. It is the perspective of the 'losers' which is in fact both more justified and objective.

Pozistorija as a project allows the 'weaker side' on all sides of a conflict, the side which was opposing the wars actively or passively, to become visible. By encouraging knowledge creation which links gendered individual experiences on an everyday life level, before and during the wars, by creating a meta-narrative which can encompass those experiences, *pozistorija* opens up a space for reconciliation on a different ground: through articulation of a narrative which could be widely shared by most of the 'ordinary' people from all the sides who actually perceive themselves as victims. This could be a ground for new solidarity and healing, beyond the boundaries of the newly formed states and ethnic affiliations.

In a political sense, it is of outmost relevance to identify the resistance to the war conflict, sometimes active, sometimes passive, and to encourage the process of healing by acknowledging the existence of this 'other' perspective. To the process of healing and reconstruction of what has been broken and destroyed by the wars, it is essential that a new meta-narrative becomes articulated, that of the powerlessness of ordinary people and alternative political actors to oppose the wars, and that it relies on some evidence, regardless of how scattered and fragmented. The issue here is that many individual experiences and historical facts exist that support this meta-narrative of powerlessness of ordinary people and alternative political (peaceful) solutions (BROZ 2004). However, these individual stories have still not been brought together to construct an alternative framework, as important as prevailing political history, in interpreting what has actually happened in the Balkans. *Pozistorija* could be a complex fabric of a load of evidence which can prove that multiculturalism in former Yugoslavia was not mainly, or only, politically and ideologically constructed, but lived, practiced and experienced by a great majority of ordinary people. The fact that the wars actually happened does not imply that they were 'logical', 'determined', 'inevitable' and therefore explicable.

In everyday life, resistance to war politics was faced with two sets of limitations: lack of institutional channels to express attitudes against the wars, with an overwhelming feeling that it was not 'us' who want the war, but 'they', and second, exhaustion of resources due to survival pressures. Nevertheless, there is much evidence of mutual help across ethnic lines during the wars. Individual testimonies, collected in a book by Svetlana Broz, for example, disclosed a whole variety of different situations when ordinary people were helping each other in life-threatening situations (BROZ 2004). What this book showed is how the war was actually perceived as some kind of a 'natural disaster' over the heads of 'normal people', causing spontaneous solidarity. In the chaos of the war many cases could be found that represent the ultimate confirmation of the power of individual agency which finds its way through a set of chaotic, dangerous, and fragile situations to *counteract* the dominant wave of animosity, hatred and destruction.

Instead of a conclusion: a work ahead...

This text is disclosing a set of arguments in favor of deconstruction and de-essentialization of both gender and nation, on one hand, as well as the Balkans, themselves, on the other hand. However, deconstruction is not enough. What is needed is a paradigm shift, offered here as a project of *pozistorija – history of living together*. But, that project is only at its beginning. Although there are growing discourses, records, testimonies, even researches which are contributing to the overall change of the dominant aggressive, hostile and conflictual discourses and 'knowledges', the process of creation of *pozistorija* is at the very beginning. Not only that there is not enough knowledge at the moment, but that knowledge is also not codified, it is not institutionalized, nor canonized. It is not part of the official history textbooks, nor part of the political programs, nor most of the TV shows and public speeches of Balkan politicians. It is still marginal, hidden, and although 'commonsensical' for the great majority of former Yugoslavs it is still not powerful nor politicized in the right way. So, what is offered here is just to bring a common name to all those growing efforts, to follow the feminist *politics of naming*, as a first step to *visibility*. But, the major work of collecting, systematizing, analyzing, is still ahead...

References

BJELIĆ, D. (2002): Introduction. Blowing Up the "Bridge". In: Bjelić, Dušan/ Obrad Savić (eds.): Balkan as Metaphor. Between Globalization and Fragmentation. London.

BLAGOJEVIĆ, MARINA (1995): Svakodnevica iz ženske perspektive – samožrtvovanje i beg u privatnost. In: Bolčić, Silvano (ed.): Društvene promene i svakodnevni život – Srbija početkom 90-tih. Belgrade.
BLAGOJEVIĆ, MARINA (1996): Društvene karakteristike etničkih grupa. Kako meriti diskriminaciju? In: Položaj manjina u Saveznoj Republici Jugoslaviji. Belgrade.
BLAGOJEVIĆ, MARINA (1999): Institutions in Serbia. From Collapse to What? In: Heinrich, Hans-Georg (ed.): Institution Building in the New Democracies. Studies in Post-Post-Communism (= Workshop series/ Collegium Budapest Institute for Advanced Study 7). Budapest.
BLAGOJEVIĆ, MARINA (2000a): The Migrations of Serbs from Kosovo during the 1970s and 1980s. Trauma and/or Catharsis. In: Popov, Nebojša (ed.): The Road to War in Serbia. Trauma and Catharsis. Budapest et al.
BLAGOJEVIĆ, MARINA (2000b): Preface. In: Nikolić-Ristanović, Vesna (ed.): Women, Violence and War. Wartime Victimization of Refugees in the Balkans. Budapest.
BLAGOJEVIĆ, MARINA (2002): Process of reconciliation. Self-fulfilling Prophecy. In: Temida 4. Belgrade.
BLAGOJEVIĆ, MARINA (2006): Serbianhood as Manhood. Politics of gender and ethnic identity in Serbia. In: Gršak, Marijana/ Ulrike Reimann/ Kathrin Franke/ Torsten Bewernitz (eds.): Frauen und Frauenorganisationen im Widerstand in Kroatien, Bosnien und Serbien. Frankfurt am Main.
BLAGOJEVIĆ, MARINA (2009a): Knowledge Production at the Semiperiphery. A Gender Perspective. Belgrade.
BLAGOJEVIĆ, MARINA (2009b): Transnationalisation and its Absence. The Balkan Semiperipheral Perspective on Masculinities. In: Harrison, Katherine/ Jeffrey L. Hearn (eds.): Deconstructing the Hegemony of Men and Masculinities. Linköping.
BLAGOJEVIĆ, MARINA (2009c): Milošević and Kosovo. Spiral of Evil. In: Pavlović, Momčilo/ Dejan Jović/ Vladimir Petrović (eds.): Slobodan Milošević. Put ka vlasti – Osma sednica CK SKS. Belgrade.
BIJELIĆ, BILJANA (2004): Lekar, majka, žena. In: Blagojević, Marina (ed.): Mapiranje mizoginije u Srbiji. Diskursi i prakse. Belgrade.
BROZ, SVETLANA (2004): Good People in an Evil Time. Portraits of Complicity and Resistance in the Bosnian War. New York.
CAMPBELL, DAVID (1998): National Deconstruction. Violence, Identity, and Justice in Bosnia. Minneapolis.
CASTELLS, MANUEL (2000): The Rise of the Network Society. Malden, Massachusetts et al.

IVEKOVIĆ, RADA (1993): Women, nationalism and war. Make love not war. In: Hypatia 8/4.
IVEKOVIĆ, RADA/ JULIE MOSTOV (2002): Introduction. From Gender to Nation. In: Iveković, Rada/ Julie Mostov (eds.): From Gender to Nation. Ravenna.
GOATI, VLADIMIR (1991): Jugoslavija na prekretnici – od monizma do građanskog rata. Belgrade.
GOLUBOVIĆ, ZAGORKA/ BORA KUZMANOVIĆ/ MIRJANA VASOVIĆ (1995): Društveni karakter i društvene promene u svetlu nacionalnih sukoba. Belgrade.
HARDING, SANDRA G. (ed.) (1997): Feminism and Methodology. Social Science Issues. Bloomington.
HARDING, SANDRA G. (1998): Is Science Multicultural? Postcolonialisms, Feminisms, and Epistemologies. Bloomington/Indianapolis.
HEARN, JEFFREY L. (2004): Gendering men and masculinities in research and scientific evaluations. In: European Commission (ed.): Gender and Excellence in the Making. Luxembourg.
JALUŠIĆ, VLASTA (2004): Gender and Victimization of the Nation as Pre- and Post-War Identity Discourse. In: Seifert, Ruth (ed.): Gender, Identität und kriegerischer Konflikt. Das Beispiel des ehemaligen Jugoslawien. Münster.
JANSEN, STEF (2005): Antinacionalizam. Etnografija otpora u Zagrebu i Beogradu. Belgrade.
LOKAR, SONJA (2003): Women Can Do It. General Lessons Learnt from Transition. In: Reysoo, Fenneke (ed.): On m'appèlle à régner. Mondalisation, pouvoirs et rapports de genre. 145–157. Genève. http://www.paix balkans.org/contributions/lokar_women%20can%20do%20it.pdf.
MEURS, MIEKE/ RASIKA RANASINGHE (2003): De-development in Post-Socialism. Conceptual and Measurement Issues. In: Politics and Society 31/1. 31–53.
NIKOLIĆ- RISTANOVIĆ, VESNA (2008): Preživeti tranziciju. Svakodnevni život i nasilje nad ženama u postkomunističkom i postratnom društvu. Belgrade.
PAPIĆ, ŽARANA (2002): Europe after 1989. Ethnic Wars, the Fascistization of Civil Society and Body Politics in Serbia. In: Griffin, Gabriele/ Rosi Braidotti (eds.): Thinking Differently. A Reader in European Women's Studies. London.
PETROVIĆ, Ruža (1987): Migracije u Jugoslaviji i etnički aspekt. Belgrade.
POPOV, NEBOJŠA (ed.) (2000): The Road to War in Serbia. Trauma and Catharsis. Budapest et al.
Popović, Srdja/ Ivan Janković/ Vesna Pešić/ Nataša Kandić/ Svetlana Slapšak (eds.) (1999): Kosovski čvor – drešiti ili seći? Belgrade.

SLAPŠAK, SVETLANA (2004): Gender and war in the Post-Socialist World. In: Seifert, Ruth (ed.): Gender, Identität und kriegerischer Konflikt. Das Beispiel des ehemaligen Jugoslawien. Münster.

SUŠAK, BOJANA (2000): An Alternative to War. In: Popov, Nebojša (ed.): The Road to War in Serbia. Trauma and Catharsis. Budapest.

TAYLOR, CHARLES (2000): Prizivanje građanskog društva. Belgrade.

TODOROVA, MARIA (1997): Imagining the Balkans. New York et al.

WALLERSTEIN, IMMANUEL (1979): The Capitalist World-Economy. Cambridge et al.

Gender Relations in Bosnia and Herzegovina between Theory and Practice

Marina Katnić-Bakaršić

Doing gender in Bosnia and Herzegovina is very complicated, even taking into account the fact that it is complicated anywhere in the world. By this I mean that in Bosnia and Herzegovina the main concern for those in power (so-called "power elites" – politicians, the media, academics...) is the *ethnic identity*. Trapped in their ethnicity and ethnic identity, women themselves sometimes forget their own Otherness in society and see the Other only in their neighbours from the other ethnicity. In the ethnically divided BiH society, dominated by the need to reduce the plurality of identities to a single, ethnic one, it is not always easy to talk about marginalization of women or about gender in general. In other words, the insistence on ethnicity "pushes gender to the background as a potential area for uniting and strengthening women as an important political factor in BiH" (MAJSTOROVIĆ/ TURJAČANIN 2006: 84). Obviously, in a situation of women's invisibility, doing gender always seems potentially subversive.

This paper aims to give a brief survey of investigating and doing gender in Bosnia for the past two decades. In order to achieve this, I shall refer to several issues here:

- development of gender studies in Bosnia and Herzegovina,
- elements of gender studies in curricula at the universities,
- language and gender,
- the role of women in literature, art and science,
- representing women in the media.

First of all, why does the title of my paper stress that gender-related activities in Bosnia are "between theory and reality"? It states so because I believe that, on the one hand, in my country gender theory has developed and even flourished since 1995. The evident improvement in raising gender awareness can be illustrated by legislation, development of gender studies, publishing books dealing with gender issues, introducing some aspects of gender studies in university curricula, as well as by literature and art in general. On the other hand, however, women still do not hold enough key positions in society; there still are only a few women in politics holding high positions; the media and advertisement representations of women are still inadequate; women are often kept from access to knowledge. The key unsolved problems, in my opinion, still remain the following ones: the status of uneducated, unemployed women, home violence and violence in general against women and various forms of "keeping women in their place" in the public sphere (at work, in politics, etc).

The Critical discourse analysis (CDA) claims that knowledge and access to knowledge can be regarded as a crucial basis for power (VAN DIJK 2003). In this regard it is especially important to say that there are still some spheres of society where women do not have access because relevant activities involve only men from work or other social groups (football, golf or basketball; informal meetings after the Friday prayer in the mosque, etc.). Apparently, the public sphere is still strongly dominated by men.

Legislation and education: a step forward in gender relations

The Gender Centre of the Federation of Bosnia and Herzegovina and the Gender Centre of Republika Srpska were established in December 2000. Even though these centres cooperate, the fact that they were established separately for both entities can serve as yet another example of the ethnical division of Bosnian society and dominance of ethnicity in all the spheres of life in Bosnia and Herzegovina. An improvement in legislation can be documented by the Law on Gender Equality in BiH, which entered into force in June 2003 (Official Gazette of BiH, No. 16/03). This law provides regulations for the promotion and protection of gender equality, guarantees equal opportunities to all citizens in all areas, and prevents direct or indirect sex discrimination. It also contains provisions on education, employment, social and health protection.

There are some positive changes in education: namely, in introducing some aspects of gender studies into curricula at the Faculty of Philosophy, University of Sarajevo (e.g. within theory of literature, philosophy, pedagogy or linguistics and stylistics). However, it is still not easy to get a job at the university for young feminist theoreticians.

The postgraduate Gender studies were established in 2006 in Sarajevo, at the Centre of International Postgraduate Studies (CIPS), owing to the great enthusiasm and expert knowledge of the late professor Nirman Moranjak-Bamburać, professor Jasna Bakšić-Muftić and professor Jasminka Babić-Avdispahić and some other colleagues. These studies are a logic consequence to the course Introduction to gender studies at the NGO Women to Women (the first lecturers were professors Nirman Moranjak-Bamburać Jasminka Babić-Avdispahić, Jasna Bakšić-Muftić and Marina Katnić-Bakaršić, joined by Zilka Šiljak-Spahić). The present postgraduate Gender studies are especially important because they brought together lecturers and students from all parts of Bosnia and Herzegovina and from different Balkan countries. This project is a major step forward in establishing gender theory and building bridges not only between different ethnicities in Bosnia and Herzegovina but also between Balkan countries in general. It can be regarded as an attempt at creating a sort of *third place* (in a sense that Homi Bhabha uses this term), where ethnic boundaries cease to exist, frontiers are in constant movement and building bridges of gender equality is strongly promoted.

Language and gender: "conquering" speech

As we know, "public power creates and reinforces private power", and those who have public power "thereby have power to make language and make definitions" (LAKOFF 1990: 199). It means that men have had power to control language use, to create the norm and exclude women from the norm.

In view of this fact, I would like to emphasize that most of gender inequalities are reproduced in language and by language; at the same time, we should not forget the role of the growing or even crucial role of images in creating and fortifying gender inequalities. Language and visual representations can be powerful means for keeping women in their place, but they can also be a powerful means for subversive changes.

First of all, the very word *gender* is often regarded in Bosnia and Herzegovina, especially by men but also by some women, as "suspicious" or imposed on them. If used in English, for some social actors and individuals it suggests something imported, even colonial. The Bosnian adaptation of the word gender as *džender* has even worse reception, and it is often laughed at. The best solution, though far from perfect, is the translation as *rod* – similarly, gender studies are translated as *rodne studije*. This adjective has caused some misogynous linguists to make puns and offensive jokes, interpreting falsely *rodni* as related to *rođenje, porod, porodiljski, ginekološki*. It is quite obvious that any word would be "problematic" for those linguists because of the concept itself.

Traditional linguists and sociolinguists, especially male linguists, are still more concerned with emphasizing differences between standard Bosnian, Croatian and Serbian languages than with investigating or changing unequal power relations in language, especially those concerning gender. In order to be accepted by their traditional male colleagues, some women linguists in BiH deny any relevance of language – gender relations. By accepting their male colleagues' position, they attempt to become "one of them", to become part of the "brotherhood of linguists".

It is clear that doing gender implies an attempt at empowering women. When applied to language, it means introducing changes into language about women and language that women use themselves. "It has long become clear that the very right to speak and be heard is the key for understanding the position of women's Otherness in culture" (KATNIĆ-BAKARŠIĆ 2009: 84). One of the most important tasks for women in Bosnia is therefore "conquering speech" (KATNIĆ-BAKARŠIĆ 2004). By this I do not mean only introducing gender sensible language in public and private communication, but also adopting pragmatic features of language that are traditionally related to power. I strongly believe that some women's attempt at adopting masculine power-style is not the right way of empowerment – it is just another form of losing women's own voice. The real goal is probably utopian – it means finding *third places* in this regard as well – developing language where both men and women feel comfortable, without domination or inequality.

In her inspiring book entitled *The Mind Has No Sex? Women in the Origins of Modern Science,* Londa SCHIEBINGER (1989) demonstrates that, in earlier periods of history, women were used as muses or as allegories of science, but they had no access to the 'fraternity' of science. It seems to me that remains of this "fraternity" are still present in contemporary BiH academia. First of all, according to my own experience and experience of my female colleagues, as well as according to my investigations, at university meetings in Bosnia women speak less than their male colleagues, they are interrupted more often, and their contributions are perceived as less important. Men are more easily promoted, whereas women, even these with internationally relevant results, especially when they are relatively young, often face obstacles in that aspect. There is an interesting new example in the Sarajevo Canton, where the new minister of science has introduced the so-called *Scientific council* without a single woman and there has been no public reaction so far.

Forms of address can also be regarded as a test for gender relations in society. It is still not rare that, in the academic or public sphere in general, women with titles are referred to as *gospođa* or *gospođica* (Mrs. or Miss), while their male colleagues are always referred to as *professor* or *doktor* (professor, PhD). It often happens at book launches, even at faculty meetings. Actually, it can be argued that in Bosnia too "the masculine and hierarchical style" of the university, seems "resistant to significant change" (LAKOFF 1990: 209), even though the number of female full professors or associate professors has increased (unlike the number of female deans or vice-deans of the faculties).

However, there are some slight changes in this respect: language awareness has become more widespread. The forms of address have gradually begun to shift towards linguistic gender equality at least in the public sphere, in some media and in the academic world. Women are often referred to as *profesorica, doktorica, voditeljica studija,* etc., even though the legislation still does not specify that usage. The shift can be documented by the example from the media referring to the American State Secretary: while Madelaine Albright was always referred to as *državni sekretar,* Hillary Clinton is as a rule *državna sekretarica* or *državna tajnica*. Some research studies have also shown a more positive attitude towards introducing parallel male and female forms of professions or titles, especially among younger population (ŠEHOVIĆ 2003). At the same time, it is still often regarded as "normal" linguistic behaviour to make fun of gender-neutral forms or address women as "ladies" or "girls" even at meetings or in other official situations, not to mention restaurants or shops.

In some parts of Bosnia and Herzegovina there still exists a way of addressing women in informal situations by the first name of their husband to which a possessive suffix is added: e.g. *Mujinica, Hadžemovica*. Even the famous *Hasanaginica* in the ballad of the same title does not have her own name – we know her only by the name of her husband (KATNIĆ-BAKARŠIĆ 2004: 96–97). This patriarchal and nowadays rather archaic form of address corresponds with forms such as *Mrs. John Smith*: in both cases women are denied the right to their own name, which can be read as denying their right to any identity apart from their identity as women.

Gender and the media

The media in Bosnia and Herzegovina strongly show or even create gender inequalities; they "mirror, represent and ultimately reify stereotypical gender roles and identities defined by conservative patriarchal ideology" (JUSIĆ 2006: 7). A very important book related to this issue is the collection of papers by authors from different countries *Stereotyping: Representation of Women in Print Media in South East Europe* (edited by Nirman MORANJAK-BAMBURAĆ, Tarik JUSIĆ and Ajla ISANOVIĆ 2006). In this book, which is another example of building bridges in the Balkans and South East Europe, the Bosnian authors have showed in their articles that dailies in BiH exclude women as actors, "stressing the masculine model of political, as well as social behaviour" (MAJSTOROVIĆ/ TURJAČANIN 2006: 84). The media represent women in stereo-typed roles – on the one hand, as mothers, wives/housewives, especially as victims, and on the other hand, as models, show business figures/starlets. In many articles "the role of victim was presupposed and inherent to the very notion of woman" (MAJSTOROVIĆ/ TURJAČANIN 2006: 97). The visual representation of women in the media and especially in advertising even more obviously shows stereotyping, representing women in passive roles or as objects of (male) desire and strongly promoting gender inequalities.[1]

---

[1] Bosnian women artists have tried to fight this representation in provocative and subversive art – e.g. Šejla Kamerić's poster *Bosnian Girl* has provoked many heated discussions (SIMMONS 2010: 25).

Gender and art: overcoming stereotypes

So far I have showed gender inequalities in various spheres of the troubled BiH society. However, there is a sphere where women have succeeded in finding *third places* – this sphere is art. Women artists in Bosnia and Herzegovina have one of the crucial roles in overcoming gender stereotypes, promoting gender equalities and empowerment of women in public spheres. Although in constant struggle for the right to be heard and become visible, even facing many obstacles from mostly male power elites in their respective arts or in society in general, women writers, filmmakers, artist and arts administrators "have entered public life" and have redirected "the public gaze onto the issues and people who have been relegated to the margins" (SIMMONS 2005: 38).

Women poets, such as Ferida Duraković, Adisa Bašić and Ajla Terzić move *beyond stereotypes* in the poetic language. Before them, Bisera Alikadić did the same in her erotic poetry and her erotic novel *Larva* [Larvae], simultaneously producing and *learning* how to speak about the erotic and *learning* how to produce the language of female desire and joy (KATNIĆ-BAKARŠIĆ 2009). A milestone in new poetic language is Ferida Duraković's poem entitled *Oleni, djevojčici bez ikoga, 2004. Tužbalica* [To Olena, a Girl All Alone, 2004. Lament], dedicated to Olena Popik, a young woman from the Ukraine who worked as a prostitute and died of AIDS in Bosnia and Herzegovina. Duraković introduces a new language into the poetry: "Frequent repetition of words like *men, transition, prostitution, trafficking in women, Christianity, Islam, Judaism, mother, sister, daughter* and some other of the same semantic field, combined in a terrific, ebullient rhythm, is in fact a cry of helpless despair, but also a cry of resistance, an expression of refusal to accede to this helplessness: as if the poet tells us that if we speak out, we are no longer the passive observer" (KATNIĆ-BAKARŠIĆ 2009: 86). At the same time, aware of the position she is writing from – from the position of the Other in two ways, for it is both female and Bosnian –

> in her series entitled *Osjećam se krivom* ["I Feel Guilty"], the poet expresses a typical, almost stereotypical, female guilt ("Umjesto da muški solidno i solidarno kriknem /J'accuse! / pa da se zatresu Državine i Historijine gaće/ Ja se onako ženski osjećam krivom, a državi se/ fućka/ što ja to tako privatno i bez javnog procesa...") ["Instead of crying /J'accuse! / like a solid, solidary man / to make the State and the History wet their pants / I feel guilty, like a woman, and the state cares not one bit / for me and my act in private, with no public hearing..."]. The position of self-irony and irony, with a mild, even post-modern distance from oneself and the world where the tragedy of Srebrenica is still possible, shows that the poet is, in fact, running away from the

stereotype of *female guilt,* even when she seems to be producing it. (KATNIĆ-BAKARŠIĆ 2009: 86)

Adisa BAŠIĆ in her awarded book *Promotivni spot za moju domovinu* (2010) speaks with ironic detachment, but at the same time emotionally, about the opposition between personal and political, between the individual women's history and collective history of Bosnia (*Rađanje nacije* [The Birth of Nation]). Her poem *Govorim* [I speak] is her poetic credo and statement: aware of the women's silence, she speaks on behalf of all poor, wounded, oppressed women. If we accept that there is a split in Western feminist thinking "between those who prioritize issues of sexual identity and sexuality, and those who focus on economic conditions and politics" (HERMAN 1998: 278), then the poetry of Adisa Bašić shows that all these issues can co-exist, creating a powerful and complex statement.

Women filmmakers and directors have received international acclaim for their films (Jasmila Žbanić for the film *Grbavica,* Aida Begić and Elma Tataragić for the film *Snijeg*). These films show all the complexity of women's life in the post-war Bosnian society. Jasmila Žbanić treated wartime rape motivated by ethnic hatred in *Grbavica*, thus breaking the silence still surrounding victims of war-rape and their children (SIMMONS 2010: 38) Aida Begić and Elma Tataragić show rural women war-survivors without men, taking their fate in their own hands and changing their role from victims and objects to subjects. This form of engaged art has significantly contributed to moving beyond stereotypes and transforming women's identities in Bosnia from passive to active ones.

Doing gender: dilemmas and challenges

Women in Bosnia and Herzegovina share many common problems and challenges; however, the shape of their lives depends on many factors: their social status, their profession, their beliefs, their marital status... As I have already pointed out, the "cloud of ethnic identity" overshadows gender identity and the status of women as the Other in BiH society.

The dilemma from the title of this paper – doing gender between theory and reality – sometimes becomes additionally complicated by some controversies of so-called "Western feminist discourses". They sometimes create their own stereotypes and participate in producing the First World – Third World differences, and are often seen "as highly detrimental to others". It means that white, Western female self-presentations "become the norms that define 'third world women'" (HERMAN 1998: 277; see also MAJSTOROVIĆ/ TURJAČANIN 2006: 85). Women in Bosnia and Herzegovina, especially Muslim women, sometimes see this as yet another form of oppression or colonialism, because they do not want to be automatically defined as religious, or as "the veiled women" (read *patriarchal, oppressed, backward*). As long as gender theory in Bosnia and Herzegovina avoids the trap of these simplifications and acknowledges the women's right to their own path to empowerment taking into account different contexts of their lives (cultural, ethnic or religious), it can give a valuable contribution to gender equality and women's role as social actors, not passive objects.

The reality of gender relations in Bosnia and Herzegovina is rather complex: there are some good examples of raising gender equality and gender awareness, crossing borders and moving beyond stereotypes; at the same time, there are still areas of life where complete ignorance of these issues prevails. Not all female children in some rural areas have access to education; moreover, it can be argued that the situation is worse than in the former socialist Yugoslavia. There are still cases of domestic violence and violence in other spheres of society against women, as well as many other unsolved problems. The most important task is combining the development of theoretical approach as well as work in practice, in the society, among different groups of women. I strongly believe that "it is time to transform both science and society so that power and privilege no longer follow gender lines" (SCHIEBINGER 1989: 277).

Sources

ALIKADIC, BISERA (2002): Ludi kamen. Zenica.
BAŠIĆ, ADISA (2010): Promotivni spot za moju domovinu (skice). Sarajevo.
DURAKOVIĆ, FERIDA (2007): Locus minoris. Sklonost Bosni kao melanholiji. Sarajevo.

References

BABIĆ-AVDISPAHIĆ, JASMINKA/ JASNA BAKŠIĆ-MUFTIĆ/ MARINA KATNIĆ-BAKARŠIĆ/ NIRMAN MORANJAK-BAMBURAĆ (eds.) (2004): Izazovi feminizma. In: Forum Bosnae 26. Sarajevo.
HERMAN, VIMALA (1998): Gender and language. In: Herman, Vimala: Dramatic Discourse. Dialogue as interaction in plays. London/New York. 245–305.
JUSIĆ, TARIK (2007): Predgovor. In: Moranjak-Bamburać, Nirman/ Tarik Jusić/ Adla Isanović (eds.): Stereotipizacija. Predstavljanje žena u štampanim medijima u jugoistočnoj Evropi. Sarajevo. 13–14.
KATNIĆ-BAKARŠIĆ, MARINA (2004): Jezik i (de)konstrukcija roda. In: Babić-Avdispahić, Jasminka/ Jasna Bakšić-Mufić/ Marina Katnić-Bakaršić/ Nirman

Moranjak-Bamburać (eds.): Izazovi feminizma. Forum Bosnae 26. Sarajevo. 69–116.

KATNIĆ-BAKARŠIĆ, MARINA (2009): Beyond Stereotypes. Representation of Women in Bosnian-Herzegovinian Literature. In: Jereb, Elza (ed.): 41. Mednarodno srečanje pisateljev, Bled, 25.03.–29.03.2009. Ljubljana. 84–88.

LAKOFF, ROBIN T. (1990): Talking Power. The Politics of Language in Our Lives. New York.

MAJSTOROVIĆ, DANIJELA/ VLADIMIR TURJAČANIN (2006): The Representation of Women in Bosnian-Herzegovinian Dailies. Gender and Ethnic Separations in Society. In: Moranjak-Bamburać, Nirman/ Tarik Jusić/ Adla Isanović (eds.): Stereotyping. Representation of Women in Print Media in South East Europe. Sarajevo. 81–110.

MORANJAK-BAMBURAĆ, NIRMAN (2006): The Unbearable Lightness of Stereotypes. In: Moranjak-Bamburać, Nirman/ Tarik Jusić/ Adla Isanović (eds.): Stereotyping: Representation of Women in Print Media in South East Europe. Sarajevo. 9–41.

SIMMONS, CYNTHIA (2010): Women Engaged/Engaged Art in Postwar Bosnia. Reconciliation, Recovery, and Civil Society. Pittsburgh.

SCHIEBINGER, LONDA (1989): The Mind Has No Sex? Women in the Origins of Modern Science. Cambridge, Massachusetts/London.

ŠEHOVIĆ, AMELA (2003): Upotreba mocionih sufiksa (u nomina agentis et professionis) u savremenom razgovornom bosanskom jeziku. Pismo 1/1. Sarajevo. 73–92.

VAN DIJK, TEUN A. (2003): The Discourse-Knowledge Interface. In: Weiss, Gilbert/ Ruth Wodak (eds.): Critical Discourse Analysis. Theory and Interdisciplinarity. Hampshire/New York. 85–109.

European Union and Western Balkans: What Prospect for Gender Equality?

Andrea Spehar

Introduction

The European Union has developed into an important actor in the field of gender equality. Beginning with the demand of equal pay for men and women, the principle of equality is now being integrated into all community policies and activities through the framework of gender mainstreaming. Large bodies of European legislative texts are also dedicated to gender equality. This is mainly made up of various treaty provisions and directives concerning access to employment, equal pay, maternity protection, parental leave, social security and occupational social security, the burden of proof in discrimination cases and self-employment. The case-law of the European Court of Justice is another key element. With good reason the EU can be defined as a gender equality actor growing in importance as it deepens its powers through a wider range of gender policy domains, enlarges the number of member countries, and has an increasingly powerful presence in world politics.[1] With regard to this, it is nonetheless important to ask whether the EU is an actor powerful enough to tackle the broader structural and institutional aspects of gender inequalities in different countries and regions.

In this article I provide empirical evidence drawn from two Western Balkan countries, Croatia and FYR Macedonia, in order to explore the effectiveness of the EU gender strategy in more detail: What are the benefits and limitations of EU gender equality policy making in the Western Balkans? While the Croatian and Macedonian EU accession processes have been beneficial for the introduction of new gender legislation and institutional mechanisms for the advancement of gender equality, the EU gender strategy in Croatia and Macedonia has also shown serious limits. Among these – and perhaps the most fundamental – is the strong contrast between stated goals and their actual implementation. Poor implementation is directly related to a lack of awareness among legislators and bureaucrats of the gender equality laws and how to implement them. Beneath a surface of legal guarantees, there are also informal social mechanisms that prevent women from utilising their rights effectively. Among the mechanisms that reduce the effectiveness of given rights in Croatia and Macedonia, political

---

[1] WALBY, SYLVIA (2004): The European Union and Gender Equality. Emergent Varieties of Gender Regime. In: Social Politics 11/1. 4–29.

and administrative corruption as well as political bigotry are the most detrimental ones, since both work against core principles of gender equality rights and democracy. I argue that unless profound institutional changes as well as changes in political culture take place in Croatia and Macedonia, the poor compliance with EU gender equality norms and policies will be hard to overcome.

European Union: a powerful gender equality actor?

Despite the wealth of research on the EU and gender, it is still unclear where the EU is heading with its policies on gender, and whether the policies actually help in bringing about more equality between women and men or whether the opposite will be true. An optimistic view of the EU's commitments and transformative potential in this policy area emphasizes the progressive deepening and widening of EU gender policy during the last few decades.[2] Today, the EU has the tools to be a polity that not only "affirms and shapes but also challenges gender power relations in several areas of its activities".[3] According to Sevil Sümer, "a basic evolution took place in EU gender policies from a focus on women's issues to an acknowledgment of gender relations and the need to transform the traditional gender contract".[4] The deepening of EU powers over gender policy in the Treaty of Amsterdam, the relatively broad interpretation of EU employment policy and the recognition of the interconnectedness of the economic with other domains within a gender regime are expected to lead to a situation where policies that affect employment will also affect many other gender relation areas.[5]

A more skeptical perspective, on the other hand, argues that despite the actions taken at the European level to eliminate discrimination, much remains to be done. Gender inequality across Europe remains elusive. Figures from

---

[2] BEVERIDGE, FIONA/ SAMANTHA VELLUTI (eds.) (2008): Gender and the Open Method of Coordination. Perspectives on Law, Governance and Equality in the EU. Dartmouth.
[3] KRONSELL, ANNICA (2005): Gender, Power and European Integration Theory. In: Journal of European Public Policy 12/6. 1022–1040, 1022.
[4] SÜMER, SEVIL (2009): European Gender Regimes and Policies. Comparative Perspectives. Farnham. 85.
[5] WALBY 2004. Three examples of such policy areas, where, by definition, the policy is under Member State competence but where EU concerns with employment policy have eventually led to gender policy innovations, are: 1. policies concerning taxation and the provision of benefits and welfare, 2. issues of fertility and sexuality; contraception, abortion, sexual preference, 3. Fighting on violence against women through policies for criminal justice and public.

2009 show that across Europe, women earn on average 17.4 % less than men.[6] Although women's participation in the paid labor force is increasing, labor markets continue to be highly segregated, with women clustering in lower paid sectors. Moreover, the increased participation of women in the labor market is largely characterized by a high proportion of part-time work.[7] This reflects the fact that women remain primarily responsible for child care, care for the elderly, and the disabled. In addition, women are underrepresented in national parliaments and other decision-making bodies. Such inequalities persist despite a deep commitment at the EU level to the achievement of gender equality, as well as a sophisticated framework of anti-discrimination laws adopted across the EU member states. This situation is the result of several reasons, the principal one being that even though gender equality is protected by law, this remains premised on a traditional notion of the gender contract. Emanuela Lombardo, who has analysed the impact of EU gender policy on Spain, argues that EU gender policy is still trapped in the "Wollstonecraft dilemma", as it generates policies which always have some negative effect on women.[8] According to Lombardo, the main problem is that policy strategies still focus on tackling the symptoms instead of giving more attention to the causes of gender inequality, such as structural obstacles in the form of a patriarchal system.[9]

Equally, Ilona Ostner describes the results of the various Directives as a double-edged sword, meaning that the legislation did not abolish discrimination but instead only required "good reasons for discriminatory practices and a minimum-means test".[10] Social policies have flourished in the process of European integration only as far as they have fitted regulatory policies of negative integration in contrast to the redistributive ones of positive integration.[11] Therefore, policies which do not focus on the centrality of the gendered division of care work and the need to share family responsibilities ultimately end up becoming market-oriented policies that encourage flexible forms of employment.[12] The opportunities and limits embedded in EU gender equality

---

[6] EUROSTAT (ed.) (2010): Reconciliation between work, private and family life in the European Union.
[7] Ibid.
[8] LOMBARDO, EMANUELA (2003): EU Gender Policy. Trapped in the 'Wollstonecraft Dilemma'? In: The European Journal of Women's Studies 10/2. 159–180.
[9] Ibid.
[10] OSTNER, ILONA (2000): From Equal Pay to Equal Employability. Four Decades of European Gender Policies. In: Rossilli, Mariagrazia (ed.): Gender Policies in the European Union. New York. 28.
[11] Ibid.
[12] SÜMER 2009.

policies have also been evaluated at the member state level. Comparative Europeanization research offers explanations for differences in national adaptation to EU legislation and policies.[13] The effect and meaning of Europeanization differs from country to country as each one is different regarding its traditions, policies and institutions.[14]

When it comes to gender equality, a review of policy formation and policy outcomes over the past few decades indicates the disjuncture between commitments at the EU level and outcomes at the member state level regarding implementation of EU gender equality guidelines.[15] The enlargement process also brought to light the issue of the impact of the EU on gender policy development in Central and Eastern European (CEE) countries. According to several empirical studies there is a tendency that the CEE countries do not formulate gender policies for the sake of improving gender equality, but rather to gain access to different EU domains. As a consequence, the implementation of adopted EU gender legislation is slow and inconsistent.[16] In this article I will give more in-depth consideration to both the benefits and limitations of EU gender equality policy in two Western Balkan countries, Croatia and Macedonia. Croatia and Macedonia belong to a region where the implementation of democracy has faced long-term obstacles much greater than those encountered by those CEE countries which have already become EU members. By analysing gender equality development making in two Western Balkan countries, this study aims

---

[13] COWLES, MARIA/ JAMES CAPORASO/ THOMAS RISSE (eds.) (2001): Transforming Europe. Europeanization and Domestic Change. Ithaca/London.

[14] LIEBERT, ULRIKE (ed.) (2003): Gendering Europeanization. Brussels; SCHIMMELFENNIG, FRANK/ ULRICH SEDELMEIER (eds.) (2005): The Europeanization of Central and Eastern Europe. Ithaca; FALKNER, GERDA/ OLIVER TREIB (2008): Three worlds of Compliance or Four? The EU 15 compared to New Member States. In: Journal of Common Market Studies 46/2. 293–314.

[15] POLLACK, MARK A./ EMILIE M. HAFNER-BURTON (2000): Mainstreaming Gender in the European Union. In: Journal of European Public Policy 7/1. 432–456; LIEBERT 2003; FAGAN, COLETTE/ DAMIAN GRIMSHAW/ JILL RUBERY (2006): The Subordination of the Gender Equality Objective. The National Reform Programmes and 'Making Work Pay' policies. In: Industrial Relations Journal 37/6. 571–575.

[16] KAKUCS, NOÉMI/ ANDREA PETÖ (2008): The impact of EU accession on gender equality in Hungary. In: Roth, Silke (ed.): Gender politics in the expanding European Union. Mobilization, inclusion, exclusion. New York; REGULSKA, JOANNA/ MAGDA GRABOWSKA (2008): Will it make a difference? EU enlargement and women's public discourse in Poland. In: Roth, Silke (ed.): Gender politics in the expanding European Union. Mobilization, inclusion, exclusion. New York; GHODSEE, KRISTEN/ STAN LAVINIA/ ELAINE WEINER (2010): Introduction: Compliance Without Commitment? The EU's Gender Equality Agenda in the Central and Eastern Europe States. In: Women's Studies International Forum 33/1. 1–2.

to broaden our knowledge about the EU's possibilities and limitations in tackling gender inequality in potential member states.

European Union and Western Balkans "facade democracies"

Since the 1990s, the EU has been steadily involved in a complex process of the stabilization and progressive integration of the Western Balkans. Today, the term "Western Balkans" is used to refer to the countries of Albania, Bosnia and Herzegovina (BiH), Croatia, the Republic of Macedonia, Serbia, Montenegro and Kosovo. All Western Balkan countries are striving for European Union membership, and in 2003 the EU declared that the future of the Balkans is within the European Union.[17] The EU's Balkan policy has shifted from an agenda dominated by security issues to an agenda focused on the Western Balkans' EU accession prospects. However, the countries of the Western Balkans are said to have a different political culture from the other East European countries.[18] The countries in this region have serious political and security problems, including the existence of intolerance, pathological nationalism and xenophobia, underdeveloped democratic political culture and lacking the art of compromise.[19] Arguably, the Western Balkans represent the most difficult set of prospective accession countries so far encountered by the EU. Most of the newly founded states are weak; the rule of law is not yet established; privatization has been done haphazardly, thus adding to the criminalization of the economy and the whole society; and corruption is still very high.[20] Economic failure had a devastating effect on standards of living and health across the region, forcing millions of people who had hitherto enjoyed a secure income into outright poverty by the late 1990s. These circumstances make the position of all citizens, especially the more vulnerable ones, very uncertain. Women from Western Balkan countries who are living with these major difficulties also experienced extremely turbulent times during and after the disintegration of Yugoslavia with conflicts and wars lasting an entire decade. With regard to gender equality policy, we can assume that the countries of the Western

---

[17] Croatia and Macedonia hold the status of candidate countries. Albania, Bosnia and Herzegovina, Kosovo, Serbia, and Montenegro hold the status of potential candidate countries.
[18] BEBLER, ANTON (2008): The Western Balkans and the International Community. In: Avrasya Dosyası 14/1. 7–22.
[19] PRIDHAM, GEOFFREY (2008): Securing Fragile Democracies in the Balkans. The European Dimension. In: Romanian Journal of European Affairs 8/2. 56–70.
[20] UNITED NATIONS OFFICE ON DRUGS AND CRIME (2011): Corruption in the Western Balkans. Bribery as Experienced by the Population. Vienna.

Balkans represent a highly unfavourable political context for the EU as a gender equality promoter. It is also essential to add the complex heritage of gender equality policy making during the communist era. It is often claimed that gender equality was one of the major achievements of the Eastern European communist regimes. Constitutional regulations provided women and men with equal rights in political, economic and social life.[21] The Communist political party equality policies such as relatively high minimum wages, generous maternity leave and child care benefits supported women's participation in gainful employment.[22] However, much of the progress in the area of gender equality under communism remained ambiguous and contradictory. Some scholars claim that the communist experiment was nothing more than an instance of "forced emancipation" and that women's incorporation into public life was "insincere" because it was motivated by economic interests, rather than by gender equality concerns.[23] In spite of the heavily propagandized gender equality in the sphere of paid employment, the reality of the labor market was far from gender-neutral since the state socialist system did not manage to challenge gendered job segregation and wage gaps.[24] In addition, under communism, gender-neutral stipulations in judicial sectors (e.g. family laws) were completely absent. Fathers, for example, were not encouraged to share responsibilities for raising children and there was no official notion of paternity leave.[25] The lack of gender-neutral legislation as well as the lack of public gender approach contributed to the strong legacy of traditionalism in attitudes towards the family and gender roles. Furthermore, some central gender equality and women's rights issues, such as sexual harassment and domestic violence, were considered "private matters" exempted from state interventions and were completely absent from public debates.

In this article the assessment of the effectiveness of EU policies in the Western Balkans will be analysed through a two-country comparison between Croatia and Macedonia.

---

[21] FUNK, NANETTE/ MAGDA MUELLER (eds.) (1993): Gender and Politics and Post-Communism. Reflections from Eastern Europe and the Former Soviet Union. New York/London; GAL, SUSAN/ GAIL KLIGMAN (eds.) (2000): Reproducing Gender. Politics, Publics and Everyday Life After Socialism. Princeton.

[22] PACI, PIERELLA (2002): Gender in Transition. Washington D.C.

[23] ASHWIN, SARAH (2006): Adopting to Russia's New Labour Market. Gender and Employment Behaviour. New York.

[24] BRAINRED, ELIZABETS (1997): Women in Transition. Changes in Gender Wage Differentials in Eastern Europe and the Former Soviet Union. In: Industrial and Labour Relations Review 54/1. 138–163.

[25] PACI 2002.

Benefits of the EU's gender equality strategy in the Western Balkans

The research conducted in this article identifies three levels of impact where Croatian and Macedonian EU accession processes have been beneficial for gender equality development in the two countries: 1. The introduction of new gender legislation, 2. the introduction of institutional mechanisms for the advancement of gender equality, 3. strengthening women's movements' legitimacy and policy influence. The issue of gender equality, being a fundamental principle of the European Union, represented an important segment of EU conditionality which required several changes in the Croatian and Macedonian laws relating in particular to labor relations and domestic violence. In Macedonia, we can even notice a positive impact of the EU *Gender Task Force of the Stability Pact*[26] on the Macedonian Electoral Law from 2002 which determines that every third place on the electoral lists for Parliament should be reserved for the less represented sex.[27] Today, 32.5% of Macedonian parliamentarians are women, which is the highest percentage in the CEE region[28], while the representation of women in the Croatian parliament is 23.5%[29].

---

[26] Since its establishment in July 1999, the Gender Task Force has been building bridges within the SEE Region as well as between the EU and the SEE Region. By targeting SEE parliaments, governments, political parties, NGO's trade unions, the GTF has been able to create a strong institutional basis for eliminating gender inequalities. The objective is improved SEE Women's active citizenship and political participation through empowerment, strategic action and capacity building (for more information see http://www.gtf.hr/).

[27] A vigorous women's NGO campaign to introduce quotas in the election law focused on political party leaders and was strengthened by the participation of women within Macedonian political parties. The efforts of the campaign bore fruit when the election law was passed by parliament with very little opposition. The law was approved by Parliament, governed by a conservative majority, on 25 June, 2002.

[28] After the first democratic elections in the beginning of the 1990s there were only 5.8 % of female representatives in the Croatian Parliament and 4.2 % female representatives in the Macedonian parliament.

[29] The advocacy of affirmative action for the political representation of women has been strongly put forward during the spring of 1999 by the Ad-hoc women's coalition, a group consisting of 28 different NGOs, political parties and female politicians. This renewed activity was linked to the (then) upcoming parliamentary elections in Croatia. The Ad-hoc coalition was asking for a minimum 40% quota of women on the party tickets for this election and for women to be placed on the lists in such a way that they would in fact enter the parliament if they should be supported. The Women's Ad-hoc Coalition demanded from parties to include women on their candidate lists proportionally and to introduce 40% women's quota into the Election Law (which was not accepted) as a temporary measure of positive discrimination to achieve gender equality in political representation. The Coalition also organized training programs for women of all parties on matters such as speaking in public, running campaigns and lobbying. Some scholars

As part of the EU membership process, the Croatian and Macedonian governments have also developed and set up national machineries for the advancement of gender equality. In Croatia, the *Parliamentary Gender Equality Committee* has been operating since 2000, the *Gender Equality Ombudsperson* since 2003, and the *Government Office for Gender Equality* since 2004. In Macedonia, the *Unit for Gender Equality* was set up by the government in 1997 within the frame of the Ministry of Labour and Social Policy (MLSP), with the purpose to influence the advancement of women's positions in conformity with international documents. Ten *Commissions on Gender Equality* within the ten Local Municipal Councils in Macedonia were established in 2000. In 2003 the *Women's MP Club* was formed, which works for the promotion of gender equality in general and for the harmonization with EU gender equality standards, as well as representing a service for elected women in the Parliament.

There are several signs of a positive impact of the EU on the development of the women's organizations in both countries. Funding support for women's organizations and for non-governmental organizations working to achieve gender equality is an important element in the EU strategy to achieve greater gender equality. Women's organizations from Croatia and Macedonia actively participate in the debate addressing the impact on women of EU accession and, to a certain extent, the future of Europe. For example, *Croatian women's network* and *Macedonian women's lobby* are members of the European women's lobby. Women's transnational advocacy networks in Europe are a source of both exchanges of knowledge and 'good practice' as well as moral support that arises from being part of a network.

Limitations of the EU's gender equality strategy in the Western Balkans

However, the EU gender policy strategy in Croatia and Macedonia has also encountered serious limits. In spite of the previously mentioned achievements, *de facto* gender equality is far from being realized. In both countries, the governments give priority to the managing of the economic and political situation, with gender issues being a much lower priority. Laws guaranteeing equal opportunities for women, in line with European standards and norms, have been adopted in both countries. However, the level of implementation of legislative measures is perceived as very low and women in both countries

---

identify women's organizations and their activities as a primary reason for the dramatic increase in women's parliamentary representation from 8 % in 1996 to 20% in 2000.

continue to face disparities in terms of jobs, wages and political representation.[30] The legal framework regarding gender equality is in place, but on the other hand, gender equality laws and policy frameworks do not have any substantial effect on the daily lives of citizens. In Croatia and Macedonia, as in most European countries, women constitute the majority of the unemployed. Among the employed, they dominate in lower-income professions such as care work, the textile industry, trade services, education, etc. Women are generally paid less than men for the same type of work, and are faced with the "glass ceiling" syndrome.[31] For example, a recent labor market assessment conducted in Macedonia by the World Bank indicates that about 83% of the gender gap in remuneration in the country is unexplained, thus pointing to discrimination against female workers.[32] Nearly 90% of employees in the textile industry, which belongs to the less-paid industries, are women. According to data from 2006, there was not a single activity where the average pay of women was higher than that of men.[33]

Besides persisting gender inequalities in Croatian and Macedonian societies, there is also other proof of poor implementation related to the EU gender directives and recommendations. Although both countries have adopted special gender equality legislation, there are still very few legal cases regarding any aspects of gender discrimination. For example, in 2009 the Macedonian Ombudsman office received only one claim based on discrimination on the grounds of sex in 2009 (European Commission 2010). This indicates, among other things, the lack of any citizen awareness about the possibilities of demanding protection and achieving their rights in the sphere of gender equality, work and employment as well as protection from domestic violence. Women NGOs in Croatia claim that many women who are subjected to rape or other forms of sexual violence abandon the idea of pressing charges for fear of social stigma or because they feel that the police, health, and judicial authorities lack experience in dealing with such cases. These NGOs also criticize some

---

[30] See for example the following national reports on gender equality: CEDAW/C/MKD/Q/1-3, Macedonia; CEDAW Shadow Report 2005, Macedonia; European Commission 2007, 2008, Macedonia; CEDAW/C/CRO/CC/2-3, Croatia; European Commission 2006, Croatia.

[31] BARKOVIC, IVANA/ MARIO VINKOVIC (2008): Gender Inequality in the Croatian Labour Market – Legal and Economic Aspects. Osijek; APOSTOLOVA, BILJANA (2010): Gender Wage Gap in Western Balkans Countries. Paper prepared for presentation at the World Bank International Conference on Poverty and Social Inclusion in the Western Balkans. Brussels.

[32] ANGEL-URDINOLA, DIEGO F. (2008): Can the Introduction of a Minimum Wage in FYR Macedonia Decrease the Gender Wage Gap? SP Discussion Paper No. 0837. Washington D.C.

[33] Ibid.

courts for passing sentences that are too lenient.[34] The problem of insufficient institutional capacity of institutions and organizations responsible for the protection and promotion of gender equality should be regarded as one of the key barriers to any serious implementation of the goal of equal pay between men and women. There are no systematic, comprehensive training programs to ensure appropriate practical implementation of the theoretical concepts by the relevant public administration. For example, an analysis of the 120 collective agreements on the Croatian labor market has shown that less than 10% of the analysed agreements include any reference to the principle of equal pay between men and women.[35] What is more, almost all of those agreements merely copied the equal pay provisions from the Labor Act. Less than 2% of the analysed agreements included certain special gender equality measures, but none was related to the issue of unequal pay. In an interview conducted for the purposes of this country report, officials of the Union of Autonomous Trade Unions of Croatia (UATUC) confirmed that the problem of gender inequality is rarely an issue of negotiations in the collective bargaining involving their association's members. As a general remark, it can be stated that the policy developments in both countries are very contradictory. On the one hand, there is formal acceptance of very advanced policies, legal changes and projects which should have an impact on the laws and institutions. Yet, these activities usually end in action plans, reports and/or conclusions which are not implemented; hence, they do not produce any actual change.

Bridging the poor compliance with EU gender equality norms and policies?

Over the last fifteen years, Croatia and Macedonia have made substantial progress in adopting new legislation and policies aimed at ensuring greater gender equality in different spheres of social life. However, Croatian and Macedonian political leadership still need to demonstrate that they respect the EU's and women's organizations' demands for gender equality and democratic institutions. The implementation of the adopted legislation in Croatia and Macedonia is slow and inconsistent. That is one of the main problems raised in examining the coherence of the EU's gender equality approaches to the Western Balkans. This is also where 'gender policy fatigue' within the EU

---

[34] B.A.B.E. (2003): Complaints on the Final Draft of the Law on Gender Equality. Zagreb.
[35] The analysis was conducted by the Croatian Office of the Ombudswoman for Gender Equality and it was published in April 2010.

meets 'accession fatigue' in the Balkans. Parallels can be drawn to similar developments in other CEE countries[36] and some of the older member states.[37]

The political elites in the region very often use verbal commitments to EU accession as a smokescreen for business as usual. Poor implementation is directly related to lack of awareness of the laws and how to implement them by both duty bearers and rights holders. Poor implementation is also symptomatic of deeply ingrained negative attitudes and gender stereotypes, which cannot be uprooted through legislation alone. The lack of litigation from below, a lack of support by governments, weak equal treatment bodies, shortcomings in the judiciary; these shortcomings lead to the fact that a lot of the transposed legislation has remained 'dead letters'. The public neglect of gender issues during the transition period in Croatia and Macedonia may be considered as one of the elements that has represented an aspect of continuity with the previous, communist system. Even back then, gender equality was important in declarative terms, but in practice it was neglected or subordinated to other policy areas considered to be of more imminent political importance.

While poor implementation can primarily be attributed to the lack of good governance in the Western Balkans, the nature of the EU strategy itself is misleading because it does not recognize the distinction between "equality of rights" and "equality of results". The fact that women and men are equal in their rights does not mean that they will achieve the same results. EU gender equality policy is confined within the limits of liberal individualism, doing little to tackle the broader structural aspects of gender inequality in different spheres of social, economic and political life. Specifically, the social dimension of ongoing changes in candidate countries needs to receive greater attention by the EU and the national political actors including the women's movement. Many women in Western Balkan countries may be better served by an emphasis on adequate housing, decent working conditions, health care, and child- and elderly care. To women whose lives are shaped by differences in class or race, gender-neutral policies may be low priorities if not meaningless symbols. While the EU and other international actors offer general norms and policies in the area of gender equality and provide basic frameworks, gender politics and policies should more frequently be adapted to specific local problems. The rule of law and openness of elites to potentially underprivileged groups, such as women, are essential to the effectiveness of given gender equality rights. However, the presence of legal guarantees for gender equality does not automatically mean that these rights work in practice. Formal democracies, such

---

[36] GHODSEE/ LAVINIA/ WEINER 2010.
[37] LOMBARDO 2003; FAGAN/ GRIMSHAW/ RUBERY 2006.

as Croatia and Macedonia, are not necessarily equal to effective democracies in which people face no social or legal barriers that prevent them from exerting their rights. Beneath a surface of legal guarantees, there are informal social mechanisms that hinder women in practicing their gender equality rights effectively. Among the mechanisms that reduce the effectiveness of given rights in Croatia and Macedonia, political and administrative corruption as well as political bigotry are the most detrimental features, since both work against core principles of human rights and democracy. Elite corruption, on the one hand, violates the rule of law and effective implementation; political bigotry, on the other hand, undermines the genuine commitment to the principle of equality of rights. Whether democracy is effective or not does not automatically follow from the institutionalization of rights. It depends on the features of a society's political elites and bureaucrats: their sensitivity to people's rights and their openness to underprivileged groups, among which women form the potentially largest one, accounting for at least half of the population in any society. Further institutional changes with regard to both legislation and political culture must take place in Croatia and Macedonia before overcoming the poor compliance with EU gender equality norms and policies will be possible. To achieve de facto equality it is necessary to invest in additional efforts in order to attain equal economic independence and prosperity between men and women, to reach a balance between work and private life, to promote equal representation in the decision-making process, to abolish gender-based violence and trafficking in human beings, and to eliminate gender stereotypes in various social areas.

Prostitution as a Profession – Searching for Answers between the Headlines

Mario Vinković

1 Introductory notes

Prostitution is a multidimensional and widespread problem that is legally treated in different ways in the national systems in Europe.[1] The complex nature of the phenomenon of prostitution has lately shifted the focus of research and the scientific approach from discussions of criminal and/or misdemeanour offence treatment of prostitutes to issues referring to discrimination, protection of human rights, economic and social implications of prostitution and the social integration of victims. Although in certain legal systems prostitution has been legalised, one should bear in mind that minors and trafficking victims are very often involved as sex service providers. In 2008, the US Department of State published that approximately 800,000 people a year are trafficked across national borders, 80% of the victims being women and girls, and that the majority of victims are females trafficked into commercial sexual exploitation.[2] The given data clearly point out the need for careful consideration of the legal treatment of prostitution and raise a question as to whether voluntary prostitution of adult persons can be treated as a profession. It is not easy at all to separate prostitution and observe it independently in relation to problems of trafficking in women and children, but also, in spite of the existing opinions and interpretations, to consider it as a mere economic activity or a form of providing services.

In this paper, we try to focus on the problem of prostitution in Europe, primarily through the prism of considerations with respect to its legal and labour elements, discriminatory features and the need for protection of the human dignity of the individual. The focus of our interest is not placed on the issues

---

[1] The findings based upon a sample of 100 countries in the world indicate that in 50% of those countries prostitution is legal, in 40% it is illegal, and in 10% it is limitedly legal (e.g. it is punishable for a person paying for sexual services, but not for a prostitute, etc.). According to the same study, prostitution is legal in Austria, Belgium, Czech Republic, Denmark, Estonia, Finland, France, Germany, Greece, Hungary, Ireland, Italy, Latvia, Luxembourg, the Netherlands, Poland, Portugal, Slovakia, Switzerland, Turkey and the United Kingdom. It is illegal in Albania, Croatia, Lithuania, Malta, Romania, Slovenia, and it has limited legality in Bulgaria, Iceland, Norway, Spain and Sweden. See: http://prostitution.procon.org/view.resource.php?resourceID=000772, retrieved 20.2.2011.

[2] U.S. DEPARTMENT OF STATE (2008): Trafficking in Persons Report 2008. 7. http://www.state.gov/g/tip/rls/tiprpt/2008/, retrieved 20.2.2011.

2 Prostitution, social environment and treatment

pertaining to the criminal law's treatment, except in the segment that deals with sex service providers and their legal position.

It may be observed that the approaches to considerations on the problem of prostitution have been changing in the last several decades with respect to the perception of national legal systems and global movements. The regulation of prostitution under the aegis of preserving the public health and combating the spread of sexually transmitted diseases started in Europe during the reign of Napoleon III, although the existence of prostitution was documented in the early days of human civilisation. The first comprehensive studies of the history of prostitution, as well as social features of prostitution and the society of the 18th century, were conducted by Dr. William Sanger, whose major work *The History of Prostitution*[3] has been reissued many times before and after his death. As an inexhaustible source of information on the history of prostitution, the book offers an excellent insight into a difficult position of prostitutes in the United Kingdom in the 19th century. Girls at the age of 11 or older were involved in prostitution. Stricken by the loss of their parents and "natural protectors", they were brought to brothels, often escorted by persons of questionable moral values, sometimes directly from school.[4] They were forcefully retained in brothels, where they were deprived of the right to go as well as the right to free movement for two or three months, or until their jailors were convinced that they had adapted to a new life.[5] At that time, a constant trade in prostitution was carried on between London and Hamburg, London and Paris, and London and the country.[6] Poverty was a direct cause of prostitution that was frequently used for the purpose of corruption and as an integral part of a profligate way of living by users.[7] Prostitutes usually originated from broken families or their

---

[3] SANGER, WILLIAM W. (1910): The history of prostitution. Its extent, causes and effects throughout the world. New York. The book was published for the first time in 1858 in New York by Harpers & Brothers, and during several decades it was reissued by various American and European publishers. In this paper, we refer to the copy of the book published in 1910.
[4] Ibid.: 313–314.
[5] Ibid.
[6] Ibid.: 315.
[7] Ibid.: 324.

parents were deceased, most frequently they were illiterate or extremely poor, in their teens and early twenties.[8]

Summing data on the social environment and background of the 19th century prostitutes clearly indicates the fundamental causes of prostitution – poverty, abuse of a difficult material situation of unprotected, uneducated and unskilled girls and women, that were often forced into prostitution, that were human trafficking victims, kept in inhumane conditions corresponding to slavery and forced labour. Moreover, the majority of sources predominantly mentions female prostitutes, since obviously there were less male prostitutes in the total population observed. This has also probably resulted in numerous definitions of prostitution, in which the female element prevails and which refer to words like promiscuity, numerous sexual partners, pay, systematic sexual offences, etc.[9] Westmarland and Gangoli point out that there are many more expressions used to describe female prostitutes than male prostitutes and that based upon the terminology like *whores, prostituted women, prostitutes, women abused through prostitution, market women, ladies of the night, madams, Natashas, working girls* etc., the author's approach may be easily and quickly identified in any text dealing with prostitution.[10] Moreover, the language used by authors to describe women involved in prostitution often says more about the authors themselves than the title of the book or the paper in question.[11]

Normative approaches to the regulation of prostitution in the 20th century are marked by the myth that prostitutes are HIV carriers[12], that is, according to Hubbard, Matthews and Scoular, not sustainable in the European Union due to the perception of prostitution as a form of gendered violence.[13] The latter approach opposes to the approach of prostitute unions stating that prostitution is actually "legitimate sex work"[14]. Such attitude is supported by the *Sex Workers in Europe Manifesto*, which defines "sex work" as a sexual-economic activity which does

---

[8] BULLOUGH, VERN L./ BONNIE BULLOUGH (1987): Women and Prostitution. A Social History. Buffalo, New York. 232–291.
[9] Ibid.: xi-xiii.
[10] WESTMARLAND, NICOLE/ GEETANJALI GANGOLI (2006): Introduction. Approaches to prostitution. In: Westmarland, Nicole/ Geetanjali Gangoli (eds.): International Approaches to Prostitution – Law and Policy in Europe and Asia. Bristol. 1.
[11] Ibid.
[12] See KILVINGTON, JUDITH/ SOPHIE DAY/ HELEN WARD (2001): Prostitution Policy in Europe. A Time of Change? In: Feminist Review 67/1. 78–93.
[13] See HUBBARD, PHIL/ ROGER MATTHEWS/ JANE SCOULAR (2008): Regulating sex work in the EU. Prostitute women and the new spaces of exclusion. In: Gender, Place and Culture 15/2. 138.
[14] Ibid.

not imply anything about identity, value systems or the participation of sex workers in the society.[15]

2.1 United Kingdom

For a long time, the United Kingdom police has thought of prostitution as a low-level job not to be dealt with by "real police officers". Such ambivalent attitude rarely encouraged the role of the police with respect to the regulation of prostitution, since the police used to get involved in the regulation of prostitution only when driven by public pressure or political demands. Particular segments of British society believe that street prostitution has a negative impact on the quality of life of local residents in certain locations, particularly young females.[16] Hence the agencies formed to help prostitutes with their problems have grown in number. However, a neo-liberal approach offers social inclusion only to those prostitutes who exit prostitution and resume normal lifestyles, while it continues to exclude those prostitutes who remain involved in the said anti-social activities, exposing them thereby to further criminalisation and marginalisation.[17] Prostitution is not a crime in England and Wales, but the exchange of sexual services for money or other rewards is subject to some form of legal control, so that street prostitution is better viewed as a problem of "disorder rather than one of quasi-criminality".[18] In the last century, trying to keep prostitution away from a wealthy neighbourhood, most urban centres in the United Kingdom established "red light districts". In such a way, the provision of sexual services became spatially contained, more available to clients and supported by an informal deal between the police and the prostitutes on receiving less police attention while providing services in the designated area, far away from a respectable neighbourhood and political focus.[19]

Recent research of experts showing that the role of male demand for commercial sexual services perpetuates and increases the sex trafficking

---

[15] See SEX WORKERS IN EUROPE Manifesto, elaborated and endorsed by 120 sex workers from 26 countries at the European Conference on Sex Work, Human Rights, Labour and Migrations, 15–17 October 2005. Brussels. http://www.sexworkeurope.org/images/phocadownload/manbrussels2005.pdf, retrieved 15.2.2011.

[16] MATTHEWS, ROGER (2005): Policing Prostitution – Ten Years On. In: British Journal of Criminology 45/6. 880.

[17] SCOULAR, JANE/ MAGGIE O'NEILL (2007): Regulating Prostitution. Social Inclusion, Responsibilization and the Politics of Prostitution Reform. In: British Journal of Criminology 47/5. 765.

[18] MATTHEWS 2005: 881–882.

[19] Ibid.: 884.

industry[20] has *inter alia* caused parliamentary debates in England and Wales on the necessity of identification and differentiation between forced and unforced prostitution. Women who are involved in the world of prostitution and work in brothels are often victims of debt bondage and most frequently they are not citizens of the United Kingdom.[21] The interpretation of prostitution as an unacceptable form of gendered exploitation is thus important for future political debates on paying for sex as a strong wind at the back of further exploitation, child prostitution and trafficking in women and children.[22] In addition, it has to be borne in mind that a survey conducted in 2004 identified a very high proportion of street prostitutes addicted to drugs and alcohol whose addiction increased by their entrance into the world of prostitution.[23]

Matthews and O'Neill point out that the historical context of prostitution policy and legislative reforms in the United Kingdom has gone through the stages of regulationism, suppression and welfarism,[24] from Victorian England to the treatment of prostitutes in the 20th and 21st century.

2.2 France

Prostitution in France has a long history, but parliamentary debates on prostitution were intensified in the 1990s. Today they have entered a completely new phase – by a recent proposal offered by French lawmakers that would like to criminalise soliciting paid sex.[25] Although prostitution is not illegal in France, procuring and soliciting other people for paid sex are.[26] According to the proposal for legislation, such persons could be sentenced to six months in jail or a fine of €3,000. The authors point out that the proposed legal solutions would "reaffirm the principle of non-commercialisation of the human body" and bury the myth that prostitution is simply the oldest profession in the world once

---

[20] YEN, IRIS (2008): Of Vice and Men. A New Approach to Eradicating Sex Trafficking by Reducing Male Demand Through Educational Programs and Abolitionist Legislation. In: Journal of Criminal Law & Criminology 98/2. 655.
[21] MATTHEWS 2005: 891–892.
[22] HUBBARD/ MATTHEWS/ SCOULAR 2008: 145.
[23] MATTHEWS 2005: 890.
[24] MATTHEWS, ROGER/ MAGGIE O'NEILL (eds.) (2003): Prostitution (= International Library of Criminology, Criminal Justice and Penology). Aldershot. xvii; SCOULAR/ O'NEILL 2007: 765.
[25] See "Sex clients could be fined, jailed under proposed law". http://www.france24.com/en/20110414prostitutes-clients-sex-trade-jailed-fined-under-proposed-law-france-busquet%20-geoffrey#, retrieved 22.4.2011.
[26] Ibid.

and for all.²⁷ Moreover, the proposal would introduce a stricter regime than the one Sarkozy's government introduced in 2003 by provisions of the Domestic Security Act pursuant to which soliciting was upgraded from minor offence to serious offence.²⁸ The French prostitutes' union STRASS believe that such proposal would have a profoundly negative impact on thousands of women and men who work in the sex "trade", since it would not reduce prostitution but put some of the most vulnerable groups of sex workers under the complete control of pimps.²⁹ A deeper knowledge of French debates on prostitution implies discernible polarisation. Some positions define prostitution as a form of violence against women and an attack on their human dignity on the one hand, and there are those who believe that the worst thing is the stigma attached to prostitution as well as poor living and working conditions for those in prostitution on the other.³⁰ Allwood stresses that it is mainly abolitionists who dominate the discourse and represent a "heterogeneous coalition of Catholics, advocates of traditional family structures, many feminists and large sections of the left". According to French government estimates, as cited by some media, about 20,000 sex workers are currently operating in France, 80% of whom originate from countries outside France.³¹ Such data clearly indicate a close relationship between prostitution and illegal immigration, which coincides with data published by the United Nations some ten years ago. It was estimated then that in the European Union there were between 200,000 and 500,000 illegal sex workers, 2/3 of whom originate from Eastern Europe, and 1/3 from other developing countries.³² It may be assumed that the global crisis as well as political and economic transitions of the last decade have also contributed to an increase in that number.

The role of French feminists, who have had an important function in political debates and the perception of prostitution as a form of men's violence towards women,³³ is still important for the social treatment of prostitution in French society, politics and legislation. It is that perception which shifted the focus of attention by the 1994 Criminal Code provisions towards clients and opened up

---

[27] Ibid.
[28] See ALLWOOD, GILL (2006): Prostitution in France. In: Westmarland, Nicole/ Geetanjali Gangoli (eds.): International Approaches to Prostitution – Law and Policy in Europe and Asia. Bristol. 52.
[29] "Sex clients could be fined, jailed under proposed law".
[30] ALLWOOD 2006: 47.
[31] HUMPHREY, HELENA (2010): Is there a Paris street prostitution boom? http://www.english.rfi.fr/france/20100810-there-paris-street-prostitution-boom, retrieved 1.5.2011.
[32] UNITED NATIONS OFFICE FOR DRUG CONTROL AND CRIME PREVENTION (1999): Global Report on Crime and Justice.
[33] ALLWOOD 2006: 48.

space for their criminal liability, classifying sex with a prostitute under the age of 18 "that belongs to a vulnerable group" as a criminal act. Although that age limit was initially set to 15 receiving thereby justified criticism that it encourages prostitution of minors, raising the age limit to 18 caused contradictory interpretations by French feminist activists. Feminist abolitionists claim that such solution points out that men do not have the right to buy sex, whereas other feminist streams believe that in that way prostitution is actually pushed underground and social support for women involved in prostitution becomes impossible.[34] Allwood also reminds that due to opposing and antagonistic attitudes within and between feminist groups, abolitionists and prostitutes' rights advocates the debates on prostitution in France are paralysed. Thus women involved in prostitution will not be the centre of attention until the parties concerned and the academic community establish the corresponding dialogue.[35]

2.3 The Netherlands

The Netherlands is a country that deserves to be paid attention to in relation to the regulation of prostitution, not only because of the general perception of prostitution in the Netherlands, but also because of the existence of elements based upon which prostitution can be considered a profession. Prostitution in the Netherlands was not legal until recently, but the organisation of prostitution or managing a brothel were subject to severe criminal penalties. The provisions referring to the general ban on brothels were repealed by changes to the Dutch Penal Code in 2000 and 2002 and an additional regulation of the protection against sexual abuse of minors. The aforementioned legislative changes and legalisation enabled the exploitation of voluntary prostitution by persons of age and in possession of the required documents. However, at the same time a sharpening up of the penalisation of any unwanted form of prostitution has taken place,[36] i.e. an application of any form of coercion. This is obviously a continuation of the Dutch political concept of "full consent to exploitation of the self", that was promoted in the beginning of the 1990s.[37] In terms of administration, amendments to legislation enabled local authorities to administer brothel licensing and control conditions set forth in the Factories Inspectorate

---

[34] Ibid.: 59.
[35] Ibid.: 60.
[36] See DAALDER, ANNELIES L. (2007): Prostitution in the Netherlands since the lifting of the brothel ban. 10–12.
[37] See LOUIS, MARIE-VICTOIRE (1997): "Legalizing Pimping, Dutch Style". In: Le Monde Diplomatique (8.3.1997).

and Tax and Custom provisions,[38] but the police still plays the most important role when it comes to monitoring the licensed sector and control of labour and other inspectors.[39] In the beginning, municipal authorities mostly used to hold on to maximum quota for doing sex business, but in 2006 the quota system was abandoned, so that now the issuing of licences for location-bound prostitution businesses is unlimited. Such an approach does not offer a solution to the problem of providing sexual services in massage parlours, clubs and sauna clubs, assumed to be disguised non-location bound prostitution businesses.[40] The primary goal of the Dutch *tippelzones* as certain "working areas" was to protect not only public order, but also the safety of prostitutes who did not have to operate at isolated and unobservable locations.

Solutions of the given model in which numerous elements of labour relations with respect to prostitutes, i.e. the issuing of permits, residence documents, the existing self-employing scheme and paying for the possibility of doing such job[41] on the one hand, and sanctioning of any form of coerced prostitution on the other, have raised numerous questions. Can this regulation prevent and eradicate coercion, human trafficking, drug use and abuse, etc.? Can prostitution be globally actually perceived as a profession, a mere provision of services or an economic activity as any other? Before we try to answer these questions we should recall that the study carried out by Daalder, that is repeatedly referred to in this paper, arrived at an estimate of 1,270 licensed sex establishments throughout the Netherlands.[42] However, it is not easy to identify the total number of prostitutes, although in 1999 it was estimated that there were some 25,000 prostitutes in the Netherlands.[43] The Dutch regulatory model undoubtedly introduces the legal order and to a great extent it ensures a certain level of government control. Women involved in prostitution *prima facie* seem to be enjoying multiple protection, and their activity is recognised as a legitimate occupation. We should not neglect the advantages of health protection, violence prevention and attempts aimed at coercing women into unwanted activities and sexual services. However, can such legal approach encourage illegal immigration, market broadening, i.e. attempts of illegal markets to provide satisfaction of criminal needs of users searching for sex with children and minors, various forms of child pornography, and other criminal acts? As in the majority of other

---

[38] See HUBBARD/ MATTHEWS/ SCOULAR 2008: 142.
[39] DAALDER 2007: 10–12.
[40] Ibid.
[41] HUBBARD/ MATTHEWS/ SCOULAR 2008: 142.
[42] DAALDER 2007: 31.
[43] See RNW ENGLISH SECTION (2009): Prostitution in the Netherlands. http://www.rnw.nl/english/article/faq-prostitution-netherlands, retrieved 1.5.2011.

European countries, prostitutes in the Netherlands are not of Dutch origin (60%); most of them originate from Latin America and work in "window prostitution", and in addition to them, an increase has been observed lately of prostitutes who do not have work permits, since they come from Russia, Romania, Bulgaria and East European countries that fall under EEA.[44] Hence our considerations cannot but be focused on illegal immigration and problems referring to trafficking in women and children in this case as well.

2.4 Sweden

The Swedish model of combat against prostitution is conceptually extremely important for our debate, since, in our opinion, it inherited the principal legal foundations and logic necessary for the perception of prostitution in the EU. After long public debate, in 1999, the Swedish Parliament passed the Act Prohibiting the Purchase of Sexual Services, which criminalises only the buyers, i.e. the users of sexual services. The Swedish government justified its adoption by the attitude that a female (male) body cannot be sold or bought, since if there were no demand for the female (male) body, there would not exist the market in which it is offered and exploited.[45] In this way Sweden became the first country in the world that criminalises exclusively buyers of commercial sexual services and treats prostitution legally as a form of male, i.e. sexual, violence perpetrated against women and girls, which violates their integrity, dignity and human rights.[46] The Act was written in gender-neutral language and it represents an inevitable part of a comprehensive Swedish strategy for combating prostitution and human trafficking. Its adoption, i.e. criminalisation of buyers of services provided by prostitutes, originally came from the Swedish women's movement, starting from the hypothesis that prostitution is yet another patriarchal tool of oppression of women who are induced and kept in prostitution.[47] Since the fight against prostitution and trafficking in human beings has been a public

---

[44] DAALDER 2007: 16, 25.
[45] Cf. SVANSTRÖM, YVONNE (2006): Prostitution in Sweden. Debates and Policies 1980–2004. In: Westmarland, Nicole/ Geetanjali Gangoli (eds.): International Approaches to Prostitution – Law and Policy in Europe and Asia. Bristol. 67.
[46] See HUGHES, DONNA M. (2004): Best Practices to Address the Demand Side of Sex Trafficking. 24–25. http://www.uri.edu/artsci/wms/hughes/demand_sex_trafficking.pdf, retrieved 1.5.2011; See also HUGHES, DONNA M. (2005): Demand for Victims of Sex Trafficking. 1–65. http://www.uri.edu/artsci/wms/hughes/demand_for_victims.pdf, retrieved 1.5.2011.
[47] See EKBERG, GUNILLA (2004): The Swedish Law that Prohibits the Purchase of Sexual Services: Best Practices for Prevention of Prostitution and Trafficking in Human Beings. In: Violence Against Women 10/10. 1191.

and political priority in Sweden for a long time, passing the Act represents an essential part of efforts to create a contemporary and democratic Swedish society, where full gender equality is a legal norm that recognises true participation of women and men.[48] However, although there are claims that after the aforementioned Act came into force, the number of women involved in street prostitution has decreased,[49] Swedish social workers suggest that the Act has been selectively enforced in Stockholm, with the focus only on highly visible spaces of street prostitution.[50] By observing the social background of prostitutes, it can be noticed that the majority of prostitutes are drug addicts, a smaller number of them are homeless, some of them have mental and physical health problems as a result of some form of sexual violence they experienced earlier.[51] Due to the existing legislation and huge public support for the Act, Sweden is not considered a good market for trafficking in human beings,[52] but there has been an increase in the number of trafficked women in the neighbouring countries like Finland and Norway.[53]

Hughes believes that the Swedish model of decriminalisation of prostitutes is actually part of the abolitionist approach that should be best understood as a transition phase or part of the process of legalisation or abolition, but it is not an endpoint in itself.[54]

2.5 South-Eastern Europe (Bosnia and Herzegovina, Croatia, Serbia)

In contrast to previously analysed Northern and Western European countries, South Eastern Europe, i.e. the Balkans, is characterised by a somewhat different approach to prostitution. Prostitution in Croatia, Serbia and Bosnia and Herzegovina is legally regulated in different ways and it is mainly treated as a misdemeanour offence, i.e. in cases of procuring, solicitation and inveiglement it is treated as a criminal act. Penalties mostly affect women, but not buyers of sexual services, so that prostitutes are said to be double victims, i.e. they are victims of both sexual abuse and social stigmatisation and prosecution that again affects the unprotected, and not the ones who create the demand for sexual services.

In those countries there hasn't been much research on prostitution, and media attention, as with cases in Croatia, is mostly focused on prostitution during the

---

[48] Ibid.: 1188.
[49] Ibid.: 1193.
[50] HUBBARD/ MATTHEWS/ SCOULAR 2008: 147.
[51] SVANSTRÖM 2006: 81.
[52] HUGHES 2004: 26–27; YEN 2008: 679.
[53] YEN 2008: 680.
[54] HUGHES 2005: 38.

tourist season or when American and NATO ships enter Croatian ports. However, by using the example of Croatia we can notice sporadic proposals by certain unions and members of the Croatian Parliament referring to the need for legalisation of prostitution. But, due to an immense influence of the Catholic Church on Croatian society as a whole, such proposal is less likely to gain significant social and political support. Historically, prostitution in Croatia has been regulated in the capital city of Zagreb since 1899. The established legal regime allowed prostitution in brothels until their abolition in 1922, when people involved in prostitution obtained the status of "publicly tolerated prostitutes" and were obliged to register in a special inquest register, which was maintained by the police.[55] Since by the year 1922 the issue of prostitution was left to the local police, there has been a different legal treatment in Croatian urban areas. Prostitution was generally allowed in brothels, where living and "working" conditions were extremely poor, and prostitutes were physically and financially abused and socially stigmatized. The police used to force them to take medical examinations, stored their identity documents, and forbade them to visit theatres, restaurants and other public facilities and events[56]. The Venereal Diseases Act of 1934 prohibited prostitution throughout the entire territory of the then Kingdom of Yugoslavia. Under communist rule, prostitution was predominantly treated as an offense against public peace and order, which was generally tolerated, whereas criminal prosecution only referred to procuring and pimping.[57] Since the independence of the Republic of Croatia in the 1990s, prostitution has never been considered an important and current topic, although the discrepancy between reality and statistical indicators on criminal acts of mediation in prostitution was noticeable.[58] People involved in prostitution were prosecuted as misdemeanants, and recent attempts to introduce criminal sanctions for service users have not been accepted but directed to further parliamentary procedure. The final draft of the new Croatian Penal Code provides for imprisonment only for inveiglement, solicitation, recruiting and encouraging the provision of sexual services, including procuring a child.[59] Such approach insists on a conservative policy of punishing only the worst forms of sexual exploitation

---

[55] ZORKO, TOMISLAV (2006): Ženska prostitucija u Zagrebu između 1899. i 1934. godine. In: Časopis za suvremenu povijest 38/1. 223–241.
[56] Ibid.: 225–227.
[57] BAČIĆ, FRANJO/ ZVONIMIR ŠEPAROVIĆ (1989): Krivično pravo – Posebni dio. Zagreb. 157–159.
[58] KANDUČ, ZORAN/ VELINKA GROZDANIĆ (1998): Prostitucija (nepoželjna tema, kažnjiva radnja i stalna pojava). In: Zbornik Pravnog fakulteta Sveučilišta u Rijeci 19/1. 26.
[59] MINISTRY OF JUSTICE (2011): Criminal Code Bill, Articles 157 and 162.

and closing eyes to everyday practice[60] rather than punishing users of services, i.e. creators of the demand for sexual exploitation.

Prostitution in Serbia is characterised by a similar genesis and historical discourse as in Croatia. According to the Statute of prostitution in Novi Sad of 1893, it was allowed to open brothels in side streets where there were no churches and schools, and prostitutes could be only girls older than 16. They were obliged to report to authorities, undergo a medical examination and obtain a health booklet, which also had to include their photograph. Moreover, a note that they were involved in prostitution was entered in the genealogy book.[61] Prostitution was banned in 1934, and in the communist Yugoslavia, the legal treatment was the same as in Croatia. Today, prostitutes are treated as having committed a misdemeanour, criminal sanctions are provided for pimping and soliciting in prostitution[62], but there is a lack of any form of sanctions for service users. Serbian media and internet portals have recently recorded numerous cases related to street and elite prostitution, but also sexual exploitation of victims of trafficking in people and minors.[63] Recent articles have actualized the subject of elite prostitution, after the disclosure of similar chains in Croatia.[64] What has been noted at the level of some women's organisations is the commitment to use the term sex worker instead of a prostitute, as well as periodic proposals for legalisation of prostitution due to economic, hygienic and health reasons.

The causes of prostitution in Bosnia and Herzegovina lie in a disastrous economic situation, the desire for quick profits, consumerism mentality and

---

[60] A series of scandals related to the provision of sexual services and elite prostitution have recently hit Croatia, as evidenced by a series of newspaper articles, such as: "Djevojke sam vozio u skupe i ekskluzivne hotele u Zagrebu". In: Večernji list (30.7.2011); Interview with Ms Rada Borić "Ovo je skandal, ali imamo i veći!". In: Magazin (supplement to Glas Slavonije) (23–24 July 2011), etc.

[61] See paragraphs 1, 2, 3, 6, and 8 of the Statute of prostitution, Novi Sad, Emil Fuks et al., 1893 (reprinted by: Futura publikacije and Ženske studije i istraživanja, 2007).

[62] See Articles 183 and 184 of the Criminal Code of Serbia.

[63] LAZIĆ, MILOŠ Ž. (2011): Prostitucija u Srbiji: Trudnica nudi seks za 15 evra. http://www.kurir-info.rs/crna-hronika/prostitucija-u-srbiji-trudnica-nudi-seks-za-15-evra-69977.php, retrieved 20.7.2011; ĐORĐEVIĆ, K. (2009): Svaka peta prostitutka u Beogradu maloletna. http://www.politika.rs/rubrike/Hronika/Svaka-peta-prostitutka-u-Beogradu-maloletna.lt.html, retrieved 20.7.2011.

[64] KOSTANJŠAK, PETRA (2011): Elitna prostitucija premrežila cijelu regiju. http://www.vjesnik.hr/Article.aspx?ID=985D5902-C956-4644-8F42-11AA54834778, retrieved 20.7.2011; ŽIGIĆ, IVANA (2011): Visoka prostitucija: Orgije za elitu po celoj Srbiji. http://www.pressonline.rs/sr/vesti/vesti_dana/story/149995/Visoka+prostitucija%3A+Orgije+za+elitu+po+celoj+Srbiji.html, retrieved 20.7.2011.

numerous migrations conditioned by the war and postwar developments.[65] Prostitutes are often trafficked from Romania, Bulgaria, Ukraine and Moldova, and in addition to the local population, trafficking in women and children for sexual exploitation also involved peacekeepers.[66] Only incitement to prostitution is punishable[67], and more serious actions on the whole national territory were undertaken in 2005 and 2006 in order to process and sanction traffickers in women and children and organisers of prostitution, i.e. procuring and soliciting for the purpose of prostitution. A comprehensive study of prostitution in Bosnia and Herzegovina carried out in 2003 pointed out real problems and the prevalence of prostitution[68], but experts estimate that, despite proposals to legalise prostitution, we should take into account the fact that legalisation would make human trafficking easier.[69]

An analysis of the approach to the problem of prostitution in Northern, Western and South-Eastern European countries, as well as their legislative solutions and experiences, raise a serious debate on the possible acceptance of prostitution as a profession. The answer to this question will be given in the sequel.

3 Prostitution as a profession, economic activity or provision of services

Past debates suggest that there are four general approaches to the regulation of prostitution in Europe, as stressed by Hughes.[70] An abolitionist approach, that is present in Sweden, treats prostitution as an activity in which women and children involved in prostitution are actually a vulnerable group and victims protected by the system, whereas the men who buy sex are all criminalised. A prohibitionist approach defines prostitution as a criminal activity and provides for criminal penalties for all subjects involved, independently of whether they sell or buy sex. Under the regulationist approach, like the one that exists in the Netherlands and some other European countries, prostitution is legalised and treated as a form of provision of sexual services. Legal regulations in the latter case precise where, when and under which circumstances prostitution can take

---

[65] ŠARIĆ, HARIZ (2006) Neki aspekti prostitucije i aktualni presjek njene /ne/legalizacije. In: Pravna misao 37/3–4. Sarajevo. 59.
[66] NEZAVISNE NOVINE (2011): Amerikanka otkrila mrežu prostitucije u BiH: Javne kuće zamaskirane u restorane. http://www.dnevnik.ba/novosti/kronika/amerikanka-otkrila-mre%C5%BEu-prostitucije-u-bih-javne-ku%C4%87e-zamaskirane-u-restorane, retrieved 20.7.2011.
[67] Article 210. of the Criminal Code of the Federation of Bosnia and Herzegovina, Official Journal of FBiH, Nos. 36/03, 37/03, 21/04, 69/04, 18/05, 42/10, 42/11.
[68] ADŽAJLIĆ-DEDOVIĆ, AZRA (2003): Prostitucija u Bosni i Hercegovini. Sarajevo.
[69] ŠARIĆ 2006: 72.
[70] HUGHES 2005: 37.

place, and under this approach prostitutes, pimps, brothel owners and men using sexual services become sex workers, managers, business people and clients, respectively. A decriminalisation approach implies the removal of criminal penalties for all participants, with the exception of children, and it is often viewed as the first step towards the regulation which means legalisation. It is, as already mentioned, best understood as a transition phase or part of the process towards either legalisation or abolition.[71] Independently of the model accepted and fostered by a particular European country, a question naturally arises as to whether prostitution can be viewed as a profession, a mere economic activity or a form of provision of services.

The Dutch model reflects all characteristics on the basis of which prostitution may generally be viewed as a profession, a legitimate occupation. Should it, or better, can it be followed? When it comes to the provision of sexual services, the sex workers have numerous characteristics, i.e. key elements of labour relations. Basically, a voluntary element is present, so that every person can freely decide to do such job. Moreover, agencies, i.e. employment services, can offer these jobs.[72] Prostitution is *inter alia* also regulated pursuant to general labour law provisions. In the case of working in brothels, there is a limiting element of subordination as an important element of labour relations, since brothel owners are mostly viewed as providing support services to self-employed sex workers. Therefore, the conclusion of employment contracts is a rare phenomenon.[73] The personal execution of labour and pay are unquestionable elements of labour relations. Sex workers have the possibility of enjoying collective rights, i.e. joining unions of sex workers, similarly to some other European countries like France, Germany, etc. The provision of sexual services is licensed pursuant to municipal regulations, what enables health and labour inspections, but also police inspections in the context of control of valid papers and permits. The Dutch legislator views the general ban on brothels as a possibility of regulating provision of sexual services and a way to improve the situation of prostitutes, i.e. sex workers.[74] But, studies conducted in the Netherlands show that due to the nature of the work, the stigma on the sector, and a weaker social and legal status prostitutes have with respect to other employees, a business owner in the prostitution sector is not like other employers.[75] Hence more than any other model, the Dutch model opens a debate on two important paradigms – human

---

[71] Ibid.: 38.
[72] See RNW ENGLISH SECTION 2009.
[73] Ibid.
[74] DAALDER 2007: 61.
[75] Ibid.

dignity and discrimination on the one hand, and the function of regulations, i.e. the boundaries of their regulation *in favorem* a general interest, ethics and morality on the other.

From the standpoint of law, the Dutch model *prima facie* seems to have its *raison d'être*, viewed through the prism of national legislation, and even part of legal logic upon which certain judicial decisions made by the European Court of Justice rely. Moreover, even during the period of validity of the Association Treaty with Poland, the Czech Republic and the Slovak Republic, in the spirit of the free movement and the provision of services, the Netherlands allowed citizens of the said countries to exercise prostitution on Dutch soil.[76] But, can it be detected easily and with security in the Netherlands whether somebody exercises voluntary or coerced prostitution, whether a prostitute is a trafficking victim or not? On the other hand, even when a legal market for sexual services is formed, a great part of its activities is illegal and outside the formal economy, since many sexual exchange procedures are illegal (soliciting, procuring, in some countries even keeping and managing brothels).[77] What is most important for this debate is that what all of us should ask ourselves when giving answers with respect to the treatment of prostitution as a profession – if prostitution were a legal profession, would we allow our children to exercise prostitution, would we think that they had chosen a right job or would we exercise prostitution ourselves? The answer here is definitely intimately negative.

Independently of the legal treatment of prostitution in a particular national legal system, its legalisation, though with certain *pro* arguments, enjoys numerous, justified and argued *contra* attitudes. In its reports, the International Labour Organisation often addresses prostitution, trafficking, debt bondage and sexual exploitation, but prostitution has never been recognised as a legitimate profession. In legal and labour terminology, prostitution cannot be treated as a profession, since, conditionally taken, in the working process we do not deal with the demonstration of certain knowledge, the intellectual capacity or skills, but with the exploitation of the human body and severe violation of personal integrity and human dignity that should be protected by every national labour and legal system during the working process (with respect to other employees and persons a worker comes into contact with during his/her work). We cannot neglect the fact that prostitution most frequently represents a relationship in which those

---

[76] Cf. DANNA, DANIELA (2011): The position of prostitutes in E.U. countries: law and practice, Paper for the 4th European Feminist Research Conference: Body, Gender, Subjectivity. Crossing borders of disciplines and institutions. http://www.danieladanna.it/wordpress/?p=211, retrieved 2.5.2011.

[77] SANDERS, TEELA (2008): Selling sex in the shadow economy. In: International Journal of Social Economics 35/10. 704–706.

having money exploit someone's situation, i.e. the condition in which that person must sell his/her own body; they exploit a difficult and unenviable social situation and the condition of poverty. Prostitution reduces the human body to an object, a thing, causing thereby a loss of subjectivity by a person. As pointed out by Scoular,[78] the highly gendered nature of commercial sex appears to undoubtedly exemplify *in favorem* "male domination exercised through the medium of sexuality". Moreover, here we deal with a form of gender-based discrimination, since in systems of legal and regulated prostitution as well as in those where prostitution is still illegal, legal solutions and practices statistically affect predominantly women. We have pointed out many times that the sexual market is formed by the prevailing male demand for sex. The legalisation of prostitution and the recognition of prostitution as a profession can only negatively influence the adjustment of the limits of demand in direction of other protected subjects, towards an increase in child prostitution and pornography, diverse types of questionable sexual behaviour, etc. Moreover, as to the European gender equality policy, although it is about the application of the principle of subsidiarity to the context of the regulation of prostitution in national systems, we have been facing further unequal gender treatment. The Swedish model, obviously increasingly influenced by radical feminism, in the context of the perception of prostitution, has gone the farthest, shifting the focus from the victim of prostitution and her/his criminal and legal treatment to subjects that encourage the sexual market and represent a constituent part of creating the demand. In addition, even in systems in which prostitution is legalised and recognised as a profession, partial legal control has been established over only a part of street prostitution; elite prostitution that takes place out of public sight is not regulated at all.[79]

In the context of European integration and various modes of legal treatment of prostitution in EU members, a question is posed as to the perception of prostitution in light of the establishing treaties and provisions with respect to four fundamental freedoms: the free movement of people (workers), goods, services and capital. In the past, certain national courts believed that prostitution could not be classified into any of the four fundamental freedoms of the

---

[78] SCOULAR, JANE (2004): The 'subject' of prostitution. Interpreting the discursive, symbolic and material position of sex/work in feminist theory. In: Feminist Theory 5/3. 343. In this text, Scoular gives an excellent overview of differences in the perception of prostitution in modern feminist theory, starting with papers written by Jo Doezema, Judith Walkowitz, Shannon Bell, Carole Pateman, Catharine MacKinnon, Andrea Dworkin to Gail Pheterson, Gayle Rubin and others. See ibid.: 343–355.

[79] See NORTON-HAWK, MAUREEN (2003): Social Class, Drugs, Gender and the Limitations of the Law. Contrasting the Elite Prostitute with the Street Prostitute. In: Studies in Law, Politics and Society 29. 123–139.

European market.[80] However, in the final judgement delivered by the European Court of Justice in the case Małgorzata Jany and Others[81] of 2001, the Court identified that the residence of Polish and Czech prostitutes was at least tolerated by the Dutch authorities and that street and window prostitution in the Netherlands are legal. In terms of law, it was important whether prostitution could be treated as economic activities in accordance with the European Agreements concluded with Poland and the Czech Republic and whether prostitutes could be viewed as self-employed persons. The Court concluded that based upon the presented arguments, prostitution falls under the category of self-employed persons in accordance with the mentioned European Agreements with Poland and the Czech Republic and it implies a provision of service for money. By taking into account all circumstances of the case, the European Court characterised prostitution as a form of the provision of services, i.e. an economic activity, thereby obviously giving an advantage to economic freedoms over the protection of human rights and balancing between various legal regimes of prostitution in the EU. An economic activity is terminologically undoubtedly defined as an economic and not a legal category. Moreover, an economic activity can be related to both legal and illegal profit-making businesses, so that it should be handled with care and not viewed as a basis for possible interpretations referring to the need for legalisation of prostitution in the EU. As regards the free movement of workers, the European Court operates *in favorem* the fundamental freedom of movement, since sex workers have a possibility for free movement between countries with legalised prostitution, but these rights are not applicable to non-citizens. This opens a complex issue of different legal treatment of sex workers who are members of the EU and those without citizenship status, i.e. migration policy issues and the concept of citizenship on the one hand, and illegal immigration and the protection of the most vulnerable groups most of the prostitutes in the majority of European countries come from on the other.

4 Concluding remarks

Prostitution is a very complex European problem that principally requires an interdisciplinary approach oriented towards human dignity and legal protection of prostitutes. Countries whose legal treatment is getting closer to equalise sex workers with workers in general, are more oriented towards the protection of

---

[80] Joined Cases 115/81 and 116/81 Adoui and Cornuaille [1982] ECR-I-1665.
[81] Case-268/99 Aldona Małgorzata Jany and others v. Staatssecretaris van Justite [2001] ECR-I-8615.

business interests of the sex industry than the issues referring to the fight against gender-based discrimination and the protection of human dignity. Since there is a cause-and-effect relation to illegal trade in human beings, especially women and children, prostitution requires a redefinition of the existing migration policy and legislative treatment of prostitution in countries that would like to turn exploitation of a difficult material and social situation into a legitimate profession. Indeed, contrary opinions should not be neglected, but from the position of legal and labour treatment, in no way can prostitution be a profession, and "an economic activity" and "the provision of services" synonyms for prostitution as a legitimate profession. Contractualists, who consider prostitution as sales of certain services, certainly would not agree with the claims presented, but, from the point of view of labour and employment, a human being cannot be reduced to a legal object, and the provision of sexual services cannot be seen as an every day or ordinary service, not even when many elements referring to employment or sex workers' union claims are present. Opposite considerations could have incalculable consequences for the perception of child pornography, the sale of narcotics or even trafficking as forms of service delivery *pro futuro*, especially in a world where economic freedom and absolute liberalisation of markets are placed above the protection of fundamental human rights. Contemporary societies should direct legal interest towards abolishing sanctions against persons involved in prostitution and the fight against the demand for sexual services (by punishing the users), rather than trying to perceive prostitution as a regular profession addressed by employment agencies. Prostitution has been, let's not forget, both in historical perspective and today, a form of sexual slavery[82], and not a profession we want for our daughters, wives, partners and friends.

---

[82] See the interview with Ms Rada Borić: BAČIĆ, IVKA (2011): Rada Borić: Prostitucija je seksualno ropstvo i ne smije se legalizirati. In: Vjesnik (29.7.2011).

Gendering Politics. The Impact of Women Politicians and NGOs in the Western Balkans

Petra Bläss-Rafajlovski

1. A spotlight from the ground: United Nations Security Council Resolution 1325 in on-road test in Kosovo

An example of a grassroots initiative

"We from the conflict regions are super creative", said Valdete Idrizi from the NGO Community Building in Mitrovica.[1] The literal bridging between Kosovo-Albanian and Serbian women in the separated city Mitrovica in Northern Kosovo is in her opinion a "criminal coalition". To come from one part of the city to the other and to meet each other the women have to overcome the bridge watched by KFOR soldiers. The often quoted peacebuilding by women – here it is practically implemented. There are simple, but also difficult steps to be made. "We simply started to speak with them." What sounds so easy makes it necessary to be creative and decided to go one's own ways behind the nationalist mainstream. Women have followed their wish to build bridges between human beings from both parts of the city and created with like-minded people an organization which is exactly trying to do that. What is prized in diplomatic language of the UNSCR 1325 as the "important role of women in combating and ending conflicts and in peace consolidation"[2] means for the women in Mitrovica to go into the field, to speak with the people and to start the dialogue. Confidence building is the key word. To get the confidence of the colleagues from the other side and to gain it themselves was, of course, the most difficult thing to do. Again and again they had to think of how the other side would understand their behaviour or statements. The binding agreement to do something together was the start of acting. The women were acting with the mutual requirement to design the coexistence of the two city parts more liveable and to make a punctual cooperation possible. "It's not politics!" – It's interesting that the women reflect their activities in this way and accent that they would be "more practical than political". But exactly this is politics, to create partnerships across ethnic barriers in an environment which is characterized by nationalism and an ongoing state of emergency.

---

[1] www.cbmitrovica.org.
[2] UNITED NATIONS SECURITY COUNCIL (2000): Resolution 1325 on Women, Peace and Security (S/RES/1325, 31.10.2000), www.un.org/events/res_1325.

Lessons learned: 1. Sustainable peace- and reconciliation-work is always starting from bottom-up and can't be ordered from outside.

2. Common problems or similar projects, especially focused on basic issues of daily life, are able to bring women from different (enemy) sides together. The so called "big politics" is staying outside.

3. Most important during the closing to each other is to create confidence. This is the basis for listening to each other and to accept and respect the history and the view of the other side.

4. It is important to be coequal at the meetings. Also the (neutral) place of meetings has to be recognized.

The Status negotiations

The long-standing negotiations about the Kosovo status until its declaration of independence in February 2008 were a clear violation of the demand of UNSCR 1325 on Women, Peace and Security "to recognize the gender perspective during negotiation and implementation of peace agreements" – besides the tireless and professional lobbying of women and peace movement activists. The (non-) participation of women in the status negotiations was and is the linchpin. All negotiation teams were male ones. All leading international negotiators and Special Representatives of the UN Secretary General were confronted with protests and catalogues of demands by women's associations and first of all the Kosova Women's Network[3], founded in 2000, uniting 90 women's organizations and initiatives across ethnic lines which is the best example of women's power at a local, regional and international level. One result of the women's strong protest against the composition of the so-called "unity team" for the negotiations 2007 was the presence of a small number of women in the working groups. Additionally to this critical assessment it seems necessary to me to scrutinize also which effects the hard fought 30% women's quota in the Kosovo Assembly and the existence of the Women's Caucus in the parliament across party-lines had and have. Attending and advising the work of women MP in the Kosovo Assembly from 2003 I was asking myself again and again why the voice of women was missed on all the plenary debates on status/ negotiation issues. But even there, a strong pressure from the women's civil society to intervene was present. In the critical moment everything was overlaid by party politics. The view of women MP was completely focused on their male party leaders. This exactly was and is the main critical point of women activists vis-à-vis the women politicians.

---

[3] www.womensnetwork.org.

Lessons learned: 1. Women have to fight for seats at negotiation tables.

2. Traditional lobbying is obviously not enough, and even some single women in institutions or power positions are no guarantee for listening to women's voice, recognizing women's perspective or dealing according to gender equality standards.

3. One key is and was the acting of women inside party structures.

4. A central challenge for all lobbyists for an adequate participation of women in conflict solution and peace processes is an offensive access to the foreign affairs, defence and security debates and to explain which concretely added value is following the recognition of the gender perspective.

My friend Vjosa Dobruna, a long-term women's grassroots movement activist, former minister of the first Kosovo interim government 1999 and former head of the RTK board, told me a characteristical story: In November 2007 the former Austrian Minister for Foreign Affairs, Ursula Plassnik, invited women from Serbia and Kosovo in leading positions in politics, economy, media and civil society themed "Designing the European future – networking of Serbian and Kosovo Women". This event was deliberately organized in parallel to the official status negotiations, the so called Troika-negotiations with Kosovo and Serbia. On the fringes of the women's event it came to a spontaneous (but obviously intended) meeting with the (exclusively male) negotiation leaders of the official status talks. One of the internationals said to the women that, in any case, the proceedings would be different ones if they would be part of the negotiation team…

Lessons learned: 1. To identify gender specific discrimination and its negative impact (in this case: the lack of progress in status negotiations) is one thing, to hand power over – the other.

2. We should always remember (as the title of a book on the history of women in civil society in Kosovo looks like): "HISTORY IS HERSTORY TOO!"[4]

2. Conclusions from my work with women politicians and NGO activists in Albania, Bosnia and Herzegovina, Kosovo and Macedonia, Montenegro and Serbia

1. The women's clear call "We want to improve our situation!" is generally remarkable. Women's grassroots movements and NGOs as well as women's

---

[4] FARNSWORTH, NICOLE (ed.) (2008): History is Herstory too. The History of Women in Civil Society in Kosovo 1980–2004. Prishtina.

national, regional and local networks are playing the key role in articulating the wish to improve both situation and structures.

2. A key demand of the women is to increase their presentation in decision making bodies. Especially during the debates on the electoral codes in the respective countries or when diplomatic negotiation teams are created this resoluteness of women to change the power balance is necessary.

3. Agreements of women across party lines should be more recognized and best practices at local and regional level offensive have to be realized. So the creation of Women's Caucuses in the national parliament (as it was the case in Macedonia or Kosovo) or local women networks (as in Albania) could push the focus on a more gender sensitive legislation and a higher presentation of women in decision making bodies.

4. It is difficult and a huge challenge to overcome traditional gender stereotypes. In view of the still well functioning patriarchal structures in the Balkans and especially in the rural areas there is a need of a continuous awareness-raising.

5. Patriarchal (in some countries even clan) structures in the political parties and especially the important role of the male leaders are the main barriers for women to enter power structures and to implement the gender quota. Additional informal decision making structures and meetings have to be more recognized and entered by women.

6. There is still a long-term need of special trainings for women who want to enter structures. They have to be tied to the concrete daily living conditions the women are confronted with and should be focused on developing messages and dealing with the media.

7. It is necessary to identify in time the right women candidates for positions at all levels and to give them a chance to develop their profile. To overcome often existing competitive attitudes and lacks of solidarity a pragmatic approach is recommended.

8. The still existing difference between urban and rural areas in all Western Balkan countries has to be noticed. This is especially relevant concerning the role of traditional patriarchal structures, an antiquated infrastructure and lack of access to information and public transport.

3. My understanding of a gender equality approach

1. Gender equality in different areas of public and political life is a huge challenge and overall goal which effects power structures at micro and macro level.

2. Gender equality, especially as, in the meantime, the term is used frequently and often as lip service, has to be defined by clear measures and translated in daily life and politics.

3. Gender equality is not a phrase or luxury, it's based in and related to daily life conditions of women and men.

4. Gender equality is not an appendix to the "big policy" and comprised cosmetic changes, it has the approach to overcome hierarchies, discrimination, exclusion, injustice and violence.

5. Gender equality is connected to the principles of human rights, self determination, emancipation, the rule of law, social justice and absence of violence.

6. The fight for gender equality at different levels is only successful if indicators are broken down to each community and into local language, if visions are translated into tangible actions.

2. Constructions of Gender in Language and the Media

Women experts – Public Disbelief in Women Professionals[1] in Serbia[2]

Zorica Mršević

The Global Network of Women in the News Media reports that there is a globally noticed permanent lack of positive media reports on professional women. The same situation is noticed when analysing the media in Serbia in the period of 2010 to September 2011. Attacks on women who are holders of public offices and state functions or who are leaders or members of opinion making intellectual elites, are always more intensive than those against men in similar positions. Even when women publicly plea for reducing discrimination and violence against women, strengthening women's access to justice or increasing women's role as decision-makers and leaders, which are not at all disputable values and goals, they are exposed to various media attacks.

Women's guilt is always twofold. Namely, together with presenting their professional mistakes, media imply as understood that they are guilty because they hold public positions in spite of the fact that they are women. High or otherwise distinguished positions are, in accordance with this patriarchal value system, almost always exclusively dedicated to men. That is the main reason

---

[1] http://iwmf.org/pioneering-change/global-research-on-women-in-the-news-media.aspx, retrieved 4.1.2011.
[2] In the period 2010–September 2011.

why women's hypothetical "guilt" is regularly exaggerated in a way that men who are targets of attacks as political actors never have to meet.

Moreover, the media space dedicated to attacks on professional women is not proportional to the importance of the issue. The media and/or the journalists sometimes actually are not the authors of the attacks; in fact the media sometimes just transfer somebody else's releases. However, the media are clearly very ready to provide more space to women as wrongdoers than the situation demands, more than they would dedicate to similar wrongs of men. In such situations the media usually engage additionally interviewed persons who are ready to support the negative attitude by means of presenting "expert" opinions.

The media clearly strive to be in accordance with the common public opinion which is set against professional women and, in that way, to gain popularity and sell well. The messages are not addressed only to attack directly one woman, but also to all women, who should be aware that public space in fact "is not a right place for women."[3] By corroborating the limits imposed to women and their marginalization to private activities far from public life, media promote such limits as "normal". By doing so, media have also an educative role in discouraging women to pursue professional careers and to have professional aspirations.[4]

Examples

1. The media promote discriminative stereotypes by reasoning that women are not born for some professions. The opinions experts search usually are those of men rivals, but in the media they are promoted as independent, even as scientific truths. One well known surgeon publicly expressed his misogynic and primitive attitude, disqualifying all his women colleagues. "Based on some reason: women are not talented for surgery. I have seen some women surgeons when operating, and all of them function the same way. It is unbelievable how rough women surgeons are! Their behavior is so unemotional and atypical for normal woman's personality. They do not cope with these tasks in the right way. They do not fit in surgery. They cannot operate just as they cannot do some

---

[3] The permanently present endecy of media is to diminish women and to reduce them to sex objects, see COLEMAN, BRENNA (2010): Female Stereotypes in the Media. Media Portrayal of Women (15.1.2010). http://www.suite101.com/content/media-portrayal-of-women-a189870, retrieved 4.1.2011.

[4] MEDIA AWARENESS NETWORK (2010): Media Portrayals of Girls and Women. Introduction. http://www.media-awareness.ca/english/issues/stereotyping/women_and_girls/index.cfm, retrieved 4.1.2011.

banal physical activities, such as parallel parking a car. In fact the best cooks worldwide are not women but men [...] Women as surgeons [...] For me, these two things are not connected."[5]

2. Media attack on a woman minister

The text is published in the journal *Kurir* with the photo of a woman minister in a short skirt, shot from below, and accompanied with typical men's taunts like "humoristic comments" on her legs – that is an example of a discriminative, diminishing media attitude towards women in politics.[6] The main message of this article is that women politicians may always be reduced to erotic objects, to legs, cleavages, etc., in a way which in media presentation is never applied to men in political functions. The message is clear, whichever function you might have, whichever responsibilities, and whichever are the results of your work, all of that is not important, this is something that is not interesting to anybody because you are always just a "piece" of female flesh, a chicken leg. As such, you are always subjected to men's estimation, comparisons, passions and wishes. This approach diminishes and negates all elements of women's professions. This clear message is aimed not only at the attacked woman, but at all women. Public space simply is not for women, perhaps only for some who have enough erotic and decorative attributes. These attributes are never demanded from male actors on the political scene, not to mention that they do not have to fear being compared or graded. Obviously, the media presentation like the *Kurir*'s is of a different type. Female politicians don't feature the results of their work, their political or professional reputation, their profile, but only their legs. In fact, they are nothing but chicken legs. Moreover, if you are a woman and dare to hold a public function, you "clearly" agree in advance to be treated differently from your male colleagues. The mentioned text in the *Kurir* legitimates the media's right to discriminate against women, to put them on their "right" places, to reduce their actual roles and that way to constantly promote gender stereotypes; moreover to create and to maintain the discriminative public opinion and public discourse in which women are only this one thing – legs. The only question remaining is whose legs are better.

3. Attack on a woman manager of a women's penitentiary

No organization for monitoring prisons, neither the autonomous women's organization nor the Protector of Citizens, who all regularly visit the women's

---

[5] TROŠELJ, SLAVKO (2010): Više od sporta: dr Boško Đukanović. Žene mogu da budu sve samo ne hirurzi. In: Politika (15.8.2010).
[6] EKIPA KURIRA (2010): Snežo, imaš najbolji batak. In: Kurir (2.12.2010).

prison, have ever noticed that the situation is as bad as described in the report prepared by the Helsinki Committee. It says: "In the women's penitentiary in Požarevac are the most brutal, the most rigorous and the most conservative implementation of the Law on Penalties regarding the inmates", said the author Ivan Kuzmanović.[7] Describing the horror in that institution, the report mentions furthermore that the woman director was deployed without previous experience, blaming her that she got the position because of her political affiliation to the ruling coalition, which of course leaves neither her nor anybody competent to manage any penitentiary institution. The political affiliations of the other penitentiaries' managers and their previous experience are not mentioned, assuming that men are always competent by the mere fact of their gender. Moreover, it is implied that the only problem in Serbia's prison administration is this one woman who manages the women's penitentiary.

4. Media lynch of Commissioner for protection of discrimination

In the beginning of 2010, the media lynch of Professor Nevena Petrušić, the candidate for the function of the Commissioner for the Protection of Equality, took place. Before her nomination in May 2010, many of her alleged professional and political mistakes and omissions were presented, which continued after her nomination when all of a sudden her main "mistake" was declared to be alleged inefficiency, from the first day of entering the position. This continues and is repeated together with the permanent stress on her purported incompatibility of her professorship with the function of a Commissioner. The ugly attacks didn't stop even when the other side didn't respond and accept the level of discussion and the whole idea of exchanging offences via public debate. It is also interesting that the attackers only paid attention to her alleged conflict of interest but not to anybody else. In fact, many professors in Serbia are engaged in numerous public functions – as members of the parliament, ministers and/or highly ranked state functionaries heading independent regulatory bodies[8], while still performing their academic or professorial duties. Obviously, this very unique but systemically conducted attacks targeting only her – the Commissioner – clearly showed that the motives were personal interests. The organizations and individuals who were engaged in the media campaign against professor Petrušić simply had another candidate for the function, and it was easy to continue and to intensify

---

[7] Public release by the Helsinki Committee (2010). The executive director of the Helsinki Committee for Human Rights in Serbia, Ivan Kuzmanović, argued that in Serbia prisons are overloaded. In: Tanjug Beograd (2.11.2010).

[8] For example, there are deputies of Protector of Citizens, whose legal status is regulated in the same manner regulating conflicts of interests.

the attacks because she is a woman. The motive behind the persistent overemphasis on her purported unsuitability was not the wish for Serbia to get the best Commissioner, but a very personal and not well hidden agenda.

But besides those personally colored attacks, this intensity of attacks and the type of criticism has never been noticed when men were attacked. The disqualifying attacks included also all supporters of professor Petrušić, and everybody who didn't share the opinion of the attackers. Coincidentally, they were all women too, who were called names and organized feminists. This model is very popular: whenever women ask for something, even much less then the men have, in public domain, they are called feminists as this is an "argument" per se.[9] The gender aspect of these attacks includes discrediting and compromising female candidates to keep them from public functions and positions. Although in this particular case, the media "only" published the attacks which were created outside the media, they are responsible for enabling and providing valuable media space whose dimensions were far above the importance of just one and, in fact, a personal conflict.

5. Attack on women NGO leaders
In the Sandžak area where the Bosniak population prevails, the local religious elite regularly organizes media attacks on female NGO activists from this region. The patriarchal model of behavior can easily be recognized. Namely, socially discriminated and frustrated men usually regain their self-esteem by beating their wives at home, politically less influential leaderships gain their stand by orchestrating public media offences, they threaten and attack their own women blaming them as traitors of national interests.

In an article published in the daily journal *Danas* (14 February 2011), there was an open hate speech against the very prominent activist leader Aide Ćorović. Ms Ćorović is also well known as the winner of the prominent media prize "Gaining Freedom"[10] for courageous public reporting and criticizing religious leaders.[11] The Commissioner for the Protection of Equality reacted by warning the perpetrators that their ways were discriminatory and menacing for the physical integrity of the attacked woman. It was also stressed that the manner of attacking was offensive to all middle-aged women when called frustrated, not successful, and in dangerous hormonal condition. On 15 September the

---

[9] Preliminary brief on the online discussion: Women and the Media. Conducted by the UN Department of Public Information, 1–28 February 2010. http://www.un.org/womenwatch/beijing15/Women_and_the_media_preliminary_brief.pdf, retrieved 4.1.2011.
[10] In: *Danas* (23.9.2011).
[11] Dani: Spomenik pozitivnim energijama [Independent review]. BH DANI – ONLINE. http://www.bhdani.com/default.asp?kat= txt& broj_id=745&tekst_rb=19.

Sandžak press[12] attacked another female NGO leader, Semiha Kačar, without any arguments and by calling her various offensive names which certainly are not suitable for public media.[13] She therefore pressed charges for the crime "public offence" against her (*Krivična prijava zbog uvrede*).[14]

In fact, the main reason is that these women are financially as independent as they are regarding their program, running their non-governmental organizations without asking the religious leaders for permission and certainly not sharing their resources with them.

Legal aspects

This media attitude offends the dignity of the (individually) attacked women, but it also, as it was said before, leads to group offence and discrimination. Moreover, maintaining this type of media reporting and promoting gender stereotypes regularly corroborate, customize and "normalize" a specific media tolerance on misogyny. Such media style is not only the issue of lack of media taste and good media manners. These are motions between deliberately not recognized misogyny and the ruthless utilization of tolerated hate and discrimination. But these media manners are also against Constitutional provisions and sanctioned as such. The Constitutional duty of everybody to "respect and protect human dignity is unquestioned" (Constitution, article 23).[15]

The law on gender equality (article 41) is also violated because its provisions stipulate the duty of the public information to develop public consciousness on equality regarding gender and to undertake adequate measures to change social and cultural models, customs and all other practices which condition stereotypes, prejudices and discrimination based on the concept that one sex is either subordinated or superior.[16] Not only do the mentioned examples not meet the legal duties, but the outputs are totally opposite: by promoting the stereotypical presentation of women, all prejudices based on the concept that women are subordinated to men are maintained.

---

[12] FEHRATOVIĆ, JAHJA (2011): Odbor za jednokratnu upotrebu. In: Elektronske novine Sandžak Press (3.9.2011). http://sandzakpress.net/odbor-za-jednokratnu-upotrebu.

[13] Kačar was accused that she took money from certain people for providing them legal aid which is meant to be free of charge. She was called very mean, corrupt, immoral – and difficult to be translated names "*opajdara, babetina* who robs other people, boot licker and sold grandmother, newly discovered boot-licker of Belgrade" (*Danas* [14.9.2011]).

[14] NOVOSEL, S. (2011): Krivična prijava zbog uvreda. In: Danas (14.09.2011). http://www.danas.rs/danasrs/drustvo/krivicna_prijava_zbog_uvreda.55.html?news_id=223645. See also http://www.sandzacke.rs/vijesti/drustvo/krivicna-prijava-zbog-uvreda-protiv-sandzak-presa/.

[15] Constitution of the Republic of Serbia, "Official Herald RS", no. 98/2006.

[16] Law on gender equality, "Official Herald RS", no. 104/2009.

It is important to pay attention to the law on public information (article 38)[17] which stipulates the ban of hate speech in its article. It forbids to publish ideas, information and opinions which stimulate discrimination against persons or groups of persons because of their sex, regardless of whether a criminal deed was committed or not.

The law on prohibiting discrimination[18] is the most effective in regard to misogynic and discriminative media attitudes against women, since it comprises various provisions by which such attitudes are sanctioned. First of all, there are provisions on hate speech in article 11 which ban the expression of ideas, information and other opinions that stimulate discrimination in public media and other publications against groups of people because of their personal characteristics – in the given situation, because of their belonging to the female sex.

The same law in article 12 bans intimidation and degrading behavior, which violates or aims to violate the dignity of groups of people because of their personal characteristics. The same law in article 20 prohibits discrimination based on sex which is in opposition to the principle of gender equality, equal rights and liberties of women and men in political and other aspects of public and professional life. Discrimination based on gender is also forbidden as well as prejudices, customs and other social patterns which are based on the concept which includes either subordination or superiority of one sex to another and/or stereotypical sex roles.

Discriminative social environment in Serbia

It should not be forgotten, that the professional women in Serbia have to live and work in a public environment which generally is very discriminative. Hate and rejection of all "others" permanently diminish women's aspirations and possibilities to realize them. Some of the professional women who are not married and have no children, not to mention who are hidden lesbians[19], are in particularly vulnerable situations and get accused of being "perverts" or "selfish" women who pursued their career rather than being mothers. In evidencing discriminative environment against non-heterosexuals the survey prepared by the Labris organization for lesbian rights should be mentioned. At the end of 2011, with the intention to evidence shortages in the implementation

---

[17] Law on public information, "Official Herald RS", no. 43/2003, 61/2005, 71/2009 and 89/2010 – decision of the Constitutional Court.
[18] Law on prohibiting discrimination, "Official Herald RS", no. 22/2009.
[19] Hidden, because being professionally successful and open lesbian is currently not yet possible in Serbia.

of the existing legal antidiscrimination provisions, Labris conducted a survey examining the public opinion, according to whom a systemic discrimination against LGBT persons[20] was obvious: About two hundred people voted on the Labris site, out of them 80% confirmed a systemic discrimination of the LGBT population in Serbia today. In the public release by Labris it is concluded that: 1. LGBT population is a minority in Serbia that isn't allowed to freely gather together and demonstrate the rights warranted by the law and the highest legal document, the Constitution. 2. LGBT persons are threatened by death if they wish to enjoy that right. 3. LGBT population is systemically discriminated against when the point at issue are the rights stemming from partnership relations, either conjugal or non-conjugal, which are governed by the law and which are available only to heterosexual persons. 4. Due to a systemic non-recognition of the same-sex partnerships, a series of laws are discriminatory towards LGBT population, including the Law on Family, the Law on Inheritance and the Law on Healthcare. 5. A systemic discrimination against LGBT persons is also obvious when the existing laws are implemented. Those laws ban discrimination on the grounds of sexual orientation and gender identity, whereas LGBT persons are regularly and mostly discriminated against in various ways at work, in educational institutions, in their families, as well as in governmental institutions, such as the police, the prosecutor's office and the court.

The greatest shortcoming of legal regulations on the position of persons with non-heterosexual orientation in Serbia is also a lack of definition of the institution of "hate crime", which would, according to the experiences of other countries and the stands of LGBT organizations, contribute to a more efficient processing of cases where people are accused of violence and other criminal offences committed against LGBT population. The Criminal Code should include the category of "hate crime", which would enable a faster and more efficient identification and processing of homophobic and trans-phobic crimes. Serbia should improve its legislative scope by adopting changes in the criminal code, by introducing "hate crime" as a specific criminal offence, or by increasing the penalties for violent criminal offences committed on the grounds of race, religion, ethnic affiliation, sexual orientation, gender, gender identity, mental or physical disability etc.

---

[20] Saopštenje Labrisa o postojanju sistemske diskriminacije (28.12.2011). Belgrade. http://www.labris.org.rs/poll-results/da-li-mislis-da-u-srbiji-postoji-sistemska-diskriminacija-lgbt-osoba.html, retrieved 22.9.2011.

Conclusion

Political, economic and cultural systems always significantly influence media contents. Media and communication technologies cannot change the lack of equality on their own, power structures in the media are just a part of an omnipresent wider social lack of gender equality.

But in that respect, media are also producers of leading values and social models, mirroring the social system. Thus, the media space in Serbia still is the domain where a misogynic discourse is produced and reproduced, where the fear of "otherness" and "changes" is clearly visible.

In fact, nobody leads an open public campaign against women professionals and their roles in public life. But a hidden moral panic can be noticed in the media. For example, there are permanent claims that the current social changes contribute to the weakening of traditional moral values, even that all moral values are totally abandoned. Among these changes, women having professional careers are, of course, perceived as main causes of the "negative" social effects, such as the changing of traditional gender relations, sexuality, and the role of women, family organization and child care. The main scenario of all moral panics is the same, from the golden age and the age of moral stability and security, changes created social degradation and ordinary people therefore are now confused and cannot differentiate between good and evil.

The role of the media is to construct pseudo events by exaggerating individual events or incidents which are not connected and by presenting them as connected and as parts of dangerous systems, threatening symptoms of widely spread problems. Women professionals or just prominent women usually are depicted as evil mistake makers, more responsible than men in similar situations.

The media have an important and – in most of the cases resulting in panic – even the main role. Still, it is not only the media creating moral panics. The media's main interest is to gain a better market position, to increase the number of their regular customers and to improve the stability of their sources. Other actors and creators of moral panics have different motives. For example, religious leaders and churches are motivated by their religious doctrines, individuals by personal interests; political leaderships conduct in fact political campaigns against other political parties and options, etc. It seems that to all of them, women professionals are easy targets.

Gender and Language in Albania[1]

Delina Binaj

Existing research

To date there has been little research on gender and language in Albania. Among the few recent scientific examinations of gender and language in Albania are the volumes *Sociolinguistika* (2003) [Sociolinguistics] and *Etnografi e të folurit të shqipes* (2004) [Ethnography of Spoken Albanian] by GJOVALIN SHKURTAJ, who addresses gender-specific differences in spoken Albanian between the categories men and women in the context of the concept of difference as treated by William Labov. In her doctoral thesis *Ligjërimi "grarisht" në qytetin e Korçës* (2007) [The Spoken Language of Women in the City of Korça], ELONA BIBA examines the subject of gender from an ethnolinguistic perspective.

The subject of female gender conceptualisation in linguistic usage became more important in linguistic research during the socialist era, however it was treated as a question of lexis and word formation. Discussion of linguistic gender equality can be traced back to the language policy aims which were current at that time: after the Second World War, political, economic and social change meant that there was an objective need to form titles for new occupations, in the context of which efforts were also made to introduce corresponding female titles which were missing from pre-standardisation dictionaries. (cf. SIMA 1972: 297f.) This linguistic shift can be regarded as a positive development, since women thus obtained a degree of visibility in and through the language; but in the same way as with the emancipation movement, which was directed by the state, this linguistic shift was not instigated by women themselves. The primary motive was an ideological one, and any considerations in relation to gender issues were secondary to that.

Since the collapse of communism, some women's NGOs in Albania have begun to discuss the subject of linguistic gender equality at their events and in various publications. Such publications include a series by the Qendra e Aleancës Gjinore për Zhvillim (MARKU 2004; MËNIKU 2007; BINAJ 2008; MARTIRI/MËNIKU/KAPLLANAJ 2009), which address the role of language in the media and call for greater public awareness of gender-sensitive language, thus

---

[1] I am grateful to Shivaun Heath for her professional support in preparing the English version of this article.

forming a starting point for further discussions on the subject of gender and language.

Terminology

Nouns in Albanian belong to one of two grammatical gender classes: feminine and masculine. Thus, the use of other words (e.g. adjectives, pronouns etc.) requires an agreement with the grammatical gender of the noun. Albanian also has a neuter gender, however this is no more than a "relic" (cf. DEMIRAJ 1985: 154; cf. AGALLIU 2002: 93). The term used in Albanian grammars to name grammatical gender is that of *gjini*, which is the term also used in everyday usage to name social gender. The monolingual dictionary *Fjalori i Gjuhës Shqipe*, published by the Academy of Sciences of Albania in 2006, thus offers the following definitions, giving gender as a social categorisation the term *seksi* [sex], and regarding social gender as natural:

> 4. tërësia e tipareve natyrore që dallojnë mashkullin nga femra; seks: *gjinia mashkull (femër)*. 5. *gjuh.* kategori leksiko-gramatikore, sipas së cilës emrat dhe disa përemra ndahen në mashkullorë e femërorë; kategori gramatikore e mbiemrave dhe e disa fjalëve të tjera, që shfaqet gjatë përshtatjes me emrat me të cilët lidhen: *gjini gramatikore; gjinia mashkullore (femërore, asnjëanëse)*. (FJALORI I GJUHË SHQIPE 2006: 357)
>
> [4. The entirety of the natural features distinguishing men from women; sex: *the male (female) gender*. 5. ling. Grammatical/lexical category, in accordance with which nouns and some pronouns are classified as masculine or feminine; grammatical category of adjectives and some other words, which expresses itself in their agreement with the nouns to which they relate: *grammatical gender; masculine (feminine, neuter) gender.*]

In the context of the examination and discussion of gender theories which followed the political changes of the 1990s, the English term "gender" has recently been introduced into Albanian public discourse. The Albanian language now includes the term *përkatesi gjinore* [gender affiliation] to denote gender as a social categorisation. The term is used primarily in publications by women's NGOs to – according to the established definition – "indicate the social attributes which are acquired in the process of socialisation as a member of a particular community, and which are thus regarded as historically alterable." (cf. ALEANCA GJINORE PËR ZHVILLIM 2009: 3)

Generic masculine and occupational titles in contemporary Albanian

When naming concrete female people, or when naming people who are known from the context to be female, standard Albanian uses feminine linguistic forms:

1. **Kryeprokurorja** *(fem.)* e Shqipërisë viziton më 26–27 mars Kosovën *(Shqip*, 25.03.2012)

    [**The female State Prosecutor** of Albania visited Kosovo on 26–27 March]

2. **Kryetarja** *(fem.)* e Kuvendit takon homologun e saj nga Turqia *(Panorama*, 16.05.2012)

    [**The female President** of Parliament meets her male counterpart from Turkey]

3. Një vepër shqiptare, e shkruar nga **autorja** *(fem.)* Edlira Gogu, e cila vjen në skenë nga **regjisorja** *(fem.)* Adelina Muça me një koncept shumë origjinal. *(Shqip*, 28.01.2012)

    [An Albanian work by the **female author** Edlira Gogu, which is being staged in a very original production by the **female director** Adelina Muça.]

As is also the case in other languages, masculine linguistic forms are used in Albanian in both gender-specific and gender-unspecific contexts. The so-called generic masculine dominates in usage and is considered by Albanian grammars as the norm. In the examples given below, therefore, it is not clear whether only men are intended, or also women. We must simply suppose that women may also be intended:

1. Nderohen **mësuesit** *(masc.)* me rastin e festës. *(Shqip* 05.03.2012)

    [**The teachers** are honoured on their day of celebration.]

2. **Konstitucionalistët** *(masc.)*: Të mos prishet tradita e shumicës së cilësuar *(Shqip*, 13.04.2012)

    [**The specialists in constitutional law**: the tradition of the substantial majority should not be broken]

Even though the use of the masculine form in occupational titles is often defended – as is often the case in other languages too – on the basis that it may include both categories men and women, the use of the generic masculine can on no account be regarded as gender-neutral. The ambiguity of masculine occupational titles puts women at a disadvantage since it gives them a smaller chance of being "meant" and directly addressed.

The use of the generic masculine in standard Albanian – in the area of official and governmental language, for example – is nevertheless viewed entirely as the norm. Reference can be made here to the public administration's online job vacancies portal, where masculine occupational titles are used in the texts of all job advertisements by the various ministries of the Republic of Albania (cf. DEPARTAMENTI I ADMINISTRATËS PUBLIKE 2012). The same is also true of other state institutions, such as the Albanian parliament (cf. KUVENDI I SHQIPËRISË 2012) and the city hall of the capital city Tirana (cf. BASHKIA E TIRANËS 2012), on whose official websites job vacancies are advertised exclusively in the generic masculine form.

Recently, positive trends have also become noticeable in Albania with regard to an increase in the visibility of the role of women in public life through language. Thus, while in 2007 all female members of the Albanian cabinet still bore a masculine title, e.g. *ministër (m.)* [male minister] or *zëvendësministër (m.)* [male deputy minister] (cf. BINAJ: 2007: 92), the Albanian government website now names the female members of the Albanian cabinet principally using feminine titles, e.g. *ministre (f.)* [female minister] or *zëvendësministre (f.)* [female deputy minister].[2]

In view of the fact that the generic masculine continues to be used without restriction in the area of official and governmental language, as described above, this form of visibility of women through language is not necessarily to be regarded as the result of a consciously gender-sensitive approach to language on the part of the institutions concerned. Rather, it is connected to the fact that women in Albania are now increasingly entering professions and holding public offices which were previously reserved for men. Thus, the corresponding feminine occupational titles are also gaining acceptance in usage, in part, no doubt, because the women successfully push for this.

In contrast to the above-outlined approach to titles in job advertisements by state institutions, new trends can be identified in the private sector employment market in Albania. An analysis of online job advertisements in the context of this article showed that although the use of masculine forms in gender-unspecific contexts still dominates, alternative linguistic forms such as the

---

[2] Research on the official website of the Albanian government showed that, of a total of nine female cabinet members, including one minister, the masculine title is now used in only one case: that of the deputy minister of justice. The remaining female cabinet members are given feminine titles on the website, though in one case the feminine form is spelled incorrectly: *Zëvendësministëre e Integrimit* instead of *Zëvendësministre e Integrimit* [female Deputy Minister for Integration]. The feminine suffix *-e* is simply "tacked on" to the masculine form *zëvendësministër (m.)* [male deputy minister], although standard Albanian requires that the vowel ë in the ending be deleted.

splitting (the use of both masculine and feminine titles) or the forward-slash option are increasingly coming into use: e.g. "ofroj vend pune menaxher/e" [vacancy for a male/female manager], "ofroj vend pune Jurist/e" [vacancy for a male/female lawyer], "ofroj vend pune Përkthyes/Përkthyese" [vacancy for a male/female translator] (cf. njoftime.com 2012). The job advertisements thus inform the reader that both categories men and women are welcome to apply for the position in question. While alternative linguistic forms such as the use of both feminine and masculine titles or the forward-slash option are not normalised in standard Albanian, they can be interpreted as indications of the beginnings of a linguistic shift in Albania towards a gender-sensitive use of language.

Media and gender-sensitive language

As a rule, gender stereotypes are as widespread in the Albanian media as they are in society as a whole. While a voluntary ethical code for journalists does exist in Albania – the *Kodi i etikës*, developed and approved by the Media Institute and journalists' professional associations – it does not take gender considerations into account, and makes no mention of avoiding sexist language. (cf. MARKU 2004: 41) In his article "Trajtimi etik i çështjeve gjinore" [The Ethical Treatment with Gender Issues], the author cited calls for a voluntary commitment by journalists to the treatment of gender issues in the media – in the form of a code of ethics or within the framework of the statutory regulations of media legislation (cf. ibid.: 43f.).

Promoting awareness of the role of journalists and the media in the advancement of gender equality and non-sexist language is a lengthy process. The relentless competition and profit seeking of a liberal market economy dictate media developments in Albania, as they do elsewhere, and lead to the reproduction in the media of those stereotypes which correspond most closely with the assumed expectations of their users. Competition for the "story of the day" which will maximise sales and viewing figures frequently leads to an unprofessional and irresponsible approach to the language and subject matter of journalistic work. (cf. GJERMENI/BREGU 2003: 86f.)

At the same time, the mass media represent an ideal platform via which to effect changes aimed at gender equality. In terms of the spreading and establishment of alternative linguistic forms such as the use of both feminine and masculine titles or the forward-slash option, the media in Albania are not only particularly suited, but indeed indispensable to a successful linguistic intervention.

Trends in language policy in Albania

In 1972, a standard written language form was defined in Albania for the first time, and also became established in other Albanian-speaking areas of the Balkans (cf. LLOSHI 2011: 38f.). The development of Albanian into a standard language and the conclusion of this process fell within the period of the communist regime, which attempted to control all aspects of life in Albania. Since the political changes of the 1990s, standard Albanian has been subject to new challenges as it evolves to reflect these changes and the political, economic, technical and cultural developments. Furthermore, standard Albanian, which is also used in other Albanian-speaking regions, has become the subject of vehement debates. The standardisation pursued by the communist state is criticised for favouring the Tosk dialect (the southern linguistic variation), while disregarding the Gheg dialect (the northern linguistic variation) for politically motivated reasons.

The combination of these manifold challenges and the distinctly political nature of some debates have led to problems such as social discrimination and sexism in language are neglected by the institutions concerned with language planning and policy in Albania. Linguistic changes aimed at gender-sensitive language remain as yet unaddressed by deliberations and reflections on language policy measures.

Outlook

As outlined above, alternative linguistic forms such as the use of both feminine and masculine titles and the forward-slash option are now increasingly being used in Albanian public discourse, which may lead to a displacement of the hitherto dominant generic masculine in Albanian. General guidelines and recommendations – which may be drawn up by state institutions, or by professional organisations, large publishing houses or expert commissions, as is the case in some European Union countries – can serve as important language policy instruments in efforts to avoid sexist linguistic usage. Lastly, it must be regarded as an immediate objective for Albanian gender and language research to offer an empirically sound basis for strategic linguistic change proposals aimed at gender-sensitive usage in the Albanian language. Currently, as mentioned, the standard language of the 1970s is faced with considerable challenges and a comprehensive linguistic reform is expected in the near future.

References

AGALLIU, FATMIR et al. (2002): Gramatika e gjuhës shqipe 1. Morfologjia. [Grammar of Albanian 1. Morphology]. Tirana.

ALEANCA GJINORE PËR ZHVILLIM (2009): Përkatësia gjinore dhe zhvillimi. Koncepte dhe përkufizime. [Gender and Development. Concepts and Definitions]. Tirana.

BIBA, ELONA (2007): Ligjërimi "grarisht" në qytetin e Korçës [The Spoken Language of Women in the City of Korça]. Doctoral thesis. Tirana.

BINAJ, DELINA (2007): Sprache und Gleichbehandlung der Geschlechter in Albanien. Genderlinguistische Begründung für eine sprachpolitische Debatte. Master's thesis. Wien.

BINAJ, DELINA (2008): Funksioni përgjithësues i gjinisë mashkullore si formë e diskriminimit gjuhësor [The Generic Masculine as an Aspect of Linguistic Discrimination]. In: Gaia 6. 43–48.

DEMIRAJ, SHABAN (1985): Gramatikë historike e gjuhës shqipe [Historical Grammar of Albanian]. Tirana.

GJERMENI, EGLANTINA / MAJLINDA BREGU (2003): Monitoring Media on Domestic Violence 2001–2002. Tirana.

LLOSHI, XHEVAT (2011): Shqipja gjuhë e hapur dhe dinamike [Albanian: An Open and Dynamic Language]. Tirana.

MARKU, MARK (2004): Trajtimi etik i çështjeve gjinore [The Ethical Treatment of Gender Issues]. In: Aleanca Gjinore për Zhvillim (ed.): Media dhe barazia gjinore [Media and Gender Equality]. Tirana. 41–49.

MARTIRI, ETLEVA/ LINDA MËNIKU/ MIGENA KAPLLANAJ (2009): Trajtimi i problematikave sociale në media. Perspektivë gjinore janar–mars 2009 [The Treatment of Social Problems in the Media. Gender Perspective January–March 2009]. Tirana.

MËNIKU, LINDA (2007): Analyzing Media Discourses on Women's Trafficking and Violence Against Them. In: Qendra e Aleancës Gjinore për Zhvillim (ed.): To Be a Woman... In Albania, after 1990. Tirana. 67–78.

SIMA, KORNELJA (1972): Vëzhgime mbi emërtimet e reja të grave sipas profesionit në fushën e prodhimit industrial pas çlirimit [Observations on New Occupational Titles for Women in the Area of Industrial Production After the Liberation]. In: Universiteti Shtetëror i Tiranës/Instituti i Gjuhësisë dhe i Letërsisë (ed.): Studime mbi leksikun dhe mbi formimin e fjalëve në gjuhën shqipe 1 [Studies on Lexis and Word Formation in the Albanian Language 1]. Tirana. 297–312.

SHKURTAJ, GJOVALIN (2003): Sociolinguistika [Sociolinguistics]. Tirana.

SHKURTAJ, GJOVALIN (2004): Etnografi e të folurit të shqipes [Ethnography of Spoken Albanian]. Tirana.

THOMAI, JANI et al. (2006): Fjalor i Gjuhës Shqipe [Dictionary of Albanian]. Tirana.

Newspapers

Shqip (28.01.2012), retrieved 28.01.2012.
Shqip (05.03.2012), retrieved 06.03.2012.
Shqip (25.03.2012), retrieved 26.03.2012.
Shqip (13.04.2012), retrieved 13.04.2012.

Websites

Newspapers

Panorama (16.05.2012), http://www.panorama.com.al/category/politike/page/7/, retrieved 06.06.2012.

Institutions

http://www.pad.gov.al/dopawebpage2/vendevakante.aspx, retrieved 06.06.2012.
http://www.parlament.al/web/Njoftime_per_vende_pune_1158_1.php, retrieved 06.06.2012.
http://www.tirana.gov.al/?cid=1,28, retrieved 06.06.2012.
http://www.keshilliministrave.al/?fq=showcabzvm, retrieved 06.06.2012.
http://www.njoftime.com/showthread.php?t=31322, retrieved 06.06.2012.
http://www.njoftime.com/showthread.php?t=11274, retrieved 06.06.2012.
http://www.njoftime.com/showthread.php?t=111212, retrieved 06.06.2012.

Language and Gender in Tertiary-Level Education

Ljiljana Marković

Introduction

The Serbian language is a grammatical-gender language, with a three-gender system (masculine, feminine and neuter) in which the masculine gender dominates. This 'masculine dominance' (PAUWELS 1998: 41) is expressed on different levels. Morphologically, masculine nouns are treated not only as dominant but also as primary since feminine forms are derived from masculine ones (*direktor$_m$* – *direktorka$_f$*). Syntactically, when there is a compound subject which includes both a feminine and a masculine noun, it is the masculine noun that determines the gender concord with other inflectional word classes (e.g. *Učenice$_f$ i učenici$_m$ su otišli$_m$ na izlet*). Semantically, masculine human agent nouns are used both in the generic and referential sense, while feminine forms are used only referentially[1].

This 'masculine dominance' in Serbian (also documented in other languages) would not present a problem if "grammatical gender [were] a mere linguistic convention and not a linguistic expression of the category of sex" (PAUWELS 1998: 68), as the opponents of the gender-sensitive language reform usually claim[2]. However, as EHRLICH and KING (1998) say, "language is not a neutral vehicle in the representation of reality and [...] it is necessarily laden with social values" (1998: 165). As a consequence, linguistic meaning is determined by the social values and attitudes of socially dominant groups and institutions, reflecting and incorporating them. For this reason, language which reflects sexist values and sexist social structure has to incorporate sexism too.

The study of ways in which language is determined by social sexism is characteristic of the 'second wave' of feminist analysis (PAUWELS 1998; MILLS 2008). Conducted in different languages, these studies show that many languages share the mechanisms employed to express linguistic sexism. PAUWELS (1998) identifies four as most common: 1) man as the norm for all human beings; 2) invisibility of women; 3) linguistic derivation of feminine forms from masculine

---

[1] The scope of this paper does not permit dwelling further on this issue, so these examples are given just as an illustration.
[2] The Serbian Language Standardization Board members often publicly present this argument. It was only recently that they accepted that "wherever it is possible, the feminine-gender nouns should be formed, but not at any cost" (Ivan Klajn, linguist, member of the Serbian Academy of Sciences and Arts and President of the Serbian Language Standardization Board in the article "Ne sveti Sava nego Sveti Save" in *Blic* 2011).

ones; and 4) stereotypical representation of women and men in language (e.g. women are 'sexual' while men are 'rational').

One of the ways in which feminists have confronted sexism so deeply rooted in language is by introducing a gender-sensitive language reform[3], implemented through guidelines for the non-sexist use of language. Although it is usually assumed that this reform takes place only on the superficial level and that essentially it is about replacing existing 'sexist' terms (e.g. *psiholog*$_m$) with newly-introduced 'non-sexist' ones (e.g. *psihološkinja*$_f$), its true goals are: denaturalizing the deeply-rooted concepts of what 'woman' and 'man' are, making women and their contribution to society more visible, and changing the ways in which men and women are linguistically represented. The common strategies used to carry out this reform are: "visibility through feminization (engendering and regendering)" (ROMAINE 2001: 156), characteristic mostly of grammatical-gender languages, and "gender neutralization (degendering)" (ROMAINE 2001: 156), mostly employed in natural-gender languages.

The success of any language reform primarily depends on the social context in which it takes place (EHRLICH/ KING 1998) and the support of socially powerful groups and institutions (EHRLICH/ KING 1998; MILLS 2008). In case of the gender-sensitive language reform, the support has often been missing and the social context unfavorable; yet, there is enough evidence that shows that in many languages the reform has been successful – sufficient enough for CRYSTAL (1984) to consider it one of "the most successful instances of prescriptivism in living memory" (in CAMERON 1995: 119).

It seems that feminists can be satisfied with the implementation of the reform because studies show that it is not carried out only on the superficial level and that it offers different options to women in the negotiation of their identity. Contrary to the usually expressed belief, research shows that this reform has far-reaching effects and that

> [b]y drawing attention to the way language is used to represent women, we also draw attention to the general and specific discrimination against women. By analyzing language, and describing the possibilities of changes in usage, we can signal to women and men that there are other ways of thinking and behaving. (MILLS 2008: 155)

Recent research also shows that those who have embraced the reform have slightly modified their relationship to its propositions. While in the past they

---

[3] Different terms are used to refer to this kind of reform: gender-sensitive, gender-neutral, non-sexist etc. In the Serbian language the frequently used term is 'rodno-osetljiv' ('gender-sensitive') (SAVIĆ 2009).

would passionately use only non-sexist terms, MILLS (2003) shows that feminist women now use both sexist and non-sexist terms, their choice as well as the meaning they inflect the terms with depending on the context and participants of the particular situation. In this way, women negotiate their identity and positions, fully aware of the implications that those choices have. Therefore, MILLS (2003) concludes that reform might not be the only response to sexism and that

> negotiating change through the interaction of individuals with their perceptions of conflicting communities of practice, strategically choosing particular options for particular contexts, and inflecting those choices positively is a more productive model than the Utopian notion that sexism can be reformed out of existence. (MILLS 2003: 104)

As for the gender-sensitive reform of Serbian, the first voices for its adoption and implementation were heard in the 1980s, their number grew in the 1990s (especially within the struggle for overall democratic social changes[4]), and these efforts were rewarded with some institutional success after the democratic changes in 2000. The work of Prof. Svenka Savić and her colleagues was particularly important in this period because they gave shape to the gender-sensitive language reform by composing guidelines for the non-sexist use of language in media and institutions (SAVIĆ 1996; SAVIĆ 2009).

The primary strategy used to undermine the effects of sexism in Serbian, just as in many other grammatical-gender languages (e.g. German, French) is "visibility through feminization" (ROMAINE 2001: 156). The main advantage of this strategy is that women are made visible through the introduction of gender-specific words (e.g. *dekanka$_f$, psihološkinja$_f$*), while its main drawback stems from the strategy itself: it may reinforce the idea (already mentioned as a mechanism in the expression of linguistic sexism) that feminine forms are derivatives and/or deviations from the male norm, since newly-formed gender-specific words are mostly morphologically derived from masculine ones. This may cause problems in the implementation of the reform, so it is necessary to monitor its progress closely and intervene when it seems not to be effective. This intervention can take the form of introducing intermediary measures – what MILLS (2008) calls "transitional strategic use of a range of different options" (2008: 95), or developing "a creative relation with language because the requirement 'make the woman visible in language in the public sphere'

---

[4] PAUWELS (1998) gives the example of Lithuania, where the feminist movement and the gender-based language reform proposal were stimulated by and part of the movement for independent Lithuania.

motivates us to find and create new language forms in our attempt to meet this requirement" (SAVIĆ 2009: 11)[5]. Both of these approaches seem to imply that the success of the language reform depends on language users' awareness that language offers many options to express gender and that it is their decision which option they will choose. This issue of language users' choices is exactly the topic of the present study.

Present study

The present study is a complex, small-scale study, consisting of three parts, each focusing on one of the following: university students' usage of, attitudes to and knowledge of gender-sensitive language. In this way we hoped to find out not only whether young generations had accepted the proposed gender-sensitive forms but also how they felt about individual instances and to what extent they were familiar with gender-sensitive language.

In this paper we will only present the results of Part I, which focuses on the use of gender-sensitive language, though occasional referencing to the findings of Parts II and III will also be made. In Part I the participants were given a writing assignment which was to elicit a language sample containing nouns of titles, positions and professions (*nomina agentis*) to denote a female person, thus exhibiting whether traditional masculine forms or newly-proposed feminine forms would be used.

The participants were 65 senior (3rd- and 4th-year) students of English language, Serbian language, Psychology and Journalism at the Niš University (Serbia) (see Appendix 1 – Table 1 for details). They were selected because, as future employees in schools and media, they would play an important role in the education, socialization and awareness-raising of future generations.

In order to elicit the language sample, the students were asked to write the candidacy of a female student – Jovana Đorđević, running for the president of a students' organization. To secure that the task was done quickly and efficiently, we provided the participants with Jovana Đorđević's CV, thus enabling them to focus on the form of the task rather than (inventing) the content. Based on the provided CV, the participants were expected to write a text of 7–13 sentences which included the information provided in Jovana Đorđević's CV. The text was expected to contain:
- an introduction (the beginning of which was also provided) ("We put Jovana Đorđević forward for the president [...]"),

---

[5] Translation from Serbian into English by Lj.M.

- the body (5–10 sentences), presenting Jovana Đorđević's career (she is a 3rd-year student with her GPA 9.84; winner of highest awards at the university; recipient of two important scholarships; member of the Psychology Students' Association; editor of a students' journal; author/co-author of papers), and
- a conclusion (1–3 sentences) ("These are the reasons why we put Jovana Đorđević forward for the president [...]").

In this text the participants were expected to use the masculine/feminine forms of the following nomina agentis[6]: *kolega/inica; predsednik/ica; student/kinja; dobitnik/ica; član/ica; urednik/ica; predstavnik/ica; (ko)autor/ka; kandidat/kinja*[7].

To avoid influencing the participants in their choice of vocabulary when doing the task, the information in the CV was expressed mostly through impersonal devices, such as: indefinite, abstract nouns (*kandidatura* = "candidacy", *u ko-autorstvo* = "coauthorship"), passive (*rad predstavljen* = "paper presented") or others, some of which are suggested in guidelines for the use of non-sexist language (SAVIĆ 2009). The participants were also given a sample biography of a male candidate running for the same position so that the obtained language samples would have the appropriate format, level of formality and language.

All these steps were taken to ensure obtaining texts which could be similar in the information they contained, the way the information was organized, the audience addressed and the sufficient number of the forms of *nomina agentis* to submit for analysis. Besides, it was believed that, by being provided with the biography of a male candidate, for whom the choice of masculine forms of *nomina agentis* is only natural, the participants would be able to choose freely the form they would normally and spontaneously use in their own writing when talking about a female person.

The obtained sample was analyzed in light of FAIRCLOUGH'S (1989) view of discourse. For Fairclough, "*discourse* [refers] to the whole process of social interaction" (FAIRCLOUGH 1989: 24) and consists of: the text, the process of text production and the process of interpretation. It is also 'ideological' but

> ideologies are brought to discourse not as explicit elements of the text but as the background assumptions which [...] lead the text producer to 'textualize' the

---

[6] The masculine forms are given first because the feminine forms are morphologically derived from them.
[7] In translation: colleague, president, student, award-winner/recipient; member, editor, representative, (co)author, candidate.

world in a particular way, and on the other hand lead the interpreter to interpret the text in a particular way. (FAIRCLOUGH 1989: 85)

In our study it was this ideological aspect that was important. The questions of particular interest were: how the participants in our sample 'textualized' the world and what 'background assumptions' they brought to the process of text productions in relation to gender.

Both quantitative and qualitative analyses were carried out on the data because we were interested in both how often the masculine/feminine forms of the *nomina agentis* were used and under what circumstances they were used. In other words, we wanted to see whether university students – future teaching and media professionals – had accepted reformed forms and, if they had, how they used them.

Quantitative analysis

In our quantitative analysis we focused on the number of masculine vs feminine forms of the *nomina agentis*. Appendix 1 – Table 2 shows the results per departments and in total.

As it can be concluded from the TOTAL column in Table 2, the gender-sensitive language reform seems to be making progress. Namely, the feminine forms were used along with masculine ones with all the nouns. However, the masculine forms overwhelmingly dominate in the majority of cases: they are from 2.5 times (*predsednik$_m$*) to 11.5 times (*predstavnik$_m$*) more often used than the corresponding feminine forms.

The only exceptions in the data were *naša koleginica$_f$* and *dobitnica$_f$*, but it seems that these two had such widespread occurrence for different reasons. The phrase *naša koleginica$_f$* was used in almost 100% of the cases because it appeared along with the name of the candidate – *naša koleginica$_f$ Jovana Đorđević*. The use of the name should also explain why the noun in the predicate was often feminine, although the masculine form of the same noun was sometimes used already in the next sentence (e.g. *Jovana Đorđević je* **studentkinja$_f$** *III godine psihologije. Važi za* **odličnog studenta$_m$**/**za jednog od najboljih studenata$_m$**). This finding that the usage of the woman's name is the key factor in (re)establishing female identity and choosing the feminine form of the noun is in line with earlier studies (MARKOVIĆ 2008). However, the other noun – *dobitnica$_f$* represents more of a puzzle. Namely, there seems to be nothing in the immediate surroundings that would explain the predominant usage of this feminine form.

When we compare the results of the students of different departments, we can notice that there are few differences between them in the usage of masculine and feminine forms respectively. However, it is noticeable that the lowest frequency of feminine forms occurred in the Serbian language students' assignments and highest in the English language students'. We can assume that the Serbian language students used such a small number of feminine forms because their choice was limited by the rules of prescriptive grammar. On the other hand, the high occurrence of feminine forms in English language students' assignments might be the result of their second language influence on the first language performance. Namely, these students are continuously exposed to gender-sensitive (English) language in the classroom (in classes, in latest literature and university textbooks, as a topic for discussion) as well as outside the classroom (newspapers, magazines, some television programs), while the influence of the prescriptive grammar of Serbian seems to be limited at this stage of their education; thus, there might be a transfer from their foreign language to mother tongue performance.

Unfortunately, during the analysis of the data another possible explanation for the great number of masculine forms emerged, located in the design of the study itself. Namely, although great efforts were taken to ensure that the participants produced spontaneous pieces of writing with the minimum influence on the part of the researcher, it turned out that the additional material (the sample biography of the male candidate and the CV of the female candidate) seems to have influenced the participants and their language. This was noticeable not only in the excessive usage of passive structures and abstract nouns worded in the exactly same way as in the biography and CV but also in the unnatural usage of some masculine forms when the referent is clearly female – Jovana (personal pronoun *ga* = "him"; possessive adjective *njegov glas* = "his voice", which were obviously slips made due to referencing back to the male student's candidacy). Consequently, this could raise the question of whether the masculine forms in the male student's candidacy had any influence on the participants' choice of the masculine form to describe the female candidate and whether they would also use it in spontaneous writing. In other words, we should ask to what extent the participants 'mirrored' not only the structure and organization of the provided text (the male student's candidacy) but also the language.[8]

In summary, quantitative analysis shows that the gender-sensitive language reform has some positive results, one of them being the occurrence of feminine nouns along with masculine ones with all the nouns in our data. However, the 'masculine dominance' is still present to a great degree since masculine nouns dominate in all cases but two. Whether this was mainly due to the effect of 'mirroring' or it was the participants' choice remained unclear after quantitative

---

[8] I'm grateful to Prof. Svenka Savić for her comments in this direction.

analysis (just as this analysis did not offer any possible explanation for the frequent occurrence of *dobitnica*$_f$). Therefore, we analyzed the data using qualitative methods, hoping that by "deploying plural research methods, combining both qualitative and quantitative techniques" (BAXTER 2003: 86), we could infer some conclusions about the circumstances in which masculine and feminine nouns are used.

Qualitative analysis

Originally, the qualitative analysis was to focus on the circumstances in the immediate surroundings – particularly the sentence – under which the feminine forms were used. This idea was, however, modified later after the analysis of the participants' attitudes to the feminine forms of some *nomina agentis* in Parts II and III. Namely, in connection with the examples where the title/ position appeared along with the name of the woman (e.g. *Ministarka*$_f$ *Dijana Dragutinović*), several students wrote: "I would use the masculine form; there is the name of the person, so I don't think I need the feminine form, it's redundant if there is the name." These comments seemed to suggest that the grammatical gender of the nouns was not important *per se* as long as there were other forms which pointed to the person's gender or, in other words, the participants seemed to react to the violation of the Gricean maxim on the quantity of information necessary for successful interaction. (GRICE 1989)[9]

This finding about how young generations perceive the question of the linguistic representation of gender slightly changed the focus of the qualitative analysis. The aim now was to establish not only in what contexts the feminine forms were used but also whether the information of the woman's gender was made prominent despite the use of the masculine form of *nomina agentis*. This sort of analysis, obviously, exceeded the level of the sentence – it had to be carried out on the level of the whole text, i.e. in discourse.

The analysis showed that the majority of the participants took the candidate's gender into account and almost regularly used a linguistic form which indicated that the person in question was female. The participants used different devices to express gender: to a certain extent they used the feminine

---

[9] That younger generations and those of researchers can have different attitudes towards the questions of gender has already been reported. Thus, Sunderland and Swann notice that the differences in "background, academic experience and perceptions of 'language and gender', along with teachers' and students' (gender) politics" (SUNDERLAND/ SWANN 2007) affect their teaching and the relationship with their students and that many issues which were important earlier are now perceived as obsolete by students.

form of *nomina agentis* (as the quantitative analysis showed), but they also used a number of morphological, lexical and even syntactic devices to convey the gender information, as the examples below will show. As long as these devices were strategically positioned – in each sentence, the reader was able to keep in mind that the text was about a female.

After the analysis, the assignments were classified in three groups: 1) the ones in which the feminine nouns were consistently used and the gender information was always kept in the foreground; 2) those in which the masculine forms were predominantly used, but the gender information was still prominent thanks to the use of other devices; and 3) those where the masculine forms were predominantly used and where the use of other devices was scarce, which led to losing the gender information at some point. Each group will be illustrated with an example and discussed below.

The first group consisted of the assignments which show how the Serbian language should work under the rules of the gender-sensitive language reform proposal: all the nouns used referentially are feminine and, as a result, the forms of all other inflectional word classes (adjectives, verb forms) are feminine too. Unfortunately, there were only three pieces in this group (4.5%) (one from the English, Journalism and Psychology Departments). Here is an example.

EXAMPLE 1[10] – Student E2[11]

(1) Mi, sa Departmana za psihologiju, predlažemo **našu koleginicu**$_f$ Jovanu Đorđević za **predsednicu**$_f$ studentske organizacije.

(2) Jovana Đorđević je **studentkinja**$_f$ III godine psihologije. (3) **Odlična** je **studentkinja**$_f$ sa prosečnom ocenom 9,84. (4) **Dobitnica**$_f$ je nagrade [...]. (5) Istovremeno Jovana je **dobitnica**$_f$ stipendije programa ASS [...] i Fonda [...].

(6) Jovana je **članica**$_f$ Udruženja studenata psihologije „Psiho" od 2007. do danas [i] **urednica**$_f$ časopisa „Psiho" od 2010. do danas. (7) Jovana je **aktivna**$_f$ i u naučnoj sferi. (8) **Autorka**$_f$ je rada „Identitet [...]", predstavljenog na Filozofijadi na Palama 2009. (9) **Koautorka**$_f$ je rada „Radne navike [...]", objavljenom u časopisu studentanta Univerziteta [...].

---

[10] In the examples, sentences are numbered at their beginning, the feminine forms of the nouns are given in bold, while the name of the person is underlined.

[11] The participants' assignments are coded at random order. The code consists of a letter and a number from 1–21. The letter stands for the department: E – English, S – Serbian, P – Psychology and J – Journalism.

(10) Smatramo da je svojim zalagenjem i učestvovanjem na naučnim skupovima <u>Jovana</u> zaslužila mesto **predsednice**$_f$ studentske organizacije. (11) Nadamo se da ćete **je**$_f$ podržati svojim glasom!

This text has 11 sentences. The name of the person is mentioned six times, while all the *nomina agentis* are feminine, which further requires gender concord in other inflectional classes. This means that each sentence contains at least one cue (usually the feminine noun) which indicates gender; if the person's name is used too, the number of cues increases and gender information is further emphasized. What is particularly striking is that the position Jovana Đorđević is running for is also expressed with the feminine form *predsednica*$_f$, though the administrative jargon and prescriptive grammar require the masculine form here (see MARKOVIĆ 2008). Thanks to the usage of all these linguistic forms, the gender of the candidate is held in the foreground throughout the passage.

The second group is the largest – it consists of 51 assignments (78.5%). In these texts there are not too many feminine nouns but, thanks to the usage of other linguistic devices, gender information is present throughout the assignments.

EXAMPLE 2 – Student J10

(1) Mi, studenti Departmana za psihologiju, predlažemo **našu koleginicu**$_f$ <u>Jovanu Đorđević</u> za predsednika$_m$ studentske organizacije. (2) <u>Jovana Đorđević</u> je student$_m$ III godine psihologije. (3) Odličan je student$_m$ sa prosečnom ocenom 9,84. (4) **Dobitnica**$_f$ je nagrade [...]. (5) Prima stipendiju programa ASS [...] i stidendiju Fonda [...]. (6) <u>Jovana</u> je član$_m$ Udruženja studenata psihologije „Psiho" [...] i uređuje časopis „Psiho". (7) **Njeni**$_f$ radovi predstavljeni su na Filizofijadi na Palama i objavljeni u časopisu studenata [...]. (8) Smatramo da je svojim radom, aktivnošću i odlučnošću <u>Jovana</u> **pokazala**$_f$ da je odličan predstavnik$_m$ studenata i da će se boriti za interese svih studenata. (9) Zato **je**$_f$ predlažemo za predsednika studentske organizacije. (10) Nadamo se da ćete podržati **njen**$_f$ glas!

There are 10 sentences in this text. The candidate's name is mentioned four times and all the *nomina agentis* – including the one indicating the position (*predsednik*$_m$) – are masculine, except for *dobitnica*$_f$. However, despite the almost consistent use of masculine nouns, the person's gender is made prominent throughout the text by means of different word classes: possessives (*njen* = "her"), gender-marked verb forms (*pokazala* = "showed"), personal pronouns (*je [nju]* = "her"), thus leaving each sentence with at least one cue that indicates that the person referred to is a female (just as in Example 1).

Of particular interest is the use of sentence structure to keep the gender information prominent, which is illustrated by Sentences 2 and 3 in Example 2. As we can see, these two sentences have the same structure: $S + be + noun_m$:
- *Jovana Đorđević je student$_m$ III godine psihologije.*
- *Odličan je **student**$_m$ sa prosečnom ocenom 9,84.*

Sentence 2 begins with the name, which is followed by the verb *jesam* (= "be") and *student$_m$* (in line with the rules of prescriptive grammar). The next sentence has the same structure though it is differently worded. Namely, Serbian being a synthetic language, there is no need for the explicit subject in Sentence 3; it is implied – 'transferred' from Sentence 2. For this reason, we can paraphrase these sentences:
- *Jovana Đorđević je **student**$_m$ III godine psihologije. (Jovana) je **odličan student** $_m$.*

In this way, using the same sentence pattern, the text producer managed to transfer the gender information into the next sentence without explicitly stating that and despite using the masculine forms in the noun phrase (*odličan student$_m$*).

As our sample shows, this 'strategy' – using the same sentence pattern, thus enabling the transfer of the gender information into the next sentence – can be used for three sentences in a row: the female name is the subject of the first sentence and then two more sentences follow having the same sentence structure and throughout the part the reader is aware that the text is (still) about a female person, although masculine nouns are used as part of the predicate. However, as will be shown below, if this becomes the only device used in a longer text, the transfer loses its function and becomes 'overpowered' by the masculine form of the nouns.

Example 2 also sheds a new light on the puzzling noun *dobitnica$_f$*, which, strangely, often appeared in the feminine form. As Appendix 1 – Table 2 shows, this noun appears somewhere in the middle of the table, which actually shows that the noun should have been used in the middle of the text. It seems that this positioning of the noun *dobitnica$_f$* was important for the participants' decision on the form to use. As the assignments in this group show, up to the place where the noun *dobitnik/ica* should appear, the participants had used different linguistic devices to keep the candidate's gender prominent (the woman's name, feminine forms of inflectional word classes, syntactic structures...), remaining at the same time true to the rules of prescriptive grammar and consistently using the masculine forms of the *nomina agentis*. At the moment the participants seemed to have exhausted all the devices at their disposal, they resorted to the last one – the feminine form of the noun, breaching the prescriptive rule but at the same time conveying the information they, obviously, found valuable in the context. Viewed in this light, it turns out that the dominance of the feminine form *dobitnica*$_f$ is not a puzzle but that its usage is discursively justified.

Finally, there is a group of 11 biographies (about 17%) in which the nouns are mostly used in the masculine form and where at one point in the text the reader loses track of the candidate's gender.

EXAMPLE 3 – Student S1

(1) Mi, studenti Departmana za psihologiju, predlažemo **našu koleginicu**$_f$ Jovanu Đorđević za **predsednicu**$_f$ studentske organizacije.

(2) Jovana Đorđević je student$_m$ III godine psihologije sa prosečnom ocenom 9,84. (3) Dobitnik$_m$ je nagrade [...] i dobitnik$_m$ je nagrade [...]. (4) Dobitnik$_m$ je stipendije programa ASS [...] i stipindije [...]. (5) Od 2007. do danas član$_m$ je Udruženja studenata [...] i urednik$_m$ časopisa „Psiho". (6) Autor$_m$ je naučnih radova „Identitet adolescenata [...]" i „Radne navike [...]".

(7) Nadamo se da ćete svojim glasom podržati Jovanu Đorđević.

Example 3 is seven sentences long. The person's name is mentioned three times: in the introductory sentence, topic sentence of the second paragraph and conclusion. All the nouns are in the masculine form, except for one – *predsednica*$_f$, which is strange: if we postulate that masculine nouns in the referential sense are used because prescriptive grammar rules require that, then it is surprising that the position, which should be masculine in administrative jargon, is not. There are no feminine forms of other word classes to refer to the candidate, while the syntactic structure as a device used to transfer the gender information to the next sentence is used at the beginning of Paragraph 2. However, as no other devices are used to reinforce that information, the focus shifts from the female person – Jovana Đorđević – onto the 'maleness' of these nouns and from then on the reader pictures the person in question as male. Finally, female identity is brought back into the reader's focus only in the conclusion with the mention of the candidate's name.

Summarizing the results of this analysis, we can say that the participants in our sample seemed to consider the gender information valuable and tried to convey it in 83% of the assignments. Though the number of those who unmistakably used feminine nouns only is rather small, the fact that the majority tried and managed to convey gender information using other linguistic devices points to some success of the gender-sensitive language reform.

Apart from these findings at the level of discourse, the assignments in this sample contained some evidence which also indicates that the gender-sensitive language reform is taking roots. For one, it is the form of the noun *predsednik/*

ica, which should be masculine when denoting the position in administrative jargon. As many as eleven participants (four students of Psychology, three of Serbian, three of Journalism and one of English) were unsure of which form to use – masculine or feminine. Obviously, they did not find the feminine form 'incorrect' in this context and yet they seemed to be aware of the prescriptive rule. For that reason, they used each: the feminine form in the introduction and the masculine form in the conclusion (or vice versa). Additionally, in several instances there is evidence of self-correction on the part of the participants, who either wrote the feminine form first and then changed it into masculine, or wrote the masculine form and then made it feminine by adding the suffix.

All these 'traces' and 'cues' show that language users (at least in our sample) are not led in their language use by the rules of official grammar only but that they seem to be sensitive to social processes and able to react in their own ways. From the point of view of the language reform proponents, it is worth noticing that their efforts are giving results.

Conclusion

In total, our study seems to show that the gender-sensitive language reform is gaining ground. The results of the quantitative analysis indicate that feminine forms are used along with the masculine ones, though the latter outnumber. The qualitative analysis, on the other hand, reveals that there are many devices in the Serbian language (morphological, lexical, syntactic) at the text producer's disposal which, used strategically, can serve as cues for the text interpreter to keep the gender information constantly in focus. This only shows that language is more resilient to the constraints of prescriptive grammar and that the text producer's message can find its way into the linguistic expression – as long as they find this message important to convey.

Even the fact that the participants were uncertain which form to use (feminine or masculine) seems to indicate that they have a growing awareness of the linguistic intervention as well as social issues behind it. In this way, the gender-sensitive language reform proves to work "on a range of different levels, consciousness-raising as well as at this more symbolic level, attempting to foreground changes in the status of women and men". (MILLS 2008: 78)

Another point in relation to the study of gender is that it should be approached from different perspectives and using different methods. In our study, thanks to a "multi-method approach" (WODAK 1996 in BAXTER 2003: 86) – the combination of quantitative and qualitative analyses and the study of the participants' use of and attitudes to gender-sensitive language, we could conclude that feminine forms were not the sole carriers of gender information. In addition, our decision to study the use of feminine forms in discourse (rather than in a sentence) shed a new light on our understanding of the linguistic construction of gender and drew attention to various linguistic devices that language users had at their disposal. This is completely in line with Romaine's stance that "reform must be directed at discourse as a whole rather than piecemeal at gendered bits of the language such as titles, forms of address, and androcentric generics". (ROMAINE 2001: 154)

Finally, one of the greatest outcomes of the gender-sensitive language reform could be the realization that, as language users change their ideas about 'woman', 'man' and gender, they look for new linguistic devices and explore new ways to express those new concepts. Thus, the participants in our study, who seemed to be aware of gender issues in language and society, did not opt for new non-sexist terms, nor did they choose to ignore gender completely; they chose to find other linguistic cues which would help them convey the gender information. In this way, applying the principle of 'action and reaction' – from the measures of awareness-raising (language reform being one of them) to new language use – and back again, "[w]orking on sexism [becomes] not a once-and-for-all process, but rather an ongoing process of attention to discrimination". (MILLS 2008: 68) The fact that young people in our sample (future professionals in education and media) have used critical thinking and re-thinking of gender issues gives hope that the work will give positive results.

References

BAXTER, JUDITH (2003): Positioning Gender in Discourse. A Feminist Methodology. Basingstoke.
CAMERON, DEBORAH (1995): Verbal Hygiene. London/New York.
CRYSTAL, DAVID (1984): Who cares about English usage? An entertaining guide to common problems of English usage. London.
EHRLICH, SUSAN/ RUTH KING (1998): Gender-based language reform and the social construction of meaning. In: Cameron, Deborah (ed.): The Feminist Critique of Language. A Reader. London et al. 164–179.
FAIRCLOUGH, NORMAN (1989): Language and Power. London et al.
GRICE, HERBERT PAUL (1989): Logic and conversation. In: Grice, H. P. (ed.): Studies in the Way of Words. Cambridge. 22–40.
MARKOVIĆ, LJILJANA (2008): Kad je ona u pitanju, da li je ona ona ili on? Predstavljanje žena u univerzitetskim dokumentima. In: Točanac, Dušanka/ Milena Jovanović (ed.): Primenjena lingvistika 9. 225–239.
MILLS, SARA (2003): Caught Between Sexism, Anti-sexism and 'Political Correctness'. Feminist Women's Negotiations with Naming Practices. In:

Discourse & Society, 14/1. 87–110. http://das.sagepub.com/content/14/1/87, retrieved 21.8.2011.

MILLS, SARA (2008): Language and sexism. Cambridge et al.

NJEŽIĆ, TATJANA (2011): Nije sveti Sava nego Sveti Sava. Dopunjeni Pravopis u školama. In: Blic (8.4.2011). 23.

PAUWELS, ANNE (1998): Women changing language. London et al.

ROMAINE SUZANNE (2001): A corpus-based view of gender in British and American English. In: Hellinger, Marlis/ Hadumod Bussmann (eds.): Gender across languages. The linguistic representation of women and men 2. Amsterdam. 153–175.

SAVIĆ, SVENKA (1998): Žena sakrivena jezikom medija: kodeks neseksističke upotrebe jezika. http://www.womenngo.org.rs/sajt/sajt/izdanja/zenske_studije/zs_s10/svenka.html, retrieved 14.08.2006.

SAVIĆ, SVENKA (2009): Rod i jezik. In: Savić, Svenka/ Marijana Čanak/ Veronika Mitro/ Gordana Štasni (ed.): Rod i jezik. Ženske studije i istraživanja i Futura publikacije. Novi Sad. 7–31.

SUNDERLAND JANE/ JOAN SWANN (2007): Teaching language and gender. http://www.llas.ac.uk/resources/gpg/2827, retrieved 9.2.2011.

WODAK, RUTH (1996): Disorders of Discourse. London.

Appendix 1 – Tables

Table 1 – The number of participants from each department and the female : male participants ratio[12]

Department	No. of participants	Female : Male ratio
English Language Dpt	11	8:3
Serbian Language Dpt	16	14:0 (2)
Journalism Dpt	17	11:5 (1)
Psychology Dpt	21	20:1
TOTAL	65	53:9 (3)

Table 2 – Frequency of masculine vs feminine forms used

NOUN Masculine/ feminine form[13]	English Dpmt	Serbian Dpmt	Journalism	Psychology	TOTAL
Naš kolega/ naša koleginica	0:10	1:10	0:12	0:17	1:49
Predsednik/ -nica	6:7	14:2	14:5	16:6	50:20
Student/-kinja 3. godine	8:3	15:0	13:4	16:4	52:11
Odličan student/-kinja	5:1	12:1	11:1	15:2	43:5
Dobitnik/-ica	1:8	8:6	6:5	5:11	20:30
Član/-ica	5:3	16:0	13:2	16:2	50:7
Urednik/-ica	3:3	4:0	3:1	2:1	12:5
Predstavnik/ -ica	5:0	5:0	6:1	7:1	23:2
(Ko)autor/-ka	0:2	1:0	3:1	3:0	7:3
Kandidat/ -kinja	2:1	0:0	4:1	1:0	6:2

---

[12] The number in brackets shows the number of students who did not mark their sex.
[13] In translation: our colleague, president, student, award-winner/ recipient; member, editor, representative, (co)author, candidate.

Appendix 2 – Translation of the examples

EXAMPLE 1[14] – Student E2[15]

(1) We, students of the Psychology Department, put **our colleague**$_f$ Jovana Đorđević forward for the **president**$_f$ of the students' organisation.

(2) Jovana Đorđević is a 3rd-year psychology **student**$_f$.(3) She is **an excellent student**$_f$ with the GPA 9,84. (4) She has been the **winner**$_f$ of [the following awards]. (5) At the same time Jovana is the **recipient**$_f$ of the scholarship of the ASS program and of the Fund [...].

(6) Jovana has been a **member**$_f$ of the Psychology Students' Association "Psycho" since 2007 and the **editor**$_f$ of the journal "Psycho" since 2010. (7) Jovana has been **active**$_f$ in the field of research as well. (8) She is the **author**$_f$ of the paper "Identity [...]", presented at the students' conference in Pale in 2009. (9) She is the **coauthor**$_f$ of the paper "Work habits [...]", published in the journal of the students of Niš University.

(10) We believe that Jovana has earned the position of the **president**$_f$ of the students' organisation with her engagement and participation in scientific meetings. (11) We hope that you will support **her**$_f$ giving your voice!

EXAMPLE 2 – Student J10

(1) We, students of the Psychology Department, put **our colleague**$_f$ Jovana Đorđević forward for the president$_m$ of the students' organisation.

(2) Jovana Đorđević is a 3rd-year psychology student$_m$. (3) She is an excellent student$_m$ with the GPA 9,84. (4) She is the **winner**$_f$ of [the awards] [...]. (5) She receives the scholarships of the ASS program [...] and of the Fund [...]. (6) Jovana is a member$_m$ of the Psychology Students' Association "Psycho" [...] and edits the journal "Psycho". (7) **Her**$_f$ papers were presented at the students' conference in Pale and and published in the students' journal [...].

(8) We believe that her work, activities and determination have shown$_f$ that Jovana is an excellent representative$_m$ of students and that she will fight for the interests of all students. (9) This is the reason why we put **her**$_f$ forward for the

---

[14] In the examples, sentences are numbered at their beginning, the feminine forms of the nouns are given in bold, while the name of the person is underlined.
[15] The participants' assignments are coded at random order. The code consists of a letter and a number from 1–21. The letter stands for the department: E – English, S – Serbian, P – Psychology and J – Journalism.

president~m~ of the students' organization. (10) We hope that you will support **her**~f~ voice!

EXAMPLE 3 – Student S1

(1) We, students of the Psychology Department, put **our colleague**~f~ Jovana Đorđević forward for the **president**~f~ of the students' organisation.

(2) Jovana Đorđević is a 3rd-year psychology student ~m~ with the GPA 9,84. (3) She is the winner ~m~ of the award [...] and winner ~m~ of the award [...]. (4) She is the recipient~m~ of the scholarship of the ASS program [...] and of the scholarship [...]. (5) Since 2007 she has been a member~m~ of the Psychology Students' Association [...] and the editor~m~ of the journal "Psycho". (6) She is the author~m~ of the papers: "The Identity of Adolescents [...]" and "The Work Habits of [...]".

(7) We hope that you will support Jovana Đorđević with your voice.

"Performing – Women" and the Socio-Political Regime: Addressing in Socialist Slovenia Compared to Today

Renata Šribar

The present discussion is dedicated to a historical and comparative study of the intersection of gender and class, with latter as a phenomenon being modified and alleviated by the now abandoned socio-political regime.[1] The elaboration of the topic is embedded in a structured interdisciplinary theoretical field derived from feminist theory and theory of discourse, anthropology, structural and feminist linguistics and semiology. The described positioning in relation to the series of possible subjects and webs of knowledge, whereby the feminisms are accentuated, is affected – and not determined – by the location in the partly still lived "transitional" period from late socialism to neoliberal capitalism; in that fluid constellation of socio-political orders and related economies, gender (a woman) and a (middle) class location co-construct the perspective – and it is marked by the feeling and awareness of gradual marginalisation and deprivation.

As the category woman/women represents the author's pivotal location in the existing context and is simultaneously a basis for theoretical positioning, it needs to be defined. This is especially crucial in relation to the poststructuralist stance, which integrates deconstruction of the epistemological grasp of the social group in question.[2] In the study women are conceptualised as a still relevant category, denoting an administratively defined and/or self-identified multitude of persons so engendered. The articulated indexation has no biological reference[3] in any interpretative manner (cf. RAHMAN/ JACKSON 2010: 119, 129, 132–133). The accompanying structural insight is rendered by thinking of women as non-homogenous, i.e. a complexly segmented social group.[4] In other words,

---

[1] The idea of the research study arose from a beneficial invitation to a conference organised by the Department of South Slavic Cultural and Linguistic Studies (in conjunction with the Centre for Transdisciplinary Gender Studies) at Humboldt University in Berlin in May 2011 entitled Doing Gender – Doing the Balkans. Dynamics and Persistence of Gender Relations in South-Eastern Europe.

[2] The fractionising of the collective subject "women" troubles feminist linguistics (CANNING 1994: 370) as much as some other fields of feminist and gender studies.

[3] On this point, we agree with Deborah Cameron who claims that feminism has been axiomatically socially constructivist (and sex/gender reflected as socially constructed) since the days and work of Simone de Beauvoir (CAMERON 1999: 121).

[4] Usually in research the intersecting axes of women's locations consist of class, race, religion, socio-political conditions, ethnicity, sexual orientation, citizenship or refugee status; in any case, there are some important but not so theoretically obvious sources of unequal societal power relations, such as bodily conditions, profession, native language and others.

by women we indicate a categorically unified but structurally diversified social group, intersected via the axes of different issues of discrimination and subjection. Thereby occurs a hierachisation of the social opportunities of women. With the described positioning we are resonating (what might be called) the late feminism of the last three decades. We are thus distancing ourselves from the narrowness of the rigid Third Wave gendered "situatedness" and "small stories", and from the stance of postmodernism: "there is no need for feminism anymore" – as well as from queer ambivalent positioning with respect to the paradigmatic exposures of women to subjection. The only queer conceptualisation which recognises the gender matrix is corporeal and economic violence (see BUTLER 2004).

As the research into differentiated addressing practices focuses on the intersections of gender, class and socio-political conditions it is obvious that we had to restrict ourselves regarding the sources of gendered hierarchies, although some of them will also be tackled as we go along. The poststructuralist and Third Wave approach will be included by reference to selected situations of language usage and by deconstructing some dominating conceptualisations of the contemporary status of women. To analyse situatedness in line with the structuralist inquiry we apply ethnographic[5] methods of participant observation, interviews and a questionnaire.

Language and societal gender division from the feminist perspective

Statements and grammar

A return to the basic question posed above in the conceptualisation of women/gender is reiterated in a reflection of the relationship between language and gender. A revision of two alternative options was performed by Sara Mills – one being the determinative role of language and the other accommodative; the author herself articulates the third possibility and defines the relationship as a dialectic one: language affirms and contests women's status in society. By referring to British feminists of the 1980s, when gender and language became an important subject in Great Britain, she actually describes their linguistic "anti-sexist" endeavours as fighting against statements which hierarchically divide two gender social groups (MILLS 2003: 88–89). But one finds it much more

---

[5] Although the piling up of disciplines seems not to contribute, it is appropriate to mention BONNIE MCELHINNY and SARA MILLS' reference to the ethnography of communication (besides e.g. pragmatics and sociolinguistics) while discussing the scope of the then new journal *Gender and Language* (2007: 6). As there are many definitions of the field, we apply a reasonably grounded one: the ethnography of communication being the application of ethnographic methods to the study of communication patterns of a group.

difficult to accept the idea that language is adaptable to societal changes with regard to gender statuses if grammar is examined. For example, the Slovenian language is extremely gender-marked morphologically and syntactically. But as the subject of the present discussion is not a systematic inquiry in the field – that has been done elsewhere, from the gender-sensitive Slovenistic perspective by Olga KUNST GNAMUŠ (1994/95) and from the feminist linguistic point of view by Paula ZUPANC (2009) – let these three examples suffice to illustrate the thesis. Some nouns in the Slovenian language denote persons with no feminine equivalent; actually, if we articulate the feminine form of a noun an item or thing is indicated and this grammatically implied rule is indicative of women's passive status: e.g. *naslovnik* (Engl. "addressee") – *naslovnica* ("front page"), *popotnik* ("traveller") – *popotnica* ("snack for a journey"). The most often cited syntactical example is one of conjugating a verb if the subject denotes one or more women and an animal of masculine gender. As probably anticipated by the readers, the verb has to be formed in masculine dual or plural. Another grammatical example of gender-biased Slovenian grammar are words of masculine gender referring to personhood and humanity: the nouns *človek, ljudje* (Engl. "man, people") and pronouns *kdo, kateri, koga, nekdo* etc. ("who", "which one", "whom", "one/somebody") (KUNST GNAMUŠ, 1994/95: 256). The unequal social gender system reflected in grammar is not inclined to change even over a longer period of vacillating gender relations. As the argumentation would be similar with other European languages, the alteration of the strategic approach from the initial discourse on "sexism in language" to the "gender-sensitive usage of language" reflects the rigidity of the socio-cultural gender system. It is much more strictly coded in grammar than in the choice of certain words and phrases taken out of the fundamental grammatical narrative of a native language. In any case, by analysing ways of addressing people we are inquiring into the sphere of *language usage* with the aim to analyse the status of women amid the changed socio-political conditions and related class divisions.

The construction of meaning

In Eva WANIEK's[6] elaboration of the structural linguistics of Ferdinand de Saussure she states that the differential meaning of "woman" depends on culturally specific connotations – semantic paradigms (2005: 61). The assertion represents the point of difference between feminist linguistics and "proper" Slovenistic

---

[6] In the referential article she selected the topic of comparing different philosophical traditions in language theories, and applied the knowledge for deconstruing the German word *Geschlecht*.

linguists, when the latter try to intervene in the contemporary feminist linguistic problematisations of "sexism in language". Even their argument of the "rationality" of language usage which should not be "overloaded" by masculine and feminine forms is based on a suppressed denial of the active/performative role of language in gender relations. Language usage and its reflection of the grammatical structure integrate a series of associations. Following the argumentation and example of Eva Waniek's "differential-semantic perspective" and the communication function of language in the case of the word "woman" (Ger. *Frau*), it is important to recognise that a sign includes *difference* as well as *similarity* in relation to other signs (ibid.: 54, 59). Thus, the meaning of the Slovenian word *ženska* is closely connected to the (truly flexible) meanings of the words and syntagms *lepa/grda/mlada/stara/seksi/huda ženska, lepši/drugi spol, punca* ("pretty/ugly/young/old/sexy/hot woman", "better/other sex", "girl") etc. The series of dominating associations and thus the prevailing meaning of the word does not only change over time (and in dependence on its socio-political and economic conditions), but also according to specific interpersonal situations where the dominance of the meaning which will prevail is induced by power relations. The process is different on the deeper level of meaning formation, with the grammatical inflection of verbs, pronouns and adjectives. The exposed example of a group of women with an accompanying dog, indicated by a verb as a masculine formation is a social power-related constellation where the inflection of the verb serves as a grammatical sign of the systemic locating of women in society, with the latter being reflected in women's unpaid work and emotional and sexual exploitations (for that see PATEMAN 1988).[7] As argued, the Slovenian language[8] is among other ones the system (with relating structures) for organising society hierarchically – gender being the starting point for analysing inequality from the feminist perspective. In certain situations this might be challenged. But the inversions of gendered meanings do not jeopardise the hierarchically organised grammatical order. The orthodoxy of Slovenistic grammarians thereby effects to some degree the powers of meaning inversions in the situated relations of language usage. They most often do not transcend importantly the dominating constructions of "femininity" and "masculinity" –

---

[7] Here I stepped a little off track by extending the thematisation of the production of meaning to the level of inflections in the syntax, but it seemed important to evolve the argumentation of Eva WANIEK (2007) to the level of the inflections produced in the syntax of the Slovenian language. The difference between producing the meaning of nouns and that of the inflections of verbs, pronouns and adjectives is the difference between associative ("latent") or paradigmatic, and syntagmatic levels of language.

[8] At least to my knowledge the same could be proven for some other native European languages: Croatian, Serbian, Bosnian, English, German, Italian, Spanish and French.

and this is also valid in cases where the gender roles of the enunciators are inversed. Some changes in dominating meanings are indicative of changes in the status of women, but they fluctuate as regards negative and positive values of womanhood in different areas of life and do not have the impact on the gender regime.

Interpersonal relations and discursive mainstream

Inversed meanings expand what is supposed to be "feminine" or "masculine", what is supposed to be a woman and a man as long as the new meanings are successfully negotiated in a "language community". Certain linguistic codes and language/discursive practices integrate the evaluation of the other person/-s' positions and thereby the self-positioning in the spectrum of (background) beliefs (see MILLS 2003: 92). In fact, the active meaning construing role is limited to the interplay of (known and guessed) social locations (such as gender, class, sexual orientation, cultural background, education, profession) of the persons and their prescribed characteristic which they "naturally" derive from them. The "speech communities", which are on the social margins, co-operate in the production of new meanings in the dominating language practice/ discourse if they succeed in *invading* the communication means or codes of those holding power positions. But such endeavours on the mainstream level rarely succeed. The thesis could be illustrated by taking the example offered by Sara MILLS of a feminist and meaning construing in mind. The author describes the imaginary situation of a feminist who has to decide if she has been the target of a sexist enunciation. She does that in consideration of the stance of her feminist comrades and her own attitude towards them (2003: 93). Her feelings provoked by the situation are not independent of the beliefs of the community and her position in it. But on reporting the event she might find her conclusion of having been sexually harassed being mocked and not easy to believe. On the contrary – if continuing Sara MILLS' emphatic imagination – her feelings and conclusions might well be misused for just another offence based on gender, sexuality and age power relations ("You should be happy that someone even takes a look at you now you are in your forties"). The dominant discourse exhibits its power here and this is not on her behalf. In contrast, the feminist campaigns against violence against women promoted by the mass media have defined the meaning of *more overt sexual harassment* of women as offensive and illegitimate. As we have learned from the study of the pornographisation of culture, when an improvement is made in one area, another is further aggravated – and the existing gender regime survives.

Against biased F/M: concepts in tackling addressing practices

Similarly as Sara MILLS reports for Great Britain (2003: 88), Slovenian feminism initially covered the gender and non-sexist language topic by focusing on naming practices and nouns. The Slovenian thematisation which first gained public and media interest was an integral part of a governmental project executed by the Office for Women's Politics; the immediate impact on the political and media discourse was not as strong, although some norms were established, e.g. the use of feminine and masculine forms of nouns denoting professionals in job advertisements in traditional news media. But the stipulation was soon largely avoided by the phrase the "generic masculine form refers to both genders alike", or with F/M in brackets, which are used with the noun in the masculine form.

At the same time, in the 1990s, gender sensibility as regards the surname of married women, whereby they keep their own one, was limited to feminist and leftist pro-feminist communities. The habit of exchanging surnames with husbands and thus keeping their own was established. Generally, women took and still are taking their husband's surname and very often in formal and informal situations they are called by the form of the surname which suggests property: *tovarišica/gospa* (Engl. "comrade/Ms") *Pahorjeva* instead of *tovarišica/gospa Pahor*. Regarding the titles of women, the feminine form was and still is a subject for negotiation.

From the concept of "woman" to embodied personhood

Referring to Eva WANIEK's argument about the connotative (associative) constructions of the meaning "woman", the difficulties of accepting the female forms of nouns denoting professions and professional statuses and mainstream unawareness or ignorance as regards the symbolic meaning of surnames and their forms reveal the continuity of a certain schism. The field of words and syntactic rules, most closely connected to the formation of the meaning of "woman/women" dictate the parameters of reifying the concept when applied to an individual or a social group. The mechanism which links paradigmatic intra-linguistic elements with the material dimension of the world narrows a woman's options in interpersonal relations. This happens by way of words/signs functioning as a means of communication and affirmation of a certain perspective/picture of life. The language dimension in question reveals a contrast between the integration of women in society on equal terms with men at least as regards the accessibility of education and work (in the EU), and the subtle mechanisms of sustaining the gender hierarchy.

Performing women by addressing

In the preceding argument we applied the Saussurian linkage of language with the (re-)production of life substantialities (for a complex explanation on the relationship between language and realities grounded in the work of Ferdinand de Saussure, see WANIEK 2005: 61). Yet in contemporary feminist theories related to the impact of symbolic exchanges in a society (discursive practices) on the level of the lived, the speech act theory and the concepts of illocutionary acts and the performative are echoed. The difference lies in the positioning – while feminist theory applies the conceptualisation of the performative and relates it to the Foucauldian concept of discourse (where native language is one of many symbolic systems), the framework presented above is primarily linguistic, Saussurian proper.

For the sake of the present research study methodology, the feminist approach needs to be explained with reference to Judith Butler and her conceptual source, John L. Austin.

The named philosopher of language considers performative (in opposition to constative) an utterance which, besides meaning, has the characteristic of an act. The latter is conceptualised as an *illocutory act* by which the difference between the act of uttering and the act of actually doing something by linguistic means is exposed (AUSTIN 1990: 14, 88–89). Feminist philosopher Judith Butler coined the syntagm gender performativity to express and explain the socio-cultural mechanism of gender construing, which is sustained by the reiteration of (symbolic and simultaneously substantiated) acting (BUTLER 2001). The instability and controversy of the individual enacting of gender is thus masked and the socio-culturally prescribed gender "roles" become naturalised and normalised.

The reiteration moment of gender performativity is the key factor in understanding addressing practices as one of the dominating discourses in the reproduction of gender dichotomy and its variances at the intersection of socio-political regimes and socio-economic class. The related and changeable set of beliefs, which give meaning to the associations induced by a specific addressing practice, is a constituent part of the semantic field of addressing. The words habitually used and understood in the prevalent way confirm the background beliefs which integrate the idea of gender hierarchy and its dichotomies. As already argued, meanings of the prevailing linguistic options in addressing implicitly revolve around, reflect, co-constitute and recycle the dominant conceptualisation of "woman", her status in the gender structure (see WANIEK 2003: 60).

Ambiguous "lady": addressing practices in socialist Slovenia

Certain hierarchically marked differences in the way women are addressed in comparison to men can be done away with or reduced in specific socio-political environments and the related socio-cultural contexts. According to the addressing practices narrative, the better status of women in a certain sphere is "adjusted" to the norms of the gender hierarchy by making it worse in another sphere. The research study, involving a survey of addressing practices in the 1970s and 1980s and in the present time, provides evidence on the thesis, although the research is limited to Slovenia and two periods of different socio-political regimes.

The subject may seem narrow to allow generalised conclusions to be drawn but, as was argued, the meanings in any discursive (thereby linguistic) practice are effected by a specific socio-cultural meta-discourse, modulated as background beliefs integrated into a certain social regime and its dominant cultural meanings, where marginalised discourses are also formulated in relation to the mainstream.

The paradigmatic, associative structure of addressing with its extra-linguistic referential dimension in the practice of utterers is constitutive of the addressing discourse. In spoken language, the integrated meanings also depend on intonation and situation, while in written language the production of meaning is affected by the typography or mode of writing, and the context. As the first part of the inquiry was a personal recollection of addressing practices during Slovenian socialism, as confirmed and corrected by two interviews and later on elaborated by a written questionnaire and some structured interviews, there is very little evidence of the mentioned phenomena, namely intonation, writing, situatedness or context. This is the reason why mostly the formal and habitual addressing practices were considered, where extra linguistic elements are of less importance.

Resumed epistemological and methodological issues

The explication of the epistemological base, the "formative theoretical framework" (SCHENSUL et al. 1999: 92) of the research study, aimed at establishing definitions of the concepts/categories which have already become some kind of academic floating currencies: women, gender, language, discourse, meaning – symbolic. These key analytical elements are contextually intertwined so it was important to indicate the relevant interrelations among them. Special attention was paid to the relation language – discourse – meaning – performative (for a more thorough yet brief insight, see BUTLER 1993). In the exposed entanglement the concept of discourse holds a privileged status of integrating the other three concepts, if considered as a *discursive formation*.[9]

After the first data were obtained (by personal recollection and two structured interviews) it was contended that the respect for women, their status and gender equity, as reflected in a certain addressing mode, might have been diminished by rudeness and gender discrimination in another addressing mode during socialism. After that, the research into addressing practices was extended and the thesis evolved: the structural inequalities, reflected and reconfirmed in the discussed usage of language, and the related discourses had different characteristics in both socio-economic regimes; the perceived and stressed inequalities appeared and are appearing in different areas of life in the two periods. Besides, Slovenian neo-liberal capitalism cannot be generalised as it is socio-culturally specific, especially when taking the gender point of view into consideration. On one hand, the employment rate of women is high and the gender differential in salaries is low compared to the EU average but, on the other, the porno-sexualisation of girls has even proliferated to kindergartens. Both issues are indirectly but indicatively implied in addressing practices.

To further develop the research, the referred to categories and concepts – gender (indeed in its dichotomic form), socio-economic class, education sphere, sexualisation – were tackled openly and directly by a questionnaire on addressing practices during socialist Slovenia. Although the first four questions, which were optional, inquired about the respondents' gender, age, socio-political status and cultural environment (urban, suburban), the selection was not representative according to the listed categories (except age) since confirmation or disagreement in recollecting was not supposed to be conditioned by the demographic characteristics of gender, class and the cultural environment if dominant public practices were in question. The relatively high number of questionnaires sent out was a consequence of contemplating the difference between memory and recollection, where the latter has the character of subjectivity and bias, of the interaction of perception and fantasy, and memory is conceptualised as a "primal" remembering of names (see KELLOGG 2001: 342). The data on contemporary addressing practices were chiefly obtained – besides writing down my own experience – on the internet, and by semi-structured interviews in informal situations where I was participating in the observing situation.

The questionnaire on addressing people in the 1970s and 1980s in socialist Slovenia consisted of 17 questions, including the optional ones on demographic

---

[9] Conceptually speaking, "discourse" is derived from the extended understanding of the linguistic production of meaning to the other systems of meaning production and thereby practices in a certain society.

data. It was sent to my colleagues, friends, secondary school peers, relatives and acquaintances, all together to 27 mail addresses; the etiquette and ethical standards were fulfilled by a request to co-operate in a minor project with a defined scientific purpose, and a guarantee of anonymity; the supposed time for filling in the answers, by indicating one or two of the indicated options and by providing some commentaries, was 10 to 15 minutes.

The questions inquiring into modes of addressing women/men formally in written and spoken language during socialism were as follows: the possibility of a woman being (old-fashionably) addressed after the profession of her husband, addressing modes at work (if already employed then), possible differences in addressing subordinates and those of a higher rank, the modes of addressing teachers in elementary, secondary and tertiary education, the meaning of the words *dama*, *baba* and *dec* ("lady", "hag" and "dude"), the mode of addressing a house-maid and a house help, and the name-calling of boys and girls due to supposed cowardice; the last two questions concerned the naming of women and men with sex appeal. The function of the initial four questions on demographic data, which were optional, was primarily psychological – to give the respondents the impression and a guarantee that they would not be treated personally in a publicised text, but as an anonymous character at the aggregate level.

The data on the modes of addressing in contemporary Slovenia were obtained by way of participant observation and writing systematised notes; reports on some addressing (and naming) practices used in communities of teenagers and young people were obtained on the web; there was also an article on the topic in the left-leaning journal *Mladina* which had collected information on that topic. The sources referred to deal with youth slang and internet slang.

For the sake of the presented study, semi-structured interviews were conducted with two relatives, a girl aged 11 and a boy aged 13, preliminarily on name-calling in the community of minors; the current practices in the education system were obtained by three structured interviews with two boys aged 17 and 22, and a girl aged 18.[10]

---

[10] These last data were obtained by two friends of mine, a journalist/media commentator and an anthropologist.

Gender roles made and remade: a comparative and historical analysis of the data obtained on addressing practices

Some general remarks

Of the initial 27 people, 18 answered the questionnaire; only one did not provide the demographic data. Two of the four men asked to respond had promised answers but did not actually provide them, so there are only two responses from men although they do not differ on any issue from those of the female respondents. The age span is from 30 years of age to over 70 (only decades were listed in the related demographic question). All respondents belong to the middle class and all three integrated socio-economic divisions are represented in that (lower middle, middle middle and higher middle class); all the respondents are highly educated,[11] one-third have a PhD, one an MA, and the others a bachelor's degree.

Qualitative and quantitative data analyses of formal addressing

In the recollection of formal addressing the prevailing option is that both forms were used in socialism: *tovarišica/tovariš* and *gospa/gospod*, depending on the status relation and circumstances. Three respondents in the two age decades from 40 to 60 claimed that only the form *tovarišica/tovariš* was used. Another three (in the three age decades from 40 to 70) claimed the opposite, that only *gospa/gospod* was the usual form (two of them stated that the exception was when school teachers were being addressed). Nowadays, formally strictly *gospa/gospod* are used beside an option with titles, with or without the surname. The popularised form is a combination of the formal *gospa/gospod* together with the homelike and local colour usage of the first name (e.g. *gospa Tina*); this is habitual in work situations, in shops, with distant (but not too much) neighbours etc. It would be of interest to obtain gender-disaggregated quantitative data on this mode of addressing, but at the moment this is beyond our task. Today, *tovarišica/tovariš* are only used informally and humorously or a little sarcastically as a sympathetic or rejecting hint at the past.

The recollections of the professional environment as regards addressing (of the 11 respondents who already had a job in the socialistic 1970s and/or 1980s) reveal the great probability that the most often used form was *tovariš/ tovarišica*. Other choices were both forms (two responses), or the use of g*ospa/*

---

[11] The only person contacted to complete the survey with a job-training education did not answer the questionnaire in spite of repeated requests.

gospod, which was only selected by two respondents (one of whom is relatively young). Besides, the strong inclination towards the socialist notion of social equality in remembrances is expressed by selecting the answer "no" for the question of whether addressing was hierarchically conditioned in the work environment (11 of 14 of those who responded to that question). In the addressing of school teachers, grammar school and university professors, the use of *gospa/gospod* and *tovarišica/tovariš* depended on the education level. More than half of the respondents (9 of 17), who were all educated at the primary and secondary level in socialism confirmed the option offered that *tovarišica/tovariš* was used in elementary school (without a surname) and, in secondary school, *gospa/gospod* with the added noun professor was the appropriate etiquette. The female form of "professor", i.e. *profesorica*, was not a rule in that syntagma. A few claimed that in grammar schools both forms were used (two), and some that only *tovarišica/tovariš* was the proper way of addressing. Two respondents suggested that exclusively addressing with *profesor/profesorica* was also a practice. Regarding tertiary education, there was an agreement that mostly *profesor/profesorica* was used with the surname added. Just like in grammar school, the female form *profesorica* was thereby often dropped, while the form of surname which suggests the idea of a woman as property was used instead (e.g. *profesor Torijeva*). Nowadays, children use various forms with teachers in elementary schools: *gospa učiteljica/gospod učitelj* ("Ms/Mr teacher")*, učitelj/učiteljica* (masculine and feminine forms of "teacher")*,* very rarely *gospa/gospod* ("Ms/Mr"). The old *tovarišica/tovariš* happens to be used with gym teachers, as reported by one of the respondents who was an elementary school teacher a few years ago. At the secondary education level the mode *gospa/gospod* accompanied by *profesor/profesorica* is still dominant, but with an important distinction: women in this role are more often addressed with the morphologically adequate and "politically correct" form *gospa profesorica* (and not *gospa profesor*, which is also grammatically correct). A similar change occurs when addressing female teachers at the tertiary level. The most common form is the "politically correct" one, at least in the social sciences and humanities: *profesorica (Grosman)*.

The narrative of addressing practices reveals that education level and associated status of teachers play a role in elementary and secondary education: the notion of equality, expressed by "comrade" in elementary schools was nearly abolished in secondary education – the connotation being evident by the trajectory of the old-school respect for the profession of professors in the traditional gymnasium. The addressing form in tertiary education in socialist Slovenia, when reduced to the title, indicates a specific function of the student–professor relationship. This mode has been emphasized in the transformed socio-economic order; it is even more stressed by the occasional new informal practice of addressing professors – mentors on the postgraduate level by their first name. The professional comradeship between students and professors had and still has a dominant role in sustaining the academic hierarchy. The expressions of internal "equalities" and comradeships, in spite of status differences, are possible on behalf of the external hierarchy, with academia being the privileged sphere of knowledge production.

The inquiry into the possibility of addressing a woman by her husband's profession confirmed the opinion that was highly unusual. Half of the obtained answers (nine) claimed that there was no such habit during socialism. The other answers consisted of a "not sure" option (three), and additional explanatory sentences: "yes, but not in my community", "yes, but not often", "only in petit-bourgeoisie". The contemporaneous use of this form does not existent.

The question on the meaning of the word "lady" had a provocative implication because of the supposition that it had been subverted in socialism. Among the three options provided of the possible meaning of "lady", there were nine answers that the word denoted a woman with distinguished manners and of a high social status, six answers referred to "women who have nothing else to do but to care for themselves", two choices indicated an "expression for prostitutes" (this was also the opinion of one of the two respondents in the preliminary oral interviews); other answers consisted of the following added comments: "snobbish jargon", "quasi gallantry", or "many meanings". It is obvious that half of the answers expressed contemporary "political correctness",[12] while the other options were ambiguous, mostly implying a pejorative connotation of the form of address in question. Nowadays, this way of addressing women is quite popular and has many different connotations with differentiated inscribed values. But, most often, when men use it this implies old-fashioned patronage and it is very rare to hear it in its original meaning (a woman of distinguished manners and a high social status). On the contrary, the associative chain here reflects "weak woman", "petit-bourgeoisie woman", "supported women", "parvenu", "just a woman".

---

[12] At the conference mentioned above, a colleague, Svenka Savić, commented on the author's presentation of the meaning of lady in socialism and nowadays by associating the word with style and attractiveness. As this option was not included, it cannot be denied or confirmed; that nobody mentioned it does not provide proof of non-existence since there was no possibility offered of adding one's own understanding as was the case with some other questions – but some ambiguity still exists here because a few comments were added anyway.

Informal interpersonal communication practices

The addressing practices described above are related to formal modes, and apart from these one of the informal modes was analysed, that is the options for orally addressing a house-maid and a house-aid[13] were checked. Among the six proposed options and the seventh allowing for individual input, eleven selected the answer that such a person was called by his/her first name. Two of them claimed that, besides this, the form with the first name preceded by *gospa/gospod* was also used (e.g. *gospa Marija, gospod Tone*). Five respondents found it impossible to answer properly since they had no experience and recollection. One of them hinted at the possibility that how paid household workers were addressed probably depended on their economic class, age and nationality, while the other respondent claimed that "social strata and age" were important. Two answers were unique, with one offering the statement that the addressing form was "aunt/uncle" and the first name (*teta Krista*). This last example was given by a respondent who claimed to belong to the higher middle class. Another one mentioned the practice of using *gospa/gospod* without the name ("because it was contextually obvious who had been addressed"). This topic has different social dimensions of which some are implied or have been already mentioned: at least that of class, which is integrated in the exposed relation of a housemaster or housemistress and a house-maid or a house help, then the gender and nationality issue. The gender perspective was not expressed openly in the answers, but three respondents referred only to a woman in this context. The domesticity implied in the addressing mode where only the first name was used might have taken its source in the described gendered working conditions, where women extended their housekeeping role to the paid work. The use of "aunt" with the first name (*teta Krista*) confirms the argument. The mode *gospa/gospod* with or without the first name in the discussed addressing practice has to be read contextually with *tovariš/tovarišica*, with the latter being the most proper and common way of addressing people who were not in one's very private realm. With the mentioned distanced and respectful mode the class difference, which officially should not have existed in socialism, was hushed up. Nowadays all of the described forms still exist, with the addition of *gospa/gospod* and a surname. The form *gospa/gospod* with a first name, which in

---

[13] Usually and indicatively from the gendered work division they were women who did paid regular work in households (PATEMAN 1988: 107). Men were involved as craftsmen. Only occasionally and usually with older households there was a habit to hire a gardener or a house painter etc. on a regular basis. But they were not in-house help as was sometimes the case with women.

socialism was restricted to the context of the paid house help, is now extended widely – and used nearly everywhere in public and in some professional environments; it connotes an ambiguous relationship, neither formal nor informal. This very popular way of addressing gives evidence of the matrix of work where the majority is homogenous from the governmentality standpoint.

Name-calling among minors

Beside practices of direct and "proper" addressing in interpersonal relations it is instructive to inquire into the differences according to socio-political background in the constructions of gender in some other naming practices. The first subject here was children's interpersonal communication and offensive language among them. The question was articulated according to the knowledge that name-calling is one of the means of the construction of masculinity and femininity, especially in relation to the imperative of courage (see PILCHER/ WHELEHAN 2004: 117), dominantly considered as a masculine virtue that is also existing in girls. Among the options offered for name-calling of a girl or a boy who was supposedly exhibiting cowardice, ten answered that *reva* (literary "poor girl/boy") was the most usual expression in the socialistic 1970s and 1980s; the second option chosen was the word *cmera* ("sissy"), while the third, which is used with boys only, is the name-calling *baba* ("hag"). The pejorative meanings of the presented words which were used by the children connoted women and the role of women, which allowed them to be weak and weeping. Today similar expressions are used; during the semi-structured interview with the two children aged 11 and 13, "lass" was indicated communicatively in the discussed usage but in the Croatian language, *"cura"*, and not in Slovenian, which would be *"punca"*. The usage of Croatisms adds a connotation of the "cool" and somewhat of a brute enunciator, and stresses the traditional dichotomy manly/womanlike. Here the gender issue intersects with a national one.

Adult expressions of friendship and sexual attraction

With adults a further inquiry was made in the questionnaire of addressing and naming practices among friends, and acclamations of the sex appeal of another person. The question on the latter was formulated in such a way that it did not imply heteronormativity in sexual and erotic relations. As regards friendly naming and addressing among men (the usual practice of using a first name excluded), the most popular choice in socialist times according to the recollections was *kolega* ("colleague") – it implied comradeship and equality. There was some popularity of the words *stari* ("old guy"), *tip* ("type"), and *dec* ("dude"). All the identified addressing and naming modes were connoting distance and humour in men's communities. According to the reporting, the case with women's comradeship was different, with the privileged mode being *punca* ("lass"). The socio-cultural prescription for women to sustain the position of the less-than-grown-ups is reflected in the chosen word, and the childish *joie de vivre*, implicated in this interpersonal communication practice is a part of it. The second most popular addressing and naming was recalled as being *baba* ("hag"). It was indicated twice (just like *dec*, its equivalent for men). *Stara*, literarily "old (one)" in English, was chosen as a usual mode a little less than *stari*, its equivalent for men. *Ženska* ("woman"), which would denote mature comradeships, was only indicated once. Today young women who speak slang very often use the word *stari* in the discussed context which is, as already explained, the masculine form of the adjective "old" in English. This grammatically inappropriate form (as regards gender) of the adjective in the function of noun has been probably impacted by various phenomena, at least queer culture and the English use of "guy" in the addressing and naming applied by women in addressing other women.

The status of an immature and thus less responsible and more playful person is now granted to both women and men alike by the often used naming or addressing with the Anglicism *bejbi* (used in this phonetic form also in written language). Apart from the influence of the queer movement on naming practices among girls and young women (i.e. *stari*), this socio-cultural margin is reflected in the pejorative slang expression *himen*[14] ("hymen"), as used in the community of young heterosexuals and aimed at people with an androgynous image.

In socialism the naming of sexually attractive persons varied regarding women and not so much with men. Seventeen answers from among the possible choices indicated the naming *dober dec/tip* ("hot dude/type"), among other options only *luštkan tip* (literally translated as "cute type") was accentuated by four answers. The naming of a sexy woman *dobra baba* ("hot hag") attracted thirteen answers, *dobra pička* (literally "good, i.e. hot, cunt") five, *dobra mrha* (literally translated as "a good, i.e. hot, scamp") was indicated twice. The disparity between the mainstream modes of naming men and women with sex appeal is transparent in revealing the traditional manly and rude heterosexist stance of enunciators referring to women and benign implications in the naming of men on the side of heterosexual women. The contemporary use of naming options maintain the described modes; new ones derive from English or new slang

---

[14] For examples of slang modes of naming and addressing, see JUD, ANA (2001): Slang First Aid. In: Mladina 18. http://webcache.googleusercontent.com/search?q=cache:MTKJ0A LLaH8J:www.mladina.si/tednik/200118/clanek/sleng/+sleng+na+internetu&cd=17&hl=sl &ct=clnk&gl=si&source=www.google.si, retrieved 10.10.2011.

words. The following are dominant expressions for a sexy woman: *bejbika* (diminutive of "baby"), *huda bejba* (literally "bad, i.e. hot, baby"), *dober komad* (literally "a good piece"), *teta* ("aunt"– the expression used for an attractive mature woman), *cukrček* ("sweety"), *prasička* ("piggy"), *bejbi* ("baby") etc. Also today there are less nouns to trendily convey the meaning of sexual attractiveness in men than in women: *hud tip* (literally "bad, i.e. hot, type"), *stric* ("uncle"– the expression used for an attractive mature man), *cukrček* ("sweety"), *pičkur* (rare usage, literally "cunt-lover"). In spite of the commoditisation of women in speech and the weakening of their grown-up status by some modes of naming, and the heteronormativity, there are two contemporary phenomena which transgress the paradigm. One is the identical naming for men and women, i.e. *bejbi*, *cukrček*, which both connote sexualised childishness in both genders, with the other being the transfer of the expression from the gay community *tetka*[15] (diminutive of *teta*, "aunt") to the domineering heterosexual community – but in its ordinary form and directed to women.

Concluding interpretation

During Slovenian socialism the formal addressing practices in public as well as in professional and educational environments connoted gender equality, promoted and implemented by the policies of what is today called "state feminism". Formally, the equivalent addressing expressions were used for women and men. The grammatical evidence reveals hidden gender discrimination on the secondary and tertiary educational levels, where the title professor (in the generic masculine form) was and still is used for both genders. In addressing women it was often accompanied by the surname in the form expressing property of a family/ husband. The same could be argued for other titling practices (e.g. *doktor Tiholetova* instead of *doktorica Tihole* for a female physician). Thus, the formal relations of equality were often strictly contextualised by the status of working women, which was subordinated in relation to that of men regarding domestic work, parenting and emotional input in intimate partnerships. Although this practice in the education environment is diminishing, it is still very persistent in professions which are devoid of social awareness from the gender perspective (e.g. technology, natural sciences). In the informal context of hired home help, where mostly women were involved, this unequal gender representation was evident in the usual practice of combining "*gospa*" ("Ms") with the first name. The gender issue was intersected with the class one, and this was the source of

---

[15] *Tetka* indicates a "feminised" gay man and degrades homosexuality, even though it is paradoxically mostly used among homosexual men.

the strange intertwining of domesticity and formality. In contemporary times, this combination of words is extended to interpersonal communication in public, often also in professional environments – which is indicative of the unified status of citizenship, especially a working one in relation to the governmentality exercised by the state, capital representatives, and transnational authorities in neoliberal capitalist Slovenia.

Comradeship expressions and claims of sexuality in addressing and naming practices among grown-ups were degrading women to the level of an immature person and rudely treated target of sexual attention, but the latter was not done often or in an imaginative variety of ways. Both practices were related to the realm which is contemporaneously defined as private. Nowadays, the options in this segment of interpersonal communications are more diversified, especially with young people and the flourishing use of slang. Nonetheless, women are still sexualised by addressing and naming practices to a greater extent than men, and the popularisation of certain forms of naming practices (*prasička*, *pička*) is derived from the pornographisation of culture, with sexuality being an area of the greatest ambiguity regarding the status of women in society. The acceptability of the ambivalent naming and addressing practices is reflected in the habit of using the word *pička* among women themselves, especially young ones. On the other hand, a strong seemingly subversive trend is evidenced by the wide circulation of the word *stari* (in the masculine form) among young women when addressing each other. Masculinity is not problematised here, but appropriated with the aim to obtain social power. The same confirmation of values, supposedly of a "masculine" origin, was detected in children's name-calling.

The degradations of women's status, mostly in non-professional but anyway in public and private environments, are paradigmatically reflected in "queering" the original high class and bourgeois meaning of the word lady, which is nowadays a popular way of patronising women. During socialism, the inversions of the meaning had mostly a class- and less gender-related motivation, while today the expressed opposition is emphasised as being primarily that of gender, but it is non-transparent in dominant perceptions.

Generally, it can be said that in the light of addressing practices the fields of education and work have been developed regarding gender relations in neoliberal capitalist Slovenia (due to feminist endeavours and some policies of gender equality on the state level). In contrast, the field of informal or less formal, private and sexualised addressing and naming practices reveals a great retrospective trend. Subversions in youth do not challenge masculinity to the degree which would jeopardise the existing gender regime.

References

AUSTIN, JOHN L. (1990): Kako napravimo kaj z besedami [How to Do Things with Words]. Ljubljana.

BUTLER, JUDITH/ PETER OSBORNE/ LYNNE SEGAL (1993): Extracts from Gender as Performance: An Interview with Judith Butler. http://webcache.google usercontent.com/search?q=cache:5BkF6ZsLP80J:www.theory.org.uk/but-int1.htm+Judith+Butler,+interview,+discourse,+1993&cd=18&hl=clnk&gl=si, retrieved 28.09.2011.

BUTLER, JUDITH (2001): Težave s spolom. Feminizem in subverzija identitete [Gender Trouble: Feminism and the Subversion of Identity]. Ljubljana.

BUTLER, JUDITH (2004): Undoing gender. New York/London.

CAMERON, DEBORAH (1999): Feminist linguistics. A response to Bent Preisler's Review Article: Deconstructing 'feminist linguistics'. In: Journal of Sociolinguistics 2. 121–139.

CANNING, KATHLEEN (1994): Feminist History after the Linguistic Turn. Historicizing Discourse and Experience. In: Signs 19/2. 368–404.

KELLOGG, CATHERINE (2001): Translating Deconstruction. In: Cultural Values 5/3. 325–348.

MCELHINNY, BONNIE/ SARA MILLS (2007): Launching studies of Gender and Language in the early 21st century. In: Gender and Language 1. 1–13.

MILLS, SARA (2003): Caught between sexism, anti-sexism and 'political correctness'. Feminist women's negotiations with naming practices. In: Discourse & Society 14/1. 87–110.

KUNST GNAMUŠ, OLGA (1994/95): Razmerje med spolom kot potezo reference in spolom kot slovnično kategorijo. In: Jezik in slovstvo 40/7. 255–262.

PATEMAN, CAROLE (1988): The Sexual Contract. Cambridge.

PILCHER, JANE/ IMELDA WHELEHAN (2004): Fifty Key Concepts in Gender Studies. London.

RAHMAN, MOMIN/ STEVI JACKSON (2010): Gender and Sexuality. Sociological Approaches. Cambridge.

SCHENSUL, STEPHEN L./ JEAN J. SCHENSUL/ MARGARET DIANE LECOMPTE (eds.) (1999): Essential Ethnographic Methods. Observations, Interviews, and Questionnaires. Walnut Creek/London/New York.

WANIEK, EVA (2005): Meaning in Gender Theory. Clarifying a Basic Problem from a Linguistic-Philosophical Perspective. In: Hypatia 20/2. 48–68.

ZUPANC, PAULA (2009): Nesimetrije izraza spolov v slovenskem jeziku in v govorih. In: Dialogi 45/11–12. 123–135.

Job Advertisements in Croatian Newspapers – Gender Perspective

Zrinjka Glovacki-Bernardi

When discussing the perspectives of a theory of culture based on pragmatics, Joachim Renn defines culture as a collective, primarily linguistic practice which determines the nature of practical collective rules, their cognitive structures as well as their re-production forms; in this process the interconnectivity of the knowledge of the world, practice and language plays a special role. The pragmatic dimension of language includes usage styles and forms of language expressions, structures or rules. For the linguistic meaning, i.e. for the understanding of the linguistic utterance, two things are of special importance: the relation between the expression, the meaning and the world and socio-cultural conventions and rules common to all the participants in the communication process, which also includes the sociolinguistic dimension (see RENN 2004). These postulates form the basis for the interpretation of the results of the job advertisements analysis conducted on a Croatian newspaper corpus focusing on the gender perspective. The formal analysis was conducted on both the morphological and the semantic level.

The debate on gender-neutral terms for occupations has been around for almost a century. In 1934 the magazine *Naš jezik* ("Our Language"), which was, as stated in the newspaper details, "recommended in all schools", published an article by Mihajlo JANJANIN (1934) entitled *Gospođa profesor* ("Mrs Professor"). Janjanin finds the usage of masculine forms for female occupations ridiculous. He starts from the basic assumption of morphology and word formation; language always creates a different form for females: *Ivan – Ivanka, Petrović – Petrovićka, pastir – pastirica, putnik – putnica*. Janjanin advocates the creation of adequate feminine forms: "[...] there is no way we can accept *'gospođa profesor'* and similar terms. This is an attempt at 'assassinating' our language. And why should we accept it? If language has created special feminine forms in all the other areas, it can also create special forms for these few words. Why should we keep these incorrect terms which are incompatible with the nature and the principles of language!"[1] Janjanin considers these words incorrect. In his opinion, there should even be different words for female occupations: *profesorica, suplentica, doktorica, inžinjerica* and for the wife of a man holding a job: *profesorka, suplentovica, doktorka* or *doktorovica, inžinjerka*.

---

[1] "[...] ni na kakav način ne možemo ostati pri nazivu gospođa professor i sl. To je atentat na naš jezik. A zašto bi ostali? Kad je jezik svuda stvorio za ženske posebne nazive, može stvoriti i za ovih nekoliko reči. Zašto bismo zadržali ove pogrešne nazive koji ne stoje u skladu s duhom i principima jezika." (JANJANIN 1934: 204)

This tradition was carried forward some 20 years later by the linguist Mate HRASTE on the example of forms for female family names (1953/54). He finds that the distinction in the forms of female family names in the standard language started to disappear even before the First World War. This practice continued throughout the interwar period, and the process came to an end after the Second World War. Hraste thinks that this change is not "in accordance with the nature of our language"[2]. This means that the rule on two forms of family names, masculine and feminine, which was rooted in systemic linguistics, disappeared.

A year later the same journal published an article *"Drugarica direktor, gospođa profesor ili drugarica direktorica, gospođa profesorica"* by Zlatko VINCE (1955). The key principle was the same as that put forward by Janjanin or Hraste – Vince pleads openly for equal use of masculine and feminine forms. He builds his argument on his view of the nature of the Croatian language: "We can [...] claim with certainty that people in denominations make a distinction between masculine and feminine. The nature of our language requires that we hold onto this principle."[3] In the same article, Vince introduces terms for female occupations, which were very unusual in those days, but which are today common unmarked nouns: "From the word *odvjetnik* [lawyer] we can coin the word *odvjetnica* [female lawyer] [...]"[4].

He also recognises certain difficulties; he sees the denomination for a female who holds the position of a judge as problematic and advocates consistent implementation of these denominations not only in the official but also in the everyday use:

> Still, we can ask ourselves [...], whether the routine of our citizens is such that it would be strange for them if we would start to use denominations relating to women in feminine forms, since so far we have not done it on a regular basis. [...] Feminine terms would also be easily accepted because their use would comply with the nature of our language, and it would expand. [...] With good will and a little consistency and patience our problem could be solved without difficulties. Of course, the best and the most successful method could be provided by our authorities; if our authorities in their regulations, appointments, transfers, etc. would use special masculine nouns for occupations held by men and special feminine nouns when these are held by women. [...] In that way, by

---

[2] "[...] ne odgovara duhu našeg jezika." (HRASTE 1953/54: 139)
[3] "Možemo [...] sa sigurnošću ustvrditi, da narod i u nazivima razlikuje redovno muško od ženskoga. Duh našeg jezika prema tome traži, da se u svemu toga načela i držimo." (VINCE 1955: 115)
[4] "Prema riječi odvjetnik mogli bismo stvoriti riječ odvjetnica [...]" (Ibid.: 116).

using feminine forms where they should be used, with a little effort and money we could demonstrate great respect for the nature of our language.[5]

Almost half a century later, the language policy based on gender equality was incorporated in the constitutional and legal provisions. The Constitution of the Republic of Croatia guarantees gender equality in two of its articles. These are Article 3:

> Freedom, equal rights, national and gender equality, peace, social justice, respect for human rights, inviolability of ownership, conservation of nature and the human environment, the rule of law and a democratic multiparty system are the highest values of the constitutional order of the Republic of Croatia and the basis for the interpretation of the Constitution.[6]

and Article 14:

> Citizens of the Republic of Croatia shall enjoy all rights and freedoms regardless of their race, colour, sex, language, religion, political or other opinion, national or social origin, property, birth, education, social status or other characteristics. All shall be equal before the law.[7]

Furthermore, the Republic of Croatia has committed itself to respect and promote gender equality by passing the Gender Equality Act and by adopting relevant international conventions and standards.

The implementation of the Gender Equality Act is monitored by the Gender Equality Ombudsperson. Special attention is given to the implementation of

---

[5] "No možemo se pitati [...] je li navika naših gradskih ljudi takva, da bi im postalo strano, kada bismo počeli upotrebljavati nazive za žene u ženskom obliku, kako to do sada nismo redovito činili. [...] Ženski nazivi bi se lako prihvatili, i zbog toga, što bi njihova upotreba bila i u duhu našega jezika, pa bi se to više proširila. Dobrom voljom i s malo dosljednosti i strpljenja moglo bi se naše pitanje povoljno riješiti. Razumije se, da bi bilo najbolje i najuspješnije, kada bi naše vlasti u svojim odredbama, postavljenjima, premještajima i sl. upotrebljavale posebne nazive u muškom rodu za zvanja, što ih obavlja muškarac, i posebne u ženskom, kada ih obavljaju žene. [...] tako bismo, upotrebljavajući ženske nazive svagdje, gdje im je mjesto, s malo truda i novčanih sredstava pokazali mnogo razumijevanja za duh našeg jezika." (Ibid.: 117–118)

[6] "Članak 3 – Sloboda, jednakost, nacionalna ravnopravnost i ravnopravnost spolova, mirotvorstvo, socijalna pravda, poštovanje prava čovjeka, nepovredivost vlasništva, očuvanje prirode i čovjekova okoliša, vladavina prava i demokratski višestranački sustav najviše su vrednote ustavnog poretka Republike Hrvatske i temelj za tumačenje Ustava." (http://www.zakon.hr/z/94/Ustav-Republike-Hrvatske, retrieved 1.8.2011)

[7] "Članak 14 – Svatko u Republici Hrvatskoj ima prava i slobode, neovisno o njegovoj rasi, boji kože, spolu, jeziku, vjeri, političkom ili drugom uvjerenju, nacionalnom i socijalnom podrijetlu, imovini, rođenju, naobrazbi, društvenom položaju ili drugim osobinama. Svi su pred zakonom jednaki." (Ibid.)

Article 13, item 2 of the Gender Equality Act which prescribes: "When advertising job positions, every advertisement has to clearly indicate that both men and women are equally eligible for the job."[8]

The first systematic analysis of job advertisements was conducted from June to December 2004. Analysed advertisements were found in *Vjesnik, Večernji list, Novi list, Slobodna Dalmacija, Glas Slavonije, Šibenski list, Dubrovački list, Dnevnik,* and in the official gazette *Narodne novine.* In all the advertisements analysed (162), the name of the position was indicated in the masculine form exclusively. Therefore, the Gender Equality Ombudsperson issued warnings of the violation of the Gender Equality Act.

This situation was vindicated in various ways: by documents which provide the basis for job advertisements (National Classification of Business Activities, *Narodne novine* 3/97, 7/97 and 11/98). In these classifications only few occupations, which are stereotypically female, are cited in feminine forms: *sekretarica* ("secretary"), *domaćica zrakoplova* ("stewardess"), *dadilja* ("nanny/nurse"), *spremačica* ("cleaning lady"), *sobarica* ("chambermaid"), *čistačica* ("cleaning lady"), *pralja* ("laundress"), *servirka* ("busgirl"). The majority of occupations is found in masculine forms. Furthermore, in all the documents issued upon completion of an education programme (diplomas and expert exam certificates), academic and expert titles are written in masculine forms. Moreover, masculine forms dominate the texts of normative legal communication, which is justified by the fact that the Croatian law relies on the principles of the Roman law, which in the area of civil law system implies that masculine forms in regulations include both genders. The Gender Equality Ombudsperson also found that a large number of employers were not familiar with Article 13 item 2 of the Gender Equality Act as well as that women applied for jobs even if they were posted in the masculine form only.

In the year 2010, from the 1st to 30th September, the Office of the Gender Equality Ombudsperson monitored job advertisements in the daily newspapers *Jutarnji list, Večernji list* and *Vjesnik* and conducted an analysis. The results were then compared to the results from previous years. In the given period 137 advertisements were analysed. 131 advertisements (or 96%) complied with the provision requiring that it should be made clear that both genders can apply for the job. In only 6 advertisements (4%) this provision was violated.

In 2006, two years after the first analysis, the percentage of advertisements abiding by the Gender Equality Act was 60%, a year later 70%, in 2008 this percentage climbed to 78%, and in 2009 it reached 88%.

---

[8] "Prilikom oglašavanja potrebe za zapošljavanjem u oglasu mora biti jasno istaknuto da se za oglašeno radno mjesto mogu javiti osobe oba spola." (*Narodne novine* 82/08)

These analyses give an insight into the level of compliance with the Gender Equality Act and enable the comparison of results. The results reveal a significant change. The percentage of advertisements in which the Act was violated in the period from 2006 to 2010 had decreased tenfold.[9]

This positive change in the area of job advertisements does not apply to gender-neutral language use. The National Classification of Business Activities consistently cites occupations in both male and female forms for all positions, for example: *biolozi/biologinje* ("biologists"), *časnici/časnice* ("officers"), *direktori/ direktorice marketinga* ("marketing directors"), *rektori/rektorice* ("rectors"), *inžinjeri/inžinjerke za okolište* ("environmental engineers"), *piloti/pilotkinje* ("pilots"), *lovci/lovkinje* ("hunters"), *ribari/ribarke* ("fishermen").[10] But when advertising a job position, the requirements of the Gender Equality Act are followed by the use of masculine forms followed by "m/ž" (m/f), for example: *regionalni direktor sektora za upravljanje nekretninama i zakupcima m/ž* ("regional director in the sector of real estates and tenant management m/f"), *voditelj projekta u službi razvoja m/ž* ("project manager in the development department m/f"). This suggests that legal regulations and the declared strategy of gender equality are not reflected in everyday language use, that women are still not represented in language.

The presence of women in language and gender-neutral language use also depend on the language policy. An institution that could and should exert its influence in this area is the Council for Standard Croatian Language Norm which was appointed by the Ministry of Science in 2005 for the purpose of providing systematic professional care for the Croatian standard language. The main objectives of the Council are to discuss current dilemmas and open issues in the Croatian standard language as well as to promote the culture of the Croatian standard language in the written and spoken communication. The presence of women in the language and gender-neutral language use unquestionably fall within the scope of the Council. However, for the first time this topic was on the Council's agenda as late as five years after it was founded, on 18th May 2010 at its 25th session, following the Parliament's request for the Council's opinion on the implementation of measures planned under the National Policy on Gender Equality Promotion 2006–2010. However, the discussion did not take place because the Council "[…] has never received a decision declaring

---

[9] http://www.prs.hr/, retrieved 1.8.2011.
[10] http://www.dzs.hr/Hrv/important/Nomen/NKZ2010, retrieved 1.8.2011.

the Council a national policy holder, nor any relevant work material".[11] This topic was again put on the Council's agenda a year later, on 9th June 2011 at its 27th session, this time upon request of the Croatian Governement Office for Gender Equality. The Council formulated *"Mišljenje Vijeća za normu hrvatskoga standardnog jezika o uporabi oblika ženskoga roda za zvanja kao izraza poštovanja ravnopravnosti spolova"* ("Opinion of the Council for Standard Croatian Language Norm on the Usage of Female Forms for Female Occupations as a Token of Respect of Gender Equality"). In the formulated Opinion it is "[…] recommended that a distinction in the gender of nouns for occupations and subjects be made wherever it is morphologically possible, and whenever they refer to an individual of a specific gender. Only these cases are relevant when we talk about respect and gender equality. The general use of nouns nominating an occupation or a subject depends only on the general structure of the language and its economy, which each educated individual has to respect. From the linguistic point of view, it is completely wrong to consider this a sign of the violation of the gender equality principle."[12] The argument of the Council is exclusively that of the language system, whereas the socio-cultural and pragmatic dimensions are completely neglected.

Language and communication are critical aspects of the production of a wide variety of identities expressed at many levels of social organisation; language and communication make up the key criteria helping members of a social group to define their group and to be defined by others. Individuals are social beings who, depending on the range of their social activity, possess a repertoire of different identities. (See KROSKRITY 2001) When construing their professional identity, especially in the areas until recently dominated by men, women must prove their professional competence and at the same time remove gender-based stereotypes in communication. Gender identity is always interrelated with other variables such as age, education, status or nationality, and thus it is important that it is expressed in language.

---

[11] "[…] nikada nije primilo odluku u kojoj je propisano da je ono određeno za nositelja te Nacionalne politike, niti su mu dostavljeni kakvi radni materijali." (http://www.ihjj.hr/dokumenti/Zapisnik_25%20sjednica.doc, retrieved 1.8.2011.)

[12] "[…] preporučuje razlikovanje spolova u rodu imenica za zanimanje i vršitelje radnje gdje je to god tvorbeno moguće i gdje se odnosi na pojedine osobe određenog spola. Jedino takvi slučajevi imaju veze s poštovanjem osobe i ravnopravnošću spola. Opća uporaba imenica za zanimanja i vršitelje radnje ima veze samo s općim ustrojem jezika i njegovom ekonomičnošću, koje svaka obrazovana osoba mora poštovati, i jezikoslovno je posve pogrješno smatrati ju izrazom nepoštovanja ravnopravnosti spolova." (http://www.ihjj.hr/dokumenti/Zapisnik_27%20sjednica.doc, retrieved 1.8.2011.)

The previous overview of job advertisements covered only some of the Croatian newspapers. Since the starting point of our analysis was socio-cultural conditionality and the pragmatic dimension of language, our intention was to investigate the situation in the newspapers that were omitted from the analysis conducted by the Gender Equality Ombudsperson. Socio-cultural patterns are adopted in the environment modelled by our way of life, occupation and in the relation to the society. Therefore, the analysis of job advertisements was conducted on the corpus which, with few exceptions, refers to the occupations or jobs requiring a lower level of qualifications. The corpus comprises job advertisements from *Oglasnik*, a three-times-a-week advertising paper. The corpus consists of 584 job advertisements: 282 advertisements by employers and 302 advertisements by job seekers. The advertisements are grouped according to business activities: catering/tourism; trade/sale; administrative occupations; personal services; household; nursing; construction/architecture; installations/repairs; transportation; electronics/informatics/engineering; business/finance/insurance; health.

The analysis was conducted at the lexical level, according to the morphological and semantic criteria.

In the advertisements posted by employers masculine forms are used for activities dominated by men – in construction and architecture: *fasader* ("plasterer"), *zidar* ("bricklayer"), *građevinski radnik* ("construction worker"), *kamenar* ("stonemason"), *keramičar* ("ceramist"), *montažer* ("assembler"), *bagerist* ("excavating machine worker"), *stolar* ("carpenter"); in transportation: *vozač* ("driver"); in electronics/informatics/engineering: *brusač* ("honer"), *tokar* ("turner").

Although business, finance and insurance are areas of activity engaging both men and women, in the analysed job advertisements exclusively masculine forms were used: *djelatnik* ("worker") and *suradnik* ("associate").

Job advertisements in the area of health care mostly indicated the required occupation:

Medicinsku sestru za rad u domu za starije tražimo ("Nurse in a nursing home for elderly people wanted").

Or the gender-unmarked noun *osoba* ("person") is used:

Osobu stariju za njegu starije muške osobe tražim ("Elderly person for nursing elderly male person wanted").

Only female forms are found in the columns Household and Babysitting. Names of occupations are rare:

Dadilju/kućnu pomoćnicu mlađu za rad u Americi na godinu dana tražim ("Younger nanny/housekeeper to work in America for a year wanted").

The gender is mostly explicitly defined:

Marljivu ženu za kućanske poslove tražim ("Diligent woman for household work wanted").

Mlađu žensku osobu bez obaveza za čuvanje djeteta u Austriji tražim ("Younger female person without obligations for babysitting in Austria wanted").

Unlike job advertisements in the area of business, finance and insurance, in which only the nouns in masculine forms are used, the structure of job advertisements in Trade and Sale is underpinned by the fact that this sector employs both women and men. Still, the advertisements targeting men differ from those targeting women. If explicitly male employees are wanted, the occupation is also stated: *komercijalist* ("sales specialist"), *djelatnik* ("worker"), *trgovac* ("salesman"). If a female worker is wanted, gender specification is mostly used:

Djevojku za prodaju pekarskih proizvoda tražim ("Girl for selling bakery products wanted").

Ženske osobe za primanje narudžbi i administraciju u uredu tražimo ("Female persons for receiving orders and administration in office wanted").

Only 25% of the analysed advertisements in this area meet the requirements of the Gender Equality Act, meaning that they clearly point out that both male and female candidates are eligible by using the abbreviation *m/ž* (m/f):

Agenta m/ž za traženje lokacija za samoposlužne aparate tražim ("Agent m/f for searching locations for vending machines wanted").

In the rest of advertisements only the neutral noun *osoba* ("person") is used:

Osobe za rad u uredu prodaje u Zagrebu tražim ("Persons to work in sales office in Zagreb wanted").

In one third of the advertisements in the Personal services area the name of the occupation in both masculine and feminine form are used: *frizer/frizerka* ("hairdresser"). In one example the abbreviation *m/ž* ("m/f") is found with the name of occupation in the feminine form: *spremačice m/ž* ("cleaning ladies m/f").

Otherwise, only feminine forms of occupations are found: *frizerke* ("female hairdressers"), *pedikerke* ("female pedicures") or gender designation is used: *djevojka* ("girl"), *gospođa* ("misses/lady").[13]

In the analysed advertisements most job offers were published in the area of Catering and Tourism – 156. In more than a half of these advertisements a specific occupation was required: *plesačica* ("female dancer"), *dostavljač* ("deliverer"), *konobar* ("waiter"), *konobarica* ("waitress"), *pekar* ("baker"), *kuhar* ("cook"), *kuharica* ("female cook").

In other advertisements jobs are offered to the specific gender:

---

[13] *Gospođa* is used in Croatian as a form of address combined with the family name, e.g. *gospođa Horvat* ("Mrs. Horvat") but it is also used by itself, e.g. *Ona je zgodna gospođa* ("She is a good looking lady").

Žensku osobu za rad u café baru tražim ("Female person to work in an espresso bar wanted").
Djevojke za rad u mirnom baru tražim ("Girls to work in a quiet bar wanted").
Ženu za rad u kemijskoj čistionici tražim ("Woman to work at a dry cleaner's wanted").
Gospođu za čišćenje tražim ("Lady for cleaning wanted").
Dečka za rad u cafe baru tražim ("Boy to work in an espresso bar wanted").
Djelatnicu za rad u novom cafe baru tražim ("Female worker to work in a new espresso bar wanted").
Djelatnika za rad u cafe baru tražim (Worker for an espresso bar wanted).
In only three advertisements the neutral specification *osoba* ("person") was used, e.g.: *Osobu za rad na recepciji u hotelu tražimo* ("Person to work at the hotel reception desk wanted").

In 70% of advertisements by job seekers the occupation was indicated by a masculine or a feminine noun; in that way job-seekers define themselves as persons, i.e. they construct their identity through the use of appropriate linguistic forms: *knjigovođa* ("bookkeeper"), *knjigovotkinja* ("female bookkeeper"), *konobar* ("waiter"), *konobarica* ("waitress"), *maser* ("masseur"), *maneken* ("male model"), *medicinska sestra* ("nurse"), *prevoditelj* ("translator").

The advertisements specifying the gender rather than the occupation were almost three times as frequent for women (94 advertisements) than for men (36 advertisements). The noun *djevojka* ("girl") is most often used (58 advertisements), followed by *gospođa* ("misses/lady" – 28 examples) and *žena* ("woman" – 8 examples). When targeting male persons, the most common noun is *muškarac* ("man" – 16 advertisements), *mladić* ("young man" – 11 advertisements) and *dečko* ("boy" – 9 advertisements).

Apart from the basic information about the job, i.e. occupation offered, in the analysed advertisements there are also some additional criteria, expressed mostly by adjectives, rarely by noun phrases. These additional criteria, which are found in a half of the advertisements, clearly indicate that the advertisement targets female persons exclusively. The age and physical appearance requirements play a crucial role in 50% of the advertisements – wanted: *atraktivne plesačice* ("attractive female dancers"), *djelatnica do 40 godina s radnim iskustvom* ("experienced female worker younger than 40"), *djevojka ili gospođa zgodna* ("pretty girl or pretty lady"), *mlađa žena* ("younger woman"), *mlađe atraktivne konobarice* ("younger attractive waitresses"). Work experience of female workers is a requirement in 15 advertisements. Positive personal traits make up an additional requirement in 18 advertisements – wanted: *ozbiljna gospođa* ("serious lady"), *odgovorna djevojka* ("responsible girl"), *uredna i vrijedna ženska osoba* ("neat and diligent female person"), *savjesna žena* ("conscientious woman"), *čistačica uredna, marljiva, razvijenih higijenskih navika* ("neat cleaning lady, diligent, with good hygiene practices"). In few advertisements (8) social competences are also a requirement, mostly in combination with physical appearance and age:

Komunikativnu mlađu vedru žensku osobu za rad u modernom dućanu muške odjeće tražimo ("Communicative younger cheerful female person to work in a modern male clothing store wanted").

Komunikativne žene za rad na zabavnim telefonskim linijama ("Communicative women to work on telephone entertainment lines").

In two advertisements there are examples of a requirement relating to private life pertaining to female employees. The first example is that of marital status implied by the use of the adjective *slobodna* ("free") in the sense of "unmarried":

Domaćica ozbiljna, slobodna i poštena ("Serious housekeeper, free [i.e. single, unmarried] and honest wanted").

In the second example the maternity status is implicitly mentioned – the syntagm *bez obaveza* ("without obligations") means without children:

Mlađu žensku osobu bez obaveza za čuvanje djeteta u Austriji tražim ("Younger female person without obligations for babysitting in Austria wanted").

The age requirement in the advertisements for male persons only (49 advertisements) is found in three advertisements. Wanted: *radnik 25–40, marljiv, organiziran, pouzdan* ("worker 25–40, diligent, organised, reliable"); *djelatnik mlađi od 30* ("worker younger than 30"); *bravar i radnik mlađi od 30* ("locksmith and worker younger than 30"). For men experience, additional skills and knowledge are listed as requirements in 35 advertisements, e.g.:

Konobara s 4 godine iskustva, 2 jezika, poznavanje vina i ribe tražim ("Waiter with 4 years of experience, 2 languages, conversance in fish and wine sorts wanted").

In seven advertisements personality traits and social competences are mentioned: *konobara ozbiljnog* ("waiter, serious"); *asistente i djelatnike komunikativne i odgovorne* ("assistants and workers, communicative and responsible"); *poštenog radnika* ("honest worker"). In one example, in the advertisement for a house painter *antialkoholičar* ("teetotaler") is wanted.

In the advertisements by job-seekers the experience is most often listed as a qualification. Women are either defining themselves by occupation or gender denotations *djevojka* ("girl") and *gospođa* ("misses/lady"), or, in most cases (17) indicate their age: *gospođa (40), gospođa (50), djevojka (24), djevojka (19)*. Personality traits are most commonly mentioned with the noun *gospođa*. The research into the forms of address of females by *gospođa* ("Mrs") or *gospođica* ("Miss") in Croatian, conducted in 2006, showed that the positive marital status for a woman is perceived by the majority of people in Croatia as a desirable social status. (See GLOVACKI-BERNARDI 2008) Therefore, the form of address and the noun *gospođa* ("misses/lady") is a prestigious lexeme because it evokes positive characteristics having to do with the traditional social role of a married woman. This is confirmed by the selection of adjectives, which in the analysed advertisements can be found next to the noun *gospođa*: *ozbiljna* ("serious"), *odgovorna* ("responsible") and *marljiva* ("diligent").

Communicativeness and social competences are mentioned in only one out of 56 advertisements in which women are looking for jobs: *komunikativna telefonistica* ("communicative telephone operator"). Language knowledge as an additional qualification is mentioned in two advertisements.

In job-search advertisements by men 58 advertisements quote both the experience and the age: *vozač (36) s iskustvom* ("experienced driver, 36"), *mladić (40) s iskustvom* ("experienced young man, 40"), *maser s iskustvom (33)* ("experienced masseur, 33"). In the advertisements by male job seekers the following characteristics are repeatedly mentioned: *samostalan* ("independent"), *ozbiljan* ("serious"), *pošten* ("honest"), *vrijedan* ("diligent"). In only one case the job seeker uses the adjective *pametan* ("clever"): *Dečko, odgovoran, pametan, traži stalni posao u Njemačkoj, odlično poznavanje njemačkog* ("Boy, responsible, clever, looking for a permanent job in Germany, excellent knowledge of German").

One job seeker is pointing out that he is a teetotaller, e.g.:

Dostavljač hrane, 53, antialkoholičar, traži stalan posao ("Food deliverer, 53, teetotaller, looking for a permanent job").

The communication between the advertiser and the recipient is based on the linguistic construction and realisation of identity. By paraphrasing the words of Ernst Cassirer we can conclude that in this process the language is not only the medium, but it actively and constitutively takes part in the formation of consciousness. (See CASSIRER 1923) In the advertisements which comply with the relevant legal provisions gender equality is assured, but only at the formal level, because it only means that the abbreviation *m/ž* ("m/f") is added to the name of occupation in the masculine form. Such a solution will not lead to overall changes of the language system, primarily at the morphological level, although in the Croatian language there is a possibility of formation of equivalent nouns in female forms. The only document in which the occupations are consistently stated in both forms is the National Classification of Business Activities. Certain changes of both the morphological and the pragmatic level could be introduced by certain measures within a systematic language policy. The institutionalised Croatian language policy takes into account only the morphological level; the socio-cultural and pragmatic levels are completely neglected.

The analysis of job advertisements published in Croatian newspapers which were not included in the monitoring of the implementation of the Gender Equality Act conducted by the Gender Equality Ombudsperson, showed that the selection of lexical means constructs and realises the identity in the specific language use following socio-cultural stereotypes of conservative male and female characteristics. By using specific nouns and adjectives employers define the identity of their targeted social group and job seekers define themselves. For female employees the nouns which denote gender are mostly used: *djevojka* ("girl"), *gospođa* ("misses/lady"), *žena* ("woman"), and *ženska osoba* ("female person"). The names of occupations in feminine forms are rarely found. For male employees the selection of nouns is completely opposite – in most cases names of occupations are found; nouns which indicate gender are rarely used: *dečko* ("boy"), *mladić* ("young man"), *muškarac* ("man"). Unlike the noun *gospođa* ("misses/lady") which is socio-culturally marked as a stereotypically prestigious noun, the noun *gospodin* ("mister") is not used at all because it is unmarked, i.e. the marital status of a man has no bearing on his social status. The noun *antialkoholičar* ("teetotaler") is used as an additional criterion, exclusively in advertisements targeting men.

The selection of adjectives is also a sign of socio-culturally conditioned male and female stereotypes. In advertising jobs targeting female workers, adjectives such as: *uredna* ("neat"), *marljiva* ("diligent"), *poštena* ("honest") and in those for male workers: *samostalan* ("independent"), *ozbiljan* ("serious"), *odgovoran* ("responsible") are used. A paradigmatic example of the realisation of male – female stereotypes in the language of analysed advertisements is repeated usage of certain adjectives. On the one hand, the adjective *atraktivna* ("attractive") is often used for female workers: *Atraktivne plesačice i hostese za erotski dance show traži erotski noćni klub* ("Attractive female dancers and hostesses for erotic dance show in erotic night club wanted"); *Atraktivnu žensku osobu za rad u cafe baru tražim* ("Attractive female person to work in an espresso bar wanted"). In the advertisements targeting male workers this adjective cannot be found. On the other hand, the adjective "clever" is found in an advertisement for male workers, but is not used when advertising jobs for female workers.

The results of the analysis also indicate that the gender identity is linguistically constructed and realised in the interrelation with other variables in different ways for women and men with the use of specific nouns and adjectives. For women, important variables are age, physical appearance and marital status, whereas for men the most important factors are education and age.

Online sources

http://www.dzs.hr/Hrv/important/Nomen/NKZ 2010, retrieved 1.8.2011.
http://www.ihjj.hr/dokumenti/Zapisnik_25%20sjednica.doc, retrieved 1.8. 2011.
http://www.ihjj.hr/dokumenti/Zapisnik_27%20sjednica.doc, retrieved 1.8. 2011.
http://www.linguistik-online.de, retrieved 1.8.2011.
http://www.prs.hr, retrieved 1.8.2011.
http://www.zakon.hr/z/94/Ustav-Republike-Hrvatske, retrieved 1.8.2011.

References

BARADA, VALERIJA/ ŽELJKA JELAVIĆ (ed.) (2004): Uostalom, diskriminaciju treba dokinuti. Zagreb.
CASSIRER, ERNST (1923): Philosophie der symbolischen Formen 1. Sprache. Berlin.
FELDMAN, ANDREA (ed.) (2004): Žene u Hrvatskoj – ženska i kulturna povijest. Zagreb.
GLOVACKI-BERNARDI, ZRINJKA (2008): Kad student zatrudni – rasprava o rodnoj perspektivi u jeziku. Zagreb.
GREVE, MELANIE/ MARION IDING/ BÄRBEL SCHMUSCH (2002): Geschlechtsspezifische Formulierungen in Stellenangeboten. In: Linguistik online 11/2. 105–162.
HRASTE, MATE (1953/54): O ženskim prezimenima. In: Jezik 2/5. 136–139.
JANJANIN, MIHAJLO (1934): Gospođa professor. In: Naš jezik 2/1. Belgrade. 201–204.
KAŠIĆ, BILJANA/ JANJA MARIJAN/ JASMINKA PEŠUT (eds.) (2005): Vodič prema politici rodne jednakosti. Zagreb.
KROSKRITY, PAUL V. (2001): Identity. In: Duranti, Alessandro (ed.): Key Terms in Language and Culture. Malden et al. 106–110.
RENN, JOACHIM (2004): Perspektiven einer sprachpragmatischen Kulturtheorie. In: Jaeger, Friedrich/ Burkhard Liebsch (eds.): Handbuch der Kulturwissenschaften 1. Stuttgart/Weimar. 430–448.
SAVIĆ, SVENKA/ MARIJANA ČANAK/ VERONIKA MITRO/ GORDANA ŠTASNI (eds.) (2009): Rod i jezik. Ženske studije i istraživanja i Futura publikacije. Novi Sad.
VINCE, ZLATKO (1955): Drugarica direktor, gospođa profesor ili drugarica direktorica, gospođa profesorica? In: Jezik 3/4. 113–118.

Creating Public Concern about a Woman's Ability to Govern the Country: The Case of Jadranka Kosor and the Media

Roswitha Kersten-Pejanić

Introductory notes

Trivialisation and marginalisation are the two key findings when women's coverage in the media is analysed. The approach towards *powerful* women in the media is often even depreciatory, although trivialisation does in these cases noticeably prevail over marginalisation, at least with regard to quantity. Furthermore, women in power often tend to contribute to the trivialisation of women in the media, either by ignoring and denying deviant provisions and existing discriminating structures or by stimulating them through displaying sexualised gender stereotypes. (See PANTTI 2007: 33) When in 2009, Jadranka Kosor became prime minister in Croatia she did neither the former nor the latter. Although she did experience negative and sexist media coverage, she evidently decided not to ignore it. Furthermore, she willingly spoke out publicly against stereotypical media coverage and highlighted persisting discriminatory terms and conditions.

So, when in September 2011, the Croatian prime minister blamed the Serbian president for sexist talk about her – after he had publicly announced that he would rather kiss her than the (male) Croatian president – it was not the first time Kosor made clear that she was not amused by any (potentially) sexist public statement. Furthermore, it seems that the first female Croatian prime minister (since the breakdown of Yugoslavia) has, ever since her assumption of office, developed a high amount of sensitivity towards any possibly pejorative or derogatory perception of women and femininity. Even more, she has not hesitated to debunk superficially complimentary remarks about herself as a woman as stereotypical and therefore biased and potentially discriminatory. Just a few months before her response to Tadić's "kissing-joke", she used her political influence to make a sexist sequence disappear from a Croatian tourist advertisement; she took part in round tables discussing women in politics while being the prime minister; she did not hesitate to publicly talk about women's issues, and she seems to have a high amount of sensibility towards androcentric views and patriarchal societal values. Nonetheless, it is a conservative we are talking about, a Croatian left-wing politician who, for example, did not falter to overtly show her sympathy for the sentenced Croatian war criminals Ante

Gotovina and Mladen Markac, probably in order to (re)gain the approval of the radical rights.[1]

The question whether women in politics as such have any effect on gender sensitive policies has often been negated for several reasons, (SAUER 2011: 34) and the term of the "critical mass" has been introduced and used to refer to the fact that it takes at least a certain number of women to observe any such effect. (See LEINERT NOVOSEL 2007) However, female politicians with a feminist stance in their political conviction are seen as strong promoters of such policies. (SAUER 2011: 36) The fact that Kosor is an HDZ[2] member and a politician with a rather nationalist attitude did not really provide much reason for expecting her to contribute to a very gender sensitive political environment as the head of the state. In conjunction with these pre-conditions, her strong self-positioning in questions of gender equality and with her repeated public statements regarding issues like sexism, the role of women in the Croatian society and the above mentioned – almost coquetting – stroke against Tadić, Kosor provides us with interesting material for the examination of different questions around stereotypical assumptions of people at different levels of analysis. Even more so, of course, since she is the first *female* prime minister of the independent Croatia and therefore an especially interesting subject of research on gender constructions and stereotypes. One of these questions is how the Croatian media treats its first female prime minister and whether her femininity is a topic in the newspaper at all. Given the presupposition that it *is* a topic in the newspaper, the subsequent questions could be related to the different ways and discourses in which the prime minister was addressed. Whether any visible changes can be traced in the conceptions and manifestations regarding Jadranka Kosor in the media at different stages of her political career, would be another interesting point.

Kosor herself repeatedly argued that ever since she became prime minister, she was subject to sexist statements and anticipations and that she was repeatedly asked "'feminine' instead of 'political' questions"[3], a fact she perceives as a clear sign of being treated differently compared to her male colleagues. The public interest in female politicians because of their gender and the corresponding neglect of their political work in the media coverage is a finding common to many empirical studies. (See SREBERNY/ VAN ZOONEN 2000: 17; ROSS/ SREBERNY 2007: 86f.) Kosor is a rather controversial public

---

[1] The fact, that this approach did not help her to stay in office, was shown in December 2011, when she and (especially) her party failed to regain the majority in the Sabor.
[2] HDZ = *Hrvatska Demokratska Zajednica* (Croatian Democratic Union).
[3] Kosor in E-NOVINE 2007.

figure in Croatia, in conservative as well as in feminist circles, and this article will clearly not help to solve any of the controversies. Nonetheless, the specific ambivalence of her reputation plus the fact that Kosor is not afraid of naming the problems that a deviant treatment of women in politics means for her personally, makes Kosor a fascinating example for the analysis of the public treatment that "public women" are facing. It is also interesting that Kosor herself points to the fact that as a divorced mother she would be suffering even more from stereotype assumptions present in peoples' minds and viewable in the media who play the role of the "world's picture apparatuses" (HOLTZ-BACHA 2007: 13) in this sense.

If we take it seriously that the ways in which people are portrayed, named, regarded, and disregarded in the media have an effect on the manner the society judges people and certain groups of people, (VIŠNJIĆ/ MIROSAVLJEVIĆ 2007: 228) the results of a study on how the Croatian media treated the country's first female prime minister may as well tell us something on how she as a woman is perceived in the broader Croatian society. At the end of such – almost circular – reasoning, of course, stays the central finding that the possible gendered construction in the media representation of the former prime minister needs to be observed very carefully in order to obtain a better understanding of societal constructions and manifestations as well as of the importance of gender identities and sex itself in talking and writing about people. Such constructions and manifested assumptions do not only harm a specific woman – in our case Kosor – but may have an effect on the ways people think about men and women that contribute to limited and limiting gender roles in society. Or, as Brown and Gardetto formulated it in their study of the picture that was established in the US news of Hillary Clinton (then still the President's wife):

> The first area that is important for feminist studies is the distinction between real, social and symbolic women. It is important to remember that we are not so much involved with a particular case but with a larger social issue – women's subordination. The way in which Clinton is represented in news coverage frames of reference is indicative, not so much for her, as it is of prevailing gender ideologies. (BROWN/ GARDETTO 2000: 44)

In this way, regarding the ways in which Croatian newspapers are talking about the first female prime minister provides us not only with a picture of how the person Jadranka Kosor (*the real woman*) was represented by the media, nor simply an insight in gender constructions when it comes to the political elite (*the social woman*), but also an idea of how femininity and femaleness (*the symbolic woman*) are perceived and assessed in the society in manners differing from the *normal* way that the *normal* politicians (namely, men) are viewed. It has been repeatedly observed in research that femaleness and politics often seem to be contradicting features that have the tendency to unsettle people, and most recognisable, journalists too.[4]

The following analysis consists of articles with certain gender stereotypes about Jadranka Kosor. They were published in Croatian daily newspapers during the days and weeks around Kosor's assumption of office on July 6th 2009 after Ivo Sanader's sudden retirement from all political mandates.[5] In order to get a more detailed picture of Jadranka Kosor's already mentioned (public) statements on aspects of gender equality, several articles from the years 2010 and 2011 are added to the corpus. Some of these articles deal with public announcements the prime minister has made concerning sexism, societal attitudes towards women or her engagement in enacting gender equality laws. Still, the main focus of this study lies on articles that contain portraits and opinions *about* her as a (female) politician.

This survey of articles is aimed at giving a (first) insight in a range of interesting matters that are often provoked by certain political events in Croatia and that enable us to examine certain aspects of the image that is conceptualised in the media of the first female prime minister and the main person studied – Kosor. It is, therefore, anything but an exhaustive analysis and, already concerning the raw quantity of the articles, not more than a launch of scientific examinations of Kosor's media coverage in Croatia.[6] Several other interesting issues will have to be studied in order to achieve a more comprehensive view on the widespread topic of this examination. For example, a closer look at Kosor's treatment in the media in 2005, when she was the main rival candidate against Stipe Mesić in the presidential election, might be able to show another important piece of the picture.[7] Empirical comparisons between the media coverage of Croatian male and female politicians would provide another interesting approach in evaluating the given practices of the (print) media. (See also KOCH/ HOLTZ-BACHA 2008; EITNER 2007) And, of course, the media

---

[4] See SREBERNY/ VAN ZOONEN 2000: 2; VAVRUS 2002: 130; STERR 1997: 114.

[5] The corpus consists of around 50 articles in July 2009 and about 20 articles in 2010 and 2011 from different newspapers.

[6] Basically, my material consists of articles from Croatia's leading daily national and regional newspapers (*Jutarnji List*, *Novi List*, *Slobodna Dalmacija*, *Večernji List* and *Vjesnik*, whereat all but *Vjesnik* were only available online for me and are therefore not representing the print versions) plus some relevant articles from one of the weeklies' newspapers, *Nacional.hr* and from some web portals. My selection was for some periods limited due to the different periods covered by the newspapers' online archives.

[7] Mesić then did his best to vilify Kosor when he contributed to the picture of her as a weak person that would even cry in public. With referring to Kosor as "Suzana" (from Croatian *suze* = "tears") he even completed this public perception of the woman not strong enough for a tough job like the president's. This image was broadly referred to again in 2009.

coverage of the days and weeks around her loss of office in the parliament elections in Croatia on December 4th 2011 provide a very interesting material to be analysed in future studies. Although a very thorough analysis on quantitative media coverage of women on the whole in Croatian media – focusing on TV – has been published in the 1990s by Leinert Novosel (1996) quantitative analyses for the last years and for other media genres would also valuably contribute to the broader question on the relation of gender and the media in Croatia. Despite being such a fascinating topic, up until now, Kosor and the media have not been in the focus of any published studies.[8]

1 The days around the assumption of office – July 2009

When on Wednesday afternoon, July 1st 2009, Ivo Sanader surprisingly announces his resignation from the post of prime minister and in the very first press conference names his deputy Jadranka Kosor as his likeliest successor, most of the (print) media reacts not just surprised but apparently taken aback, before switching to "concern" about the quality of Kosor's political talents as well as about her abilities to lead the government and the country. For a better overview of the, subtly or overtly shown, gendered, and sometimes sexist, media (re)presentation of the days around her assumption of office, I will distinguish different issues the print media focused on.

The sample of analysed articles from the days around her assumption of office can be assigned to two major topics (firstly, her *weakness* and secondly, the *very fact that she is a woman* and the first *female* prime minister) and some less significant but still very telling areas of (public) interest (her *private life*, her *fashion appearance/style* and her *cold-heartedness and nepotism*). The list therefore starts with the statements soon after Sanader's resignation announcement that mainly dealt with the perception of Kosor as a politician without political and personal backbone due to her openly shown loyalty to Sanader as well as to her engagement with family and social politics, seen as *soft* politics.

---

[8] I would like to thank Prof. Dr. Smiljana Leinert Novosel and Sanja Sarnavka very much for their friendly affirmation of this non-existence of any such studies when I was starting to think that it was due to my external perspective from Germany that I could not find any such work.

1.1 Kosor's *weakness*

On July 2nd, in *Jutarnji List*, the well-known novelist and journalist Jurica Pavičić provides an unusual analysis of Jadranka Kosor's political professionalism when he paraphrases her work as the minister of family, veteran's affairs and intergenerational solidarity as "uloga oficijelnog ramena za plakanje" ("the role as the official shoulder to cry on") (PAVIČIĆ 2009). In line with such underlying assumption and accordingly actively contributing in building a discourse on Kosor's "weak" politics as contrary to the "real" daily business that a party and government leader has to deal with, there is a range of similar articles tending to classify not only Kosor as a person but also her style in politics during the previous years as *soft* and mostly in Sanader's shadow. *Slobodna Dalmacija* is quoting political analysts who are announcing that the Croatian government will basically be without a leader even after Kosor's assumption of office because of her "lack in charisma". The same people presage her term of office to be a very short one, since they are certain that there will soon be new elections. (KARLOVIĆ-SABOLIĆ 2009) More subtle, but still evident enough, are the questions about Kosor put to leading party members, like Darko Milinović in *Jutarnji list* (BARILAR 2009) or Andrija Hebrang in *Vjesnik* (LIPOVAC 2009: 7) when the interviewer wants them to comment on their personal assessment of Kosor's authority and of her ability (as a woman) to lead the party and the country. In *Slobodna Dalmacija*, a journalist expresses her "concern" that the extreme right wing of the party around Andrija Hebrang might not be able to stand this female leadership and, by giving many different scenarios other than Kosor's assumption of office, makes it clear to the reader that Kosor is not the right candidate because of her "weakness":

> Dosadašnjim radom Jadranka Kosor nije se nametnula kao samosvojna, neovisna osoba sa stavom i gardom. Naprotiv, djelovala je poslužnički i odano do poniznosti. Kad krenu pritisci sa svih strana, nije vjerojatno da će im se znati oduprijeti [...][9] (BLAŽEVIĆ 2009)

The circular emphasis of Kosor's weakness due to the nature of her previous political involvement, due to her close relationship to Ivo Sanader, due to the fact that Sanader announced her candidacy and that she did not take the office after a parliamentarian election, creates the picture of a very weak politician in

---

[9] "With her previous work Jadranka Kosor has not shown up as a self-confident and autonomous person with her own stance. Quite the contrary, she appeared subservient and obedient to subjectedness. When the all-round pressure will start it is not likely that she will be able to bear it [...]"

a very weak political situation. Furthermore, the construction of a *weak woman* is highlighted by another very interesting aspect: some of the newspapers are (at that point) searching for advice and expertise from feminist and women's groups. It goes without saying that women's and feminist groups need to be much more in the media focus and I would claim it to be definitely always right to enquire expert opinion on all issues of societal inequality and that there is very much to be further analysed by feminists and women's experts all around, but it seems heavily doubtful whether this was the motive of any of the articles in the given context. I will come back to the issue of feminism in portraying Kosor as a person and as a politician in the next part of this survey, but I will give some examples of these articles here, since – intended or not – some of these comments by feminist experts seem to have contributed greatly to the constructed media image of a certain weakness of Kosor in the days around her assumption of office.[10] Since newspaper articles are only able to show extracts of the conversations and interviews, it appears rather due to the choice of these extracts made by the journalists (or editors) than to the statements of the experts that the picture of a *feminist attack* on the first prime minister evolves. It contributes to the impression of a "concerned" public when journalists at that early state of Kosor's inauguration ask feminist experts questions about the effect that a powerless female head of government might have for the progression of gender equality in Croatian society.

1.1.1 Feminists bashing the first female prime minister?

On July 6th 2009, *Jutarnji List* titles: "Ženske udruge: Sanader želi ostati šef jer zna da će Kosor biti poslušna" ("Women's organisations: Sanader wants to stay the boss because he knows that Kosor is at his beck and call") (ŽUŽIĆ 2009a): The article that goes with this title is an analysis of the fact that the constructed public picture of Kosor in these first days after Sanader's resignation is at least awkward. The article contains some very differentiated quotes and thoughts, formulated by the author herself and by three leading Croatian gender experts. The only negative comment occurring in the article functions as its title, which in the given context shows quite clearly that the prevailing public picture of the female prime minister as shown by the print media is above all the product of a very clear – and to a great extent gendered – construction of Kosor.

The article could easily be titled: "Ženske udruge: u hrvatskoj javnosti prema političarkama i dalje odnosi s predrasudama i stereotipima" ("Women's

---

[10] See Leinert Novosel's comments criticising the lack of feminist solidarity when it came to evaluating Kosor's candidacy and assumption of office in ORUČ IVOŠ 2009a: 22.

organisations: In Croatia the public still treats female politicians with preconceptions and stereotypes"), or "Ženske udruge: žene se u politici ocjenjuju na drukčiji način" ("Women's organisations: Women in politics are evaluated differently"), or "Ženske udruge: važno je da Hrvatska ima premijerku" ("Women's organisations: It is crucial that Croatia has a female prime minister"), since these are all quotes deriving from the same article. But instead, by choosing the only negative remark by one of the gender experts, a picture of *feminist bashing* of Kosor is constructed that gives way to roundly critique for all doubting citizens, whether a woman in such a position is necessary or valuable at all. "If even the feminists say so..." And although the feminist experts have of course every right to criticise politicians, especially if they contribute to traditional and consequently often limiting gender roles, this is not the case in the articles analysed (and the question the author dealt with). Interestingly enough, *Slobodna Dalmacija* is also publishing two articles on the same topic, and here also the rare negative statements given by the group of women and gender experts are used for the titles. (See PODRUG 2009; ŽUŽIĆ 2009b)

By focusing on Kosor's potential political as well as personal *weakness* for some of the mentioned (and some other) reasons, the person Jadranka Kosor is clearly trivialised. It does not seem far-fetched that this is connected to her being the first *female* prime minister of Croatia, and it becomes very obvious by the fact that the journalists themselves refer to the *women's question* and are thereby framing the articles in a gender specific context. Interestingly, it is a journalist from *Jutarnji List* too, who as one of the first of her peers, reflects on the fact that Kosor's *weakness* might, if at all, be above all due to the fact that she appears to be the typical "human sacrifice" in politics. In line with a framework of gendered societal conceptions, Jelena Lovrić contextualises the whole process around Sanader and Kosor in those days as "[k]lasično spašavanje kralja žrtvovanjem kraljice" ("the classical rescue of the King through the sacrifice of the Queen") (LOVRIĆ 2009).

Gender specialists have already pointed out this problem. Sanja Sarnavka, e.g., on that score was quoted in *Jutarnji List* making the very plain statement: "Kad žena u ovakvim uvjetima postaje premijerka, to znači da smo ne u banani, nego u dubokom bunaru!"[11]

---

[11] "If in such terms and conditions a woman becomes the prime minister, this means we are not only in a banana republic but in a deep well!" (ŽUŽIĆ 2009a)

1.2 It is a woman! Coverage of "female" topics and the prime minister's private life

On July 3rd, a *Vjesnik* headline reads "Prva žena na čelu Vlasti" ("First woman as head of government") accompanying a detailed article about Kosor's achievements, abilities, her political experience and the statement by the journalist writing the article that her nomination could have hardly surprised anyone since it would simply be logically consistent – but with no further comments on her femaleness: „Jadranka Kosor na novu funkciju dolazi s golemim kapitalom, odnosno političkim iskustvom koje je stekla predanim i upornim radom".[12]

Apart from *Vjesnik*, who seems to play a special and deviant part in this respect,[13] the news coverage on Kosor appears in many cases much more biased and considerably less issue-related:

Jutarnji List "reveals" Kosor's childhood dream of becoming Queen in a rather depreciatory way and reminds the reader of public scenes where Kosor had been reacting emotionally and thin-skinned in the past when it came to talking about her father who had left the family when she was a toddler. In the same article, the journalist tells us who Kosor would like to share a romantic evening with and other "facts" that have at least a doubtable newsworthiness, not even to speak of their evidence. (See TURČIN 2009) The next day, *Jutarnji List* publishes statements by an anonymous staff member of the then-president, Stipe Mesić, saying that the President will – grudgingly, though – work together with Kosor, who he and his staff like to call *Suzana*[14], alluding to the fact that Kosor had some emotional moments in public in the past. (NEZIROVIĆ 2009) *Jutarnji List* also gives an overview on Kosor's dress style, calling her hats too romantic and advises Kosor to dress more stylishly. (MIRKOVIĆ 2009) Another long comment on Kosor's style during her first important political meetings as a prime minister follows ten days later. (VALENTIĆ 2009)

---

[12] "Jadranka Kosor comes to her new function with giant capital and political experience which she has achieved through devoted and laborious work." (ORUČ IVOŠ 2009b: 4)

[13] There were hardly any stereotype articles in *Vjesnik* in the period analysed, but a very high coverage of the politician Kosor – not only as a prime minister but also before as a minister in Sanader's government. Furthermore, *Vjesnik* even published articles about the bad media coverage Jadranka Kosor suffered, plus a very well-balanced interview with the political analyst and gender expert Smiljana Leinert Novosel on questions of women in politics. See MILANOVIĆ 2009: 20f.; ORUČ IVOŠ 2009a: 22f.

[14] The allusion stems from the Croatian word *suze* for "tears", see above.

Slobodna Dalmacija tops it off with a highly pejoratively slanted article disclosing that the "apparently humanitarian" politician Kosor would in reality be prepared to raise her voice and even get rid of unpopular staff:

> [...] dosadašnja potpredsjednica Vlade, koju javnost percipira kao uplakanu humanitarku koja se voli slikati dodjeljujući ključeve stanova i posjećujući domove teško bolesne i ostavljene djece, i te kako zna povisiti glas i glatko se riješiti neposlušnih suradnika.[15] (BELAK KRILE 2009)

The discourse behind such remarks – in this case, even formulated as a deconstruction of the asserted prevailing public picture of Kosor as the "whining humanitarian" – is not only trivialising and vilifying by (re)painting the picture of an easily tear-filled and therefore weak politician. Such comments also contain and transport assumptions and thoughts about the norms of politicians as well as of men and women. Being emotional *and* conscious of one's power, plus (maybe) a poor boss is, as it seems, not what people should want their first female chief of government to be. This points to a special expectation in Kosor because of her gender. Any deviation from the norm bears the danger of a problematic categorization since well-known prototypes and stereotypes fail to help labelling the given person, leaving the commentator alone with no "normal" classification to use. Kosor, not only as a woman of power, but also because of her ambivalent appearance in public leaves the journalists alone with a set of inapplicable conceptions. This can be true when it comes to showing normality as well in politics as in assumptions about public-private divisions in society as in manifested ways of dealing with femaleness, maleness and gender altogether.

It is, at this early stage, another politician from the conservative party spectrum, Đurđa Adlešić, who points to the fact that the way the news about Kosor's assumption of office are shaped, formulated and contextualised has a strong sexist connotation. In an article in *Slobodna Dalmacija* she is quoted saying that the repeatedly asked question about Kosor's capability to lead the country would not have been asked as often and by as many people had the candidate been a man. (See "Hrvatska ima premijerku" 2009) In another article, Adlešić states that her own party and most of the other leading political parties would not be ready to cope with a woman at their top, pointing not only at discriminatory tendencies in the media but in politics as well. (BARILAR/ PAVIĆ

---

[15] "[...] the present vice-president of the government, who the public perceives as a snivelling humanitarian that likes to be taken pictures of when giving out apartment keys and while visiting homes of critically ill and left children, just as well knows how to raise her voice and smoothly gets rid of disobedient staff members."

2009) Similarly, Holtz-Bacha points to the frequently repeated question by journalists about Germany's capability to have a female chancellor in 2005, when Merkel was appointed as the candidate of the CDU[16]. Holtz-Bacha concludes that it is probably much rather the media who is not ready for a female chancellor and not the people they seem so concerned about. (HOLTZ-BACHA 2007: 9) But, and that is the problem of such a commentatorship, the repeatedly spread unsettledness that accompanies such questioning must have an effect on the people reading the news. Namely, they might perceive a female candidate as less eligible, due to her political weakness, her lack in experience, the worry that the other – male – politicians might not take her seriously, or whatever.

In the same way as the media in the beginning of July seemed "concerned" about Kosor's effect on gender equality (see above Chapter 1.1.1) for the country, the media also expressed doubts about her, as a woman, being able to achieve the needed amount of authority in the party, the government and politics at large. This is an ostentatious way of trivialising her as a public person and a practice that has been often observed in other national backgrounds as a common tool of creating a certain discourse of discomfort with powerful women and female politicians altogether. (See FOWLER 1991: 105; MRŠEVIĆ 2008: 80) In the same sense, in a public-opinion poll people were asked about their evaluation of Kosor's possible authority over the ministers of her future government; with the result of only about eight percent of the participants believing that she would have the "final say" in government meetings.[17] For this again is true what Adlešić stated earlier: it is highly doubtable whether this question would have been posed, had it been one of Kosor's male fellows that had been chosen as Sanader's successor.

Interesting in itself though is the fact that already at that same time not only the person concerned, Kosor, but many others started raising their voices against a prevailing sexist tendency in the media as well as among the politicians when it comes to commenting on Kosor's assumption of office. (See "Slučaj premijerka – seksizam na djelu" 2009)

After Andrija Hebrang as one of the leading politicians of the HDZ publicly announced that he and his party would be ready to back up the new prime minister "not only as if she was a man but even more so as if she was a real he-

---

[16] The Christian Democratic Union in Germany.
[17] See the short film on the poll at: http://manjgura.hr/politika/glas-gradana-kosor-ce-biti-losija-od-sanadera-a-on-ce-vladati-iz-sjene-dnevnik-nove-tv-i-puls/, retrieved 20.8.2011 and BIBIĆ MOSOR 2009.

man"[18], Kosor, in her first speech in the Croatian *Sabor* after her announcement, declares that she will rule the government with an "iron female fist"[19].

In an interview with *Jutarnji List* on the following day, she makes one of her first comments on her deviant treatment as a woman in public; the first in a series of public statements of the sexist treatment she experiences. Very adeptly, again, she makes use of the interviewer's predictable question why, in her mind, she has a problem with authority, answering in terms of female solidarity by saying that it would have meant a backlash for the emancipation of Croatian women if she had not used this opportunity of becoming prime minister and thereby giving herself a rather feminist explanation of the current gender system when it comes to politics:

> "Zato što sam žena. Živimo u društvu u kojem se misli da je politika prvorazredan posao za muškarce, da žene mogu promatrati, ali odluke donose muškarci. I to je jedan od razloga zbog kojih sam prihvatila ponudu premijera i šefa stranke. Ako odbijem, mislila sam, učinit ću korak unatrag za žene u Hrvatskoj."[20] (PLIŠIĆ 2009)

It is this kind of rhetoric that makes Kosor such a very interesting subject of feminist media analyses since she herself points to an amount of illustrative material on gender stereotype and sexism in the media. And with her keen sense of discriminatory manners and practices, she developed a very clear standing against any sexist tendencies in the media coverage of her person and of women altogether.

---

[18] The, very telling, quote goes as follows: "Mi u HDZ-u smo ponosni da je na red za tu funkciju došla jedna žena. Ja joj osobno poručujem: Stajat ćemo svi uz tebe, ne kao da si muško nego kao da si muškarčina. U svom radu i u politici i u zdravstvu i u obrazovanju sam se uvjerio da su žene vrlo često kvalitetnije od muškaraca." ("We in the HDZ are proud that it is the time of a woman coming to that position. I advise her personally of the following: We will all back you up, not as if you were a man but as if you were a he-man. During my work as well as in politics, in health and in education I have seen for myself that women are very often of higher quality than men.") (IVIĆ 2009)

[19] This pronouncement, of course, found its way into television too: Dnevnik on HRT 1 (4.7.2009). http://dnevnik.hr/vijesti/hrvatska/hdz-i-vladu-vodit-cu-cvrstom-zenskom-rukom.html, retrieved 20.8.2011. See also "Vodit ću Vladu čvrstom ženskom rukom" 2009.

[20] "Because I am a woman. We live in a society where it is commonly assumed that politics is first and foremost men's work, which women may observe, but men are the ones taking decisions. And that is one of the reasons why I have accepted the offer of becoming the prime minister and the leader of the party. Would I reject it, I thought, I would make a step backwards for the women in Croatia."

2 The Prime Minister openly reacts to sexism – 2010/2011

With this acute awareness of derogatory public coverage of her as a politician because of her sex and the drive to stand up against it, Kosor quite obviously takes on a special position in comparison with other politicians:

The British politicians interviewed by Ross and Sreberny, e.g., did not perceive a particular sexism in the media coverage of their person and rather stated that the media had a special interest in them due to the fact that they as women were a minority in politics, although they had previously in the interviews named a range of clearly sexist incidents in the media concerning the ways of reporting about them. (ROSS/ SREBERNY 2007: 93f.) And for Angela Merkel seems to be true what LUENENBORG et al. state, namely that she has established a certain "gender-neutral appearance" (2011: 70), and one of her – often criticized – practices in handling the fact that she is the first female chancellor (and the first East German as well) in that position is simply not to speak of this feature in public. (See JOURNALISTINNENBUND n.d.) It is also very interesting in this context that in the USA a project to fight sexist media coverage of female politicians and calling upon the politicians to no longer ignore such treatment has been established in 2010 only.[21] That gives reason for the assumption that there is not only a big problem with sexist media coverage but also a tendency by the concerned politicians to avoid striking back in such incidents and to rather hush it up and try to avoid to actively negate discriminatory practices.

A trained journalist herself, Kosor seems to be very well aware of the ways in which media "help to construct gender identity and subjectivity" (CARTER 2012: 375) and is, obviously, not willing to accept any such constructed public coverage of her own person without resistance. From the very beginning of her nomination for the function as the next prime minister after Sanader's resignation, she seemed very pugnacious and not hesitating to name issues of sexism. Be it in the media coverage of her person, be it in general societal matters – mostly, of course, within the scope of her political affiliation but with a considerable tendency of challenging her conservative peers. Already on July 4th, two days before her assumption of office, she talks in the Croatian parliament (*Sabor*) of her special experience as a woman in politics, calling for solidarity among women – especially in her own party. ("Vodit ću Vladu čvrstom ženskom rukom" 2009) In the following two years of her government,

---

[21] See PAGE 2010. The project has created a blog with reports on sexist media coverage and information about the possible (political) harm done by sexist comments. See http://www.nameitchangeit.org/, retrieved 20.8.2011.

Kosor uses other events to articulate her disapproval when it comes to public sexism, but does not hesitate to take her own person as an example to personalise general statements.

In an article in *Slobodna Dalmacija* on May 7th 2010, Kosor was labelled as "uvrijeđena premijerka" ("the offended prime minister") after she had talked at a roundtable on gender equality and the media about her own – negative – experiences as a woman in the media focus. In the quotations of the given article, Kosor gives several incidents of mistreatment that she has suffered ever since becoming prime minister: She names different fields of deviant media coverage of her person because of her being a woman, such as: her fashion style, her charm in political discussions with other – male – heads of state or government, and the usage of giving her nicknames like "Jaca" while male colleagues are named correctly, with their full or at least their real names. Apart from these features, Kosor states that women as such face many more difficultties in being successful in politics due to prevailing and persisting stereotypes and gendered assumptions, and that it was especially hard for women if they were not married. (See BELAK-KRILE 2010)

Over and above the fact that the latter might also need some more empirical evidence, it has become clear by now that Kosor is, more than others, willing to draw attention to sexist treatment of herself and her peers and does not follow Merkel's example of hushing-up and ignoring unequal treatment of herself in comparison to leading male politicians due to her gender. Which of these two approaches might be the better practice when it comes to building-up political authority and public invulnerability becomes quite clear after reading the comments beneath the mentioned article, which are predominantly very derogatory and do not only contain even more sexist assaults but above all question her political strength and her responsibility to act as a politician while worrying about seemingly secondary matters like gender equality and equal treatment in the media.[22] On the other hand, it is important to know that at this time, Kosor is already at a very high position in public polls on the popularity of politicians, (MOSKALJOV 2010) only beaten by the new president, Mesić's successor, Ivo Josipović, which seems surprising after her very difficult start only half a year before.

Previous to this rather personal statement *Slobodna Dalmacija* reports, Kosor had already in April of the same year called for public attention to sexist matters when she asked the people in charge of the HTZ (*Hrvatska turistička zajednica* – Croatian Tourist Agency) to reconsider broadcasting an advertising

---

[22] See all the comments, altogether more than 40, at: http://www.slobodnadalmacija.hr/Hrvatska/tabid/66/articleType/ArticleView/articleId/101752/Default.aspx, retrieved 20.8.2011.

spot for Croatia that contained a short sequence with the bottom of a woman, alluding to "Croatia's beauty". After mentioning her and her collaborationist's work on putting the *Zakon o ravnopravnosti spolova* (Gender Equality Act) through, she is quoted saying:

> "Predlažem da iz spota u kojem se govori o turističkim vrijednostima izostavi kadar dijelova ženskoga tijela jer je to na neki način seksistički. [...] To je moja primjedba, ne naredba, i molim razmotrite je [...]"[23] (TUŠKAN 2010)

Of course, Kosor receives negative feedback for this intervention, not only due to interpretations showing that sexism is sometimes not easily defined but very easily dismissed; (TOMIĆ 2010) and a pretty lucid commentary by Jelena Lovrić, again, claiming that Kosor would really need to be aware of persistent sexist attitudes among her own ministers and not only focus on sexism outside her direct sphere of influence. (LOVRIĆ 2010) This seems to be a very frequent way of devaluating Kosor's public statements about deviant treatment towards women from men (as a norm), claiming her inconsistency and shallowness when it comes to feminist declarations.[24] There is also some public support, for instance from gender expert Sanja Sarnavka, who, however, takes the opportunity to say that she would really appreciate if the prime minister would address other inadequacies as promptly and effectively as well. (BANJEGLAV 2010)

Kosor herself tops the prevailing discussion in the media off when she uses the tense relationship with the Eastern neighbour state, Serbia, as one of her – by now already customary – clarifications of sexist attitudes. As a consequence of Kosor's public greeting to the just before sentenced war criminals and former Croatian generals Ante Gotovina and Mladen Markac at the Croatian Victory Day (August 5th, the celebration day of the military operation "Oluja" that took place in 1995), the official relations with Serbia cooled down. When the two presidents, Boris Tadić and Ivo Josipović, met some weeks later with other regional political leaders in Belgrade, they seemed to have a good time together. Later on, journalists asked the Serbian president whether he would like to kiss Josipović and whether he would do the same with Kosor (probably an awkward way of asking about their personal contact and relation), the president answered that he would like to kiss Kosor, but would not kiss Josipović. A few months earlier he had, answering a similar awkward question, already publicly announced that he would like to be the witness to a marriage between Jadranka

---

[23] "I recommend that we leave the shoot of the parts of a female body out of the spot which is about touristic values, since it is in a certain way sexist. [...] That is my plea, not an order, and I kindly ask you to consider it [...]"

[24] See, e.g., BROZ 2010 plus the comments underneath the article.

Kosor and Borut Pahor (another issue of very disputable media coverage regarding Kosor's skills in foreign politics after she and her Slovenian colleague agreed on resolutions in the border-discussion). ("Boris Tadić otkriva" 2011) There is no doubt that both, the questions posed by the journalists and the answers provided by Tadić, contain an aspect of shadiness and are highly questionable. Clearly, Kosor has every right to say that she will not leave public statements about her person uncommented, when they are along such a sexualized line. But Kosor does not only ask her colleague to refrain from any such salacious remarks about her person derived from her gender and sexual orientation. Instead, she is quoted in Serbian news saying: "Ja ga podsećam da mi u Hrvatskoj imamo zakon koji zabranjuje takav odnos prema ženama."[25] (BETA 2011b) Using her criticism of the Serbian president's sexist remarks about her person for a boastful counterstrike with a nationalist side blow, very much reveals again, why Kosor is such a highly disputed public person, as it shows her special way of using generally rather disconnected discourses for her own, sometimes very heterogonous political approach.

Concluding remarks

There is not only a clear ambivalence due to the way Kosor is perceived as a politician and a public person but also due to her own frequent remarks on discriminatory and especially sexist matters in Croatian society, in politics and in the media, since these do not seem to harmonize with her strong conservative political background. Not only the public person Kosor (a divorced, single mother, a woman at the head of an often very unprogressive party with strong links to the catholic church etc.), but also the politician Kosor (with a rather weak start due to the external settings around her assumption of office, a sympathiser of sentenced generals and war criminals, a rather liberal figure within her party – in some matters –, a strong and demanding leader in the economical crisis etc.), and even more so the "feminist" Kosor (as a member of the HDZ an opponent of abortion rights, but a declared fighter for women's rights and women's political participation, with only a negligible number of women in her own government, etc.), suggests a very controversial public person that likes to have several things on the go at once. This might be unpleasant, especially when one might easily support some of these things but oppose others – however it is hardly a substantial allegation. The bare fact that Kosor, as a prime minister, as the head of a conservative party, as a woman in top

---

[25] "I remind him that we, in Croatia, have a law prohibiting such behaviour against women." See also "Kosor: Tadić govori seksistički o meni" 2011; BETA 2011a.

politics is still willing to talk about women's rights, should be taken as a great advance and a point that really sets her apart from other female political leaders who often tend to neglect the fact that their way into top politics was – maybe – different, longer or more demanding because of their sex and the societal stereotypes regarding sex and gender that might have gotten in their way.

Whether the former prime minister Kosor really has a strong feminist conviction or not, might not be so relevant in this regard; the certainty that she was treated differently from her male colleagues from the very beginning in most of the media and with a certain gendered approach, which became clear from my data analysis, definitely gives her every right to oppose any deviant and very often derogatory treatment. And even more so, since during her government, she was willingly and decidedly outspoken against other matters she regarded as sexist and discriminatory and definitely made people aware of sexism in society as such, as well as of existing sexist attitudes and behaviours. If only she made citizens discuss the way people are perceived because of their sex and/or gender controversially and made some journalists think about the way they talk and write about men and women in politics, she made a valuable contribution to the discussion about the perception and construction of gender as a category of discriminatory action in society.

References

BROWN, MARY ELLEN/ DARLAINE C. GARDETTO, REPRESENTING HILLARY RODHAM CLINTON (2000): Gender, Meaning, and News Media. In: Sreberny, Annabelle/ Liesbet van Zoonen (eds.): Gender, Politics and Communication. Cresskill. 21–51.

CARTER, CYNTHIA (2012): Sex/Gender and the Media. From Sex Roles to Social Construction and Beyond. In: Ross, Karen (ed.): The Handbook of Gender, Sex, and Media. Malden. 365–382.

EITNER, JANIS (2007): Macht Macht männlich? Das Bild von Angela Merkel und Gerhard Schröder in der deutschen Tagespresse. Marburg.

FOWLER, ROGER (1991): Language in the News. Discourse and Ideology in the Press. London/New York.

HOLTZ-BACHA, CHRISTINA (2007): Zur Einführung: Politikerinnen in den Medien. In: Holtz-Bach, Christina/ Nina König-Reiling (eds.): Warum nicht gleich? Wie die Medien mit Frauen in der Politik umgehen. Wiesbaden. 7–16.

JOURNALISTINNENBUND (n.d.): Is' was, Kanzlerin? Das Besondere an weiblicher Macht oder wie Männer wieder richtige Männer wurden. Eine Analyse des Journalistinnenbundes zur Darstellung von Angela Merkel in den Medien. http://www.journalistinnen.de/verein/pdf/jb_angelawatch.pdf, retrieved 20.8.2011.

KOCH, THOMAS/ CHRISTINA HOLTZ-BACHA (2008): Der Merkel-Faktor – Die Berichterstattung der Printmedien über Merkel und Schröder im Bundeswahlkampf. In: Holtz-Bach, Christina (ed.): Frauen, Politik und Medien. Wiesbaden. 49–71.

LEINERT NOVOSEL, SMILJANA (2007): Politika ravnopravnosti spolova: kako do „kritične mase" žena u parlamentima? In: Politička Misao 3. 85–102.

LEINERT NOVOSEL, SMILJANA (1996): Women in Croatian Media, In: Politička misao 5. 136–147.

LUENENBORG, MARGRETH/ JUTTA ROESER/ TANJA MAIER/ KATHRIN MUELLER (2011): Gender Analysis of Mediated Politics in Germany. In: Krijnen, Tonny/ Claudia Alvares/ Sofie van Bauwel (eds.): Gendered Transformations. Theory and Practices on Gender and Media. Bristol. 57–75.

MRŠEVIĆ, ZORICA (2008): Žene u medijima: 2010 u Srbiji, In: Genero 12. 69–93.

PAGE, SUSAN (2010): Study: Sexist insults hurt female politicians. In: USA today (23.9.2010). http://www.usatoday.com/news/politics/2010-09-22-sexist-insults-female-politicians_N.htm, retrieved 20.8.2011.

PANTTI, MERVI (2007): Portraying Politics. Gender, Politik und Medien. In: Holtz-Bach, Christina/ Nina König-Reiling (eds.): Warum nicht gleich? Wie die Medien mit Frauen in der Politik umgehen. Wiesbaden. 17–51.

ROSS, KAREN/ ANNABELLE SREBERNY (2007): Women in the House. Media Representation of British Politicians. In: Sreberny, Annabelle/ Liesbet van Zoonen (eds.): Gender, politics and communication. Cresskill. 79–99.

SAUER, BIRGIT (2011): Die Allgegenwart der „Androkratie". Feministische Anmerkungen zur „Postdemokratie". In: Aus Politik und Zeitgeschichte, 1–2. 32–36.

SREBERNY, ANNABELLE/ LIESBET VAN ZOONEN (2000): Gender, Politics and Communication. An Introduction. In: Sreberny, Annabelle/ van Zoonen, Liesbet (eds.): Gender, politics and communication. Cresskill. 1–19.

STERR, LISA (1997): Frauen und Männer auf der Titelseite. Strukturen und Muster der Berichterstattung am Beispiel einer Tageszeitung. Pfaffenweiler.

VAVRUS, MARY D. (2002): Postfeminist News. Political Women in Media Culture. New York.

VIŠNJIĆ, JELENA/ MIRJANA MIROSAVLJEVIĆ (2007): Problem reprezentacije roda u medijima. In: Zaharijević, Adriana (ed.): Neko je rekao feminizam? Kako je feminizam uticao na žene XXI veka. Belgrade. 227–243.

ŽIKIĆ, BILJANA (2009): Gendered Representations in Slovenian and Serbian Media Discourses. In: CAS Working Papers Series 2. Sofia. 3–20.

Articles/Sources

BANJEGLAV, GORANA (2010): Sporna Guza u spotu. Sarnavka: Često gledam porniće, jako me zanimaju. In: dalje.com (12.4.2010). http://dalje.com/hr-hrvatska/sarnavka--cesto-gledam-pornice-jako-me-zanimaju/301711, retrieved 20.8.2010.

BARILAR, SUZANA (2009): Sanader nam je rekao: Evo, dečki, pokažite što možete. In: Jutarnji List (4.7.2009). http://www.jutarnji.hr/sanader-nam-je-rekao--evo--decki--pokazite-sto-mozete/301870/, retrieved 20.8.2011.

BARILAR, SUZANA/ SNJEŽANA PAVIĆ (2009): Adlešič: Moja se stranka nije usudila izabrati ženu za premijera. In: Jutarnji List (4.7.2009). http://www.jutarnji.hr/adlesic--moja-se-stranka-nije-usudila-izabrati-zenu-za-premijera/301916/, retrieved 20.8.2011.

BELAK-KRILE, ANITA (2010): Jadranka Kosor nezadovoljna medijskim tretmanom. Uvrijeđena premijerka: Nisam vam ja Jaca. In: Slobodna Dalmacija (7.5.2010). http://www.slobodnadalmacija.hr/Hrvatska/tabid/66/articleType/ArticleView/articleId/101752/Default.aspx, retrieved 20.8.2011.

BELAK KRILE, ANITA (2009): Jadranka bez maske: oštra šefica ispod blaga lica. In: Slobodna Dalmacija (3.7.2009). http://www.slobodnadalmacija.hr/Hrvatska/tabid/66/articleType/ArticleView/articleId/60517/Default.aspx, retrieved 20.8.2011.

BETA (2011a): Kosor: Tadić daje seksističke izjave. Hrvatska premijerka se poziva na zakon o zaštiti prava žena. In: Blic online (3.9.2011). http://www.blic.rs/Vesti/Politika/275000/Kosor-Tadic-daje-seksisticke-izjave, retrieved 30.9.2011.

BETA (2011b): Kosorova: Tadićeva izjava seksizam, no author given. In: B92.net (3.9.2011). http://www.b92.net/info/vesti/index.php?yyyy=2011&mm=09&dd=03&nav_category=11&nav_id=539476, retrieved 30.9.2011.

BIBIĆ MOSOR, MILORAD (2009): Imamo premijerku! Sabor dao povjerenje Vladi Jadranke Kosor. In: Slobodna Dalmacija (6.7.2009). http://web2.slobodnadalmacija.hr/Mosorova-pitalica/tabid/208/articleType/ArticleView/articleId/60887/Default.aspx, retrieved 20.8.2011.

BLAŽEVIĆ, DAVORKA (2009): Što čeka Hrvatsku nakon odlaska najmoćnijeg čovjeka? Što nakon odlaska Sanadera: Predsjedniče, Vi ste na potezu. In: Slobodna Dalmacija (4.7.2009). http://www.slobodnadalmacija.hr/Spektar/tabid/94/articleType/ArticleView/articleId/60480/Default.aspx, retrieved 20.8.2011.

Boris Tadić otkriva: S Josipovićem se neću ljubiti, a s Jadrankom uvijek. No author given. In: Jutarnji List (2.9.2011). http://www.jutarnji.hr/josipovic-i-tadic-uz-tamburase-zapjevali-u-beogradu/970411/, retrieved 30.9.2011.

BROZ, TAJANA (2010): Trebam li se ispričati Premijerki? In: Libela – portal o rodu, spolu i demokraciji (10.5.2010). http://www.libela.org/sa-stavom/1447-trebam-li-se-ispricati-premijerki/, retrieved 20.8.2011.

E-NOVINE (2010): Žene godine po izboru američkog magazina Glamour. Fergie, Julia Roberts, Jadranka Kosor... In: e-Novine (3.11.2010). http://www.e-novine.com/entertainment/entertainment-licnosti/41946-Fergie-Julia-Roberts-Jadranka-Kosor.html, retrieved 20.8.2011.

Hrvatska ima premijerku: Mesić dao mandat Jadranki Kosor. No author given. In: Slobodna Dalmacija (3.7.2009). http://www.slobodnadalmacija.hr/Hrvatska/tabid/66/articleType/ArticleView/articleId/60496/Default.aspx, retrieved 20.8.2011.

IVIĆ, SNJEŽANA (2009): Intervju, Andrija Hebrang: Jadranka, stat ćemo uz tebe kao da si muškarčina! In: Dalje.com (2.7.2009). http://dalje.com/hr-hrvatska/jadranka-stat-cemo-uz-tebe-kao-da-si-muskarcina/268623, retrieved 20.8.2011.

KARLOVIĆ-SABOLIĆ, MARINA (2009): Riječ stručnjaka: Jadranka Kosor ne može povezati koaliciju. In: Slobodna Dalmacija (3.7.2009). http://www.slobodnadalmacija.hr/Mozaik/tabid/80/articleType/ArticleView/articleId/60447/Default.aspx, retrieved 20.8.2011.

Kosor: Tadić govori seksistički o meni, a mi imamo dva zakona protiv toga. No author given. In: Jutarnji List (3.9.2011). http://www. jutarnji.hr/jadranka-kosor--tadic-govori-seksisticki-o-meni--a-mi-u-rh-imamo-zakon-protiv-toga/970818/, retrieved 30.9.2011.

LIPOVAC, MARIJAN (2009): HDZ nastavlja u Sanaderovu smjeru. In: Vjesnik (3.7.2009). 7.

LOVRIĆ, JELENA (2010): Seksizam ministra Milinovića. In: Jutarnji List (20.4.2010). http://www.jutarnji.hr/seksizam-ministra-milinovica/730653/, retrieved 20.8.2011.

LOVRIĆ, JELENA (2009): Premijerka ili žrtva kraljice. In: Jutarnji List (7.7.2009). http://www.jutarnji.hr/premijerka-ili-zrtva-kraljice/302175/, retrieved 20.8. 2011.

MILANOVIĆ, ZORAN (2009): Jadranki Kosor, unatoč medijskoj hajci, hrvatski građani vjeruju. In: Sedam dana [supplement to *Vjesnik*] (25./26.7.2009). 20–21.

MIRKOVIĆ, NADA (2009): Premijerka se mora odreći svojih šešira. In: Jutarnji List (2.7.2009). http://www.jutarnji.hr/template/article/article-print.jsp?id=301658, retrieved 20.8.2011.

MOSKALJOV, VANJA (2010): Ivo Josipović najpozitivniji političar, Ivo Sanader najveći „negativac". In: Večernji List (3.2.2010). http://www.vecernji.hr/vijesti/ivo-josipovic-najpozitivniji-politicar-ivo-sanader-najveci-negativac-clanak-91455, retrieved 20.8.2011.

NEZIROVIĆ, VANJA (2009): Predsjednikov suradnik: Mesić će surađivati sa „Suzanom" iako to nikada nije htio. In: Jutarnji List (3.7.2009). http://www.jutarnji.hr/predsjednikov-suradnik--mesic-ce-suradivati-sa--suzanom--iako-to-nikada-nije-htio/301777/, retrieved 20.8.2011.

ORUČ IVOŠ, SILVANA (2009a): Dolazak prve žene na čelo Vlade izrazito je pozitivan demokratski iskorak. Razgovor: Smiljana Leinert Novosel. In: Sedam dana [supplement to *Vjesnik*] (18./19.7.2009). 22–23.

ORUČ IVOŠ, SILVANA (2009b): Prva žena na čelu Vlasti: Jadranka Kosor kao jamac kontinuiteta i sigurnosti. In: Vjesnik (3.7.2009). 4.

PAVIČIĆ, JURICA (2009): Pavičić o Jadranki Kosor: Dugo u centrima moći, sveprisutna, ali nevidljiva. In: Jutarnji List (2.7.2009). http://www.jutarnji.hr/pavicic-o-jadranki-kosor--dugo-u-centrima-moci--sveprisutna--ali-nevidljiva/301666/, retrieved 20.8.2011.

PLIŠIĆ, ANA (2009): Kosor: Moja će biti zadnja! In: Jutarnji List (4.7.2009). http://www.jutarnji.hr/kosor--moja-ce-biti-zadnja-/302011/, retrieved 20.8.2011.

PODRUG, A. (2009): Aktivistice o Jadranki Kosor: Ženama ne pomaže „ćaćin izbor". In: Slobodna Dalmacija (5.7.2009). http://web2.slobodnadalmacija.hr/Hrvatska/tabid/66/articleType/ArticleView/articleId/60638/Default.aspx, retrieved 20.8.2011.

Slučaj premijerka – seksizam na djelu. No author given. In: CESI (4.7.2009). http://www.cesi.hr/hr/za-medije/1216-slucaj-premijerka-seksizam-na-djelu/, retrieved 20.8.2011.

TOMIĆ, ANTE (2010): Tomić: Djevojka se, valjda, trebala sunčati u suknji do koljena. In: Jutarnji List (11.4.2010). http://www.jutarnji.hr/ante-tomic--djevojka-se--valjda--trebala-suncati-u-suknji-do-koljena/707094/, retrieved 20.8.2011.

TURČIN, KRISTINA (2009): Jadranka Kosor: Kao dijete je maštala da postane kraljica. In: Jutarnji List (2.7.2009). http://www.jutarnji.hr/jadranka-kosor--kao-dijete-je-mastala-da-postane-kraljica/301656/, retrieved 20.8.2011.

TUŠKAN, DANIJEL (2010): Kosor: Izbacite žensku stražnjicu iz turističkog spota za Hrvatsku! In: Jutarnji List (10.4.2010). http://www.jutarnji.hr/seksizam--premijerka-jadranka-kosor-zatrazila-da-se-iz-promotivnog-spota-htz-a-makne-gola-zenska-guza/704783/, retrieved 20.8.2011.

VALENTIĆ, JELENA (2009): Najvažniji premijerkin modni detalj. In: Jutarnji List (12.7.2009). http://www.jutarnji.hr/najvazniji-premijerkin-modni-detalj/302713/, retrieved 20.8.2011.

Vodit ću Vladu čvrstom ženskom rukom. No author given. In: Jutarnji List (4.7.2009). http://www.jutarnji.hr/vodit-cu-vladu-cvrstom-zenskom-rukom/301932/, retrieved 20.7.2011.

ŽUŽIĆ, BRANKA (2009a): Ženske udruge: Sanader želi ostati šef jer zna da će Kosor biti poslušna. In: Jutarnji List (6.7.2009). http://www.jutarnji.hr/zenske-udruge--sanader-zeli-ostati-sef-jer-zna-da-ce-kosor-biti-poslusna/302099/, retrieved 20.8.2011.

ŽUŽIĆ, BRANKA (2009b): Ženske udruge: Ostat će Sanaderova mala od kužine. In: Slobodna Dalmacija (6.7.2009). http://web2.slobodnadalmacija.hr/Hrvatska/tabid/66/articleType/ArticleView/articleId/60881/Default.aspx, retrieved 20.8.2011.

3. History and Anthropology

Reproduction, Nation, and Masculinity: Serbia in the 1990s[1]

Rada Drezgić

Introduction

Biological reproduction plays a key role in the (re-)production of ethnic and other social groups. Anthropologists have stressed the central role of kinship as an ideological concept that organizes social relations within groups and through the control of reproduction regulates ethnic boundaries. These organizing structures of kinship are important not only for families and lineages, but also for political entities (for example the state), and for the construction of femininities and masculinities (MCCLINTOCK 1993).

This article explores how within the neo-traditionalist narratives patrilineage served as an organizing principle of the nation-state in Serbia in the 1990s, and discusses the production of marginalized rural masculinity against this background. The focus of the article is a failed attempt in international matchmaking launched by the social organization *Village Hearth*. Even though this organization started a matchmaking project, it was not a typical international match-making agency. To begin with, *Village Hearth* was a non-profit organization, and second, unlike the for-profit agencies in the West which respond to a market demand, so to speak, catering to differential needs of classes of individual women in the East and men in the West, *Village Hearth* was catering to what its leadership perceived to be the needs of the Serbian nation (DREZGIĆ 2002). They believed that the Serbian nation was in a desperate need for renewal, which was a common trope within the neo-traditionalist narratives (see NAUMOVIĆ 2009: 157–178) and were convinced that national renewal begins with the rural family renewal.

This article is based on a discourse analysis of media reports about activities of the social organization *Village Hearth*, the discourse analysis of the documents issued by this organization, and on a participant observation of a week long visit of eight women from Ukraine to a Serbian village. The visit was organized by *Village Hearth* in an attempt to find potential marital partners for middle-aged rural bachelors in Serbia.

The visit started on a cold February morning in 1997 when a dusty, white minibus arrived to a picturesque mountainous village in western Serbia. Eight visibly tired women who came out of the bus were greeted by a small number

---

[1] This paper was realized as a part of the projects no. 41004 and 43007, financed by the Ministry of Education and Science of the Republic of Serbia within the framework of integrated and interdisciplinary research for the period 2011–2014.

of elderly villagers, representatives of the local and national media and by representatives of the social organization *Village Hearth*. As everyone gathered in a spacious former pub (*kafana*), temporarily reopened for this occasion, breakfast was served. It consisted of traditional homemade offerings brought in by villagers: various dairy products, pastries, smoked meat, tea, coffee and fruit brandy. In no time, a cordial and festive atmosphere was created while an ancient wood furnace heated the room managing only to take the edge off of the freezing cold, but no one seemed to care.

Lidija[2], who accompanied the group on behalf of the Association of Ukrainian-Serbian Friendship, was busy. Being a professor of Serbo-Croatian, she was the only person present on this occasion who could facilitate communication between the guests and the welcoming crowd. Thus she was translating everything – from welcoming speeches given by the representatives of the organization *Village Hearth*, to journalists' interviews and introductions between guests and the locals. Missing on the occasion, however, were middle-aged bachelors, purportedly the main reason of this visit.

Out of 48 unmarried middle aged men who at the time lived in the village not a single one came to greet the visitors. Why they did not show up, what were the motives of the organizers of this failed attempt in international match-making, what were the expectations and attitudes of various social agents – those directly involved and those at the margin of the event? The answers to these questions weave a story which serves as a backdrop against which I examine how reproduction, masculinity and nationhood intersected within the neo-traditionalist narratives and conceptions of the nation in Serbia in the 1990s. The story of marrying off rural men was part of neo-traditionalist narratives on the national fall and renewal (see NAUMOVIĆ 2009). This story tells about the demographic fall of the nation, about its biological survival that is threatened by the lack of births. Here, low fertility symbolizes 'unnatural' gender relations and the lack of masculine power. Thus the national fall is considered a consequence of an alleged masculinity crisis. Consequently, the renewal of the nation presupposes a return to 'natural' gender relations while the rural family is seen as the most 'natural' place for that process to begin.

The first part of the article situates the organization *Village Hearth* and its matchmaking project within the brother discourses on 'population decline' and threatened biological survival of the nation. It is argued that there was a widespread perception that Serbian women were the main culprits for such a state of the nation and thus they became main targets of various discourses

---

[2] The name is a pseudonym given by the author.

aimed at stimulating birth rates. What makes the *Village Hearth's* project unusual and interesting is its attention to men.

The second section discusses the symbolic place of the rural in the national. It is argued that the *Village Hearth* reproduced discourses about rural Serbia as the hearth of the nation and as the place where the national renewal should begin. The renewal of rural family, restoration of the patriarchal order and traditional masculinity were considered prerequisites of the renewal of rural Serbia and the nation.

The following section examines how the rule of patrilineage was supposed to salvage the threatened way of life of the nation and the men alike. Relying on CAMPBELL and BELL (2000), this section discusses the ambiguous role of the rural within the hegemonic masculinity. It is also argued that the neo-traditionalist assumption of reproducing the nation rested upon the mutual constitution of masculinity and rurality and their naturalized association. The rule of patrilineage designated masculinity as the carrier of the national. Thus, it is argued, the idea of saving Serbian rural family life by women from Ukraine was a logical consequence of rules of patrilineage, according to which only 'Serbian men' could sire 'Serbian children'.

In the final section, the article discusses the process of marginalization of the rural bachelors' masculinity through the failed matchmaking project. Through the project, their masculinity was constructed as subordinate vis-à-vis hegemonic masculinity, masculinity of married rural men and vis-à-vis femininity of mostly urban Ukrainian women who visited the village.

The article concludes arguing that while the idea to replace Serbian women by foreign women made a perfect sense within the urban-born neo-traditionalist conceptions of the nation, the resulting matchmaking project designed to marry off middle-aged bachelors was destined to fail because it was based on an urban-rural hierarchy and had very little to do with the living realities of those involved in it.

The vacant nation

During the 1990s there was a widespread perception in Serbia that the nation and its very biological survival were threatened by the 'population decline'. This perception – that was produced by political, religious and expert discourses – prompted an outpour of grass-roots and local initiatives designed to stimulate births and improve child care in Serbia. Grass-roots agents and local level initiatives, from concerned individuals to NGOs, and local governments, created discourses and, to a lesser degree, practices targeting primarily Serbian women in an attempt to increase the number of Serbian babies (see DREZGIĆ 2004).

The *Village Hearth* stood out with an apparently paradoxical strategy: it circumvented Serbian women as a target group for intervention and turned its attention to Serbian men. Not just any men, though – this organization was primarily concerned with rural men. Ignored by rural women as potential marital partners, rural men, it was argued, were deprived of the possibility to reproduce: The program of the organization states: "[In rural areas] there are many men aged between 20 and 40 who have no perspective of marrying and forming a family because there are almost no girls around them. The girls leave for the city in search of a nicer and easier life."

This representation of Serbian rural men as victims of Serbian rural women's actions echoed the discourses created by experts, politicians and religious leaders, which represented Serbian women, and their reproductive behavior, as the inimical to the nation.[3] Here, rural women that were leaving villages were added to the list. The leadership of the organization came up with the idea to find a replacement and fill in the void created by outmigration of rural women.

Nation as rural family

The organization *Village Hearth* was founded in the town of Užice in western Serbia, in the fall of 1996. Its name, *Village Threshold* (*Seoski prag*), evokes ideals of family and belonging. Thus, the very name of the organization carries a multiple symbolism: on the one hand, the village replaces the home and as an idealized community becomes an extended family. On the other hand, the organization's focus on 'Serbian' villages extrapolates the family and the community into the nation and designates 'rural' Serbia – and not any other – as the hearth of the nation.

This multiple symbolism is evident in the organization's written documents. For example, in a letter issued in 1998, to solicit donations and public support, it was stated that "[we] can halt the dying of Serbia only if we build young families, tie people to villages and create conditions for those who have a difficult life in the cities to return to the hearth of their ancestors." This statement simultaneously defines the organization's aims and creates a romantic image of the true Serbianhood as 'rural' and 'family' life. "The overall prosperity of Serbia" – states the letter further – "depend[s] on the survival and progress of the rural family" (VILLAGE HEARTH 1996). It is worth noting that the family assumed here is the classical heteronormative, reproductive unit with a married couple. It is not a family of a single parent such as a divorced woman, or a woman with a child born outside of 'wedlock'.

---

[3] More on this in DREZGIĆ 2010.

Most of their time, energy and resources the leadership of the organization invested in the project of Serbian-Ukrainian marriages. Still, they rarely failed to depict these activities as anything but a segment in a much broader and complex plan, for the revitalization of rural Serbia.

But the marriage and the starting of the family, and the revitalization of the Serbian village(s), were actually two inter-related discourses that weaved a narrative of an endangered, falling nation: a nation represented by the (broken) ideals of the rural life and Serbian men and women who, each in their own way, did not live up to their expected gender roles, and national duties. This was the nation in a desperate need of renewal. Since the rural Serbia was represented as the hearth of the nation, that is where the renewal was supposed to begin. The precondition of the rural renewal was the renewal of rural family and restoration of the patriarchal order and traditional masculinity which implied, among other things, reproducibility and continuation of the family line.

Apparently, *Village Hearth* espoused a neo-traditionalist conception of the nation, within which rural areas are constructed as spaces of "health, normal gender relations and naturally high fertility" (HORN 1994). Thus the revitalization of rural family was considered a precondition for the revitalization of the Serbian nation. But this family was dying out because "women are leaving villages for a better and easier life in the city" (VILLAGE HEARTH 1996). Women were thus considered responsible for creating unnatural conditions in this natural rural environment. Moreover, they deprived, it was argued, rural men of the possibility to reproduce at a time when reproduction was considered a national/patriotic duty.

Rural masculinity and the rules of patrilineage

This story of marrying off middle-aged rural bachelors, as a precondition for 'revitalizing' the village and the nation, is an example not only of the ambiguous place of the rural within the national but also of the complex relationship between rural and hegemonic masculinity – which is inherent to most nationalist projects.

According to CAMPBELL and BELL, "masculine rural" refers to masculine identities of rural men, while "rural masculine" signifies rural aspects of the dominant (hegemonic) concept of masculine identity in a specific society (2000: 532).

They argue that rural "images and realities of the lives of rural men play central roles in the social construction of masculinities of all sorts, as well as in the gendered construction of rural life" (ibid.: 540). Rural images are often used in images of "real men": a logger cutting a tree, the Marlboro cowboy cantering over the plains, the hairy warrior, the soldier defending the fields of the motherland... At the same time, this specific type of masculinity becomes a symbol of rurality. Especially important in all these images is how the "association with the rurality brings an air of the natural to masculinity legitimizing it as allegedly in touch with truths that are deeper than the merely social" (ibid.: 540). Thus, rural "images and realities of the lives of rural men play central roles in the social construction of masculinities of all sorts, as well as in the gendered construction of rural life" (ibid.: 540).

The mutual constitution of masculinity and rurality and their naturalized association are the grounds upon which rests the assumption of reproducing the nation. In other words, as much as the rural is extended into the national, masculinity is the carrier of the national. In the discourses created by *Village Hearth* the nation was constructed trough the classical assumptions about territory and blood. But clearly, not just any blood.

Serbian blood could be reproduced primarily through the male blood line; thus only 'Serbian men' can sire 'Serbian children'. Since the nation in such discourses is represented by metaphors of family (see McCLINTOCK 1993; VERDERY 1996) that family is a patrilineage and as in a true patrilineage, women are, and can be, brought in from outside, i.e. from other patrilineages. Even though belonging to the family is determined exclusively through birth, the role of the mother in this matter is rendered insignificant by the dominant kinship ideology. Thus, the apparent paradox of saving Serbian rural family life by women from Ukraine is not a paradox after all: it is a logical consequence of an assumption about patrilineage.

Since marriages serve to establish alliances between patrilineages (see DENICH 1974; ERLICH 1966), it is far from insignificant where the wife comes from. The marriages between foreign women and Serbian men were supposed to establish an alliance between Serbia and another state-cum-patrilineage creating kinship ties between men and organizing them into networks for exchanging favors and obligations (DREZGIĆ 2002). Given that both ethnicity and faith were constitutive of nationhood, men of Slavic ethnic stock and Orthodox background were considered the most 'natural' allies.

Thus, for the *Village Hearth* representatives Russia was their first choice. In addition to being predominantly Slavic and Orthodox, Russia was also a military power and a major player on the international political scene. The latter feature made Russia a perfect and desirable 'kin-state' at the time when Serbia's international standing and reputation was very low due to its role in the wars through which Yugoslavia disintegrated.

However, *Village Hearth* could not find support for its matchmaking project in Russia, and Ukraine turned out to be the second best choice: also a Slavic country and while religiously more diverse than Russia, still predominantly

Orthodox. Whereas no organization in Russia expressed an interest to partake in *Village Hearth*'s matchmaking project, the Association of Ukrainian-Serbian Friendship in Ukraine offered its assistance.

The *Village Hearth*'s perception of the Serbian nation was that of a patriarchal, *zadruga* type family. This type of family produces gender images according to which women are inherently polluting and represent a constant threat for the group's cohesion. In this context, Ukrainian women had an advantage. While inherently dangerous and polluting, unlike Serbian women they had not been corrupted by "too much modernization".[4] In addition, as their nationality was irrelevant, their main task was to secure the married and reproductive status of the Serbian men and thus restore the patriarchal order. The Ukrainian women might have presented a lesser threat for the patriarchal order because they were – apparently – willing to marry Serbian men, while Serbian women were not. Better yet, they were able to restore the patriarchal order through their perceived inferior and hence submissive status within an orientalized hierarchy of nations on the west-east and north-south axes.

The structures of gender relations and specific notions of masculinity and femininity are firmly embedded in the notions and ideals of the nation. In the case of the failed marriage arrangement of Serbian men and Ukrainian women, the national and gender identities met in a specific way: the rule of patrilineage was supposed to salvage the threatened way of life of the nation and the men alike.

Subordination of rural masculinities

The neo-traditionalist conceptions which imagine the nation as a rural family represent rural men as physically strong and superior but simpleminded and deficient in intellectual capacities as compared to their urban compatriots:

> Farm work affords the farmer with his exceptional physical characteristics, his robust, muscular body. But farm work is also responsible for his lack of skills that require a finer adjustment of the muscles. Because his physical work dominates his life, the farmer does not use his full intellectual potential and for that reason he represents more of a muscular than of a brain type [...] The countryside has primarily material-reproductive function because it produces

---

[4] Within the discourses on 'population decline', the socialist project of women's emancipation, i.e. over-modernization of Serbian women was often blamed for low birth rates. More on this in DREZGIĆ 2004.

food for the national community [...] It also regenerates society culturally and morally [...] (VOJNOVIĆ 1995: 114)[5]

This kind of marginalization of rural masculinity was implicit to discourses created by the organization *Village Hearth*. The whole matchmaking project was actually founded against a backdrop of urban-rural hierarchy. Its creators, while prizing the "purity" of rural life and its potential for rejuvenating the nation and its essence were at the same time denying agency to the rural population – including the rural men who otherwise, in nationalist discourses. stand as pillars of protection and provision for the family. For the creators of the marriage project, only the city had the potential for creating and leading progress, while the village was assigned "material-reproductive function". Since, middle-aged rural bachelors were deprived of the possibility to reproduce and continue the family line, their masculinity was at stake. The *Village Hearth*'s matchmaking project was meant to restore their masculinity. However, it only contributed to its further subordination and marginalization.

The masculinity of the village bachelors was actually challenged every step on the way during the visit of the women from Ukraine. To begin with, they were ridiculed in the Serbian national press for not showing up at the welcoming ceremony. This prompted some unbecoming titles in the Serbian press implying their skittishness as a reason: "Ukrainian [Women] Have Arrived, Bachelors not to be Seen" (*Blic* [11.2.1997]: 1); "Brides have arrived, Bachelors not to be Seen" (*Blic* [11.2.1997]: 9); "The Prospective Brides from Ukraine Have Arrived, Serbian Guys Not to be Seen" (*Dnevni Telegraf* [11.2.1998]: 10).

At the local level, many villagers believed that that majority of the 48 middle-aged bachelors in the village were not suitable marital partners for anyone any more, being long past their prime and deeply engrained in their bachelor habits. Drinking was often mentioned among those.

The description that villagers gave resembled those found in Lévi-Strauss's descriptions of bachelors in a central Brazilian village – one of his deepest impressions was that of a man who looked pathetic and unkempt, almost excluded from the community, only because he was not married (LÉVI-STRAUSS 1969: 46).[6]

---

[5] This quotation is from a book that elsewhere (DREZGIĆ 2010), I designate as pseudo-science. It was written by a university professor but did not adhere to the usual scientific standards regarding methods, rigor and supporting evidence.
[6] Cited according to PAPIĆ 1997: 269.

"I don't know, child, but the girls are too nice [/fine] for those lads of ours," replied an elderly women when I asked her opinion regarding the matchmaking attempt.[7]

"I would not give my sister in marriage to any of them", said a young man in his mid twenties and added: "This arrival of potential brides opens up a conflict between the older, unmarried lads and the young men of my generation. The old guys are afraid that we young guys will pick up [*pokupiti*] all the girls." In a way, this turned out to be true at the party that was organized in the village on the second day after the arrival of the Ukrainians. The aim of the organizer was to provide an opportunity for local, unmarried middle-aged men and Ukrainian women to meet and socialize.

The party was attended by the Ukrainians, young and middle-aged single men from the village, elderly men and women, mostly those who hosted the Ukrainians, a few elderly relatives of the middle-aged bachelors who were too shy and/or uninterested to attend, and the organizers.

The evening started off in a rather uncomfortable atmosphere with little or no communication between the locals and the guests.

For the generation of the middle-aged bachelors the *kafana* is a space where they primarily communicate with other men, and in various ways assert their masculinity vis-à-vis one another. This includes heavy drinking and bragging about (hetero-)sexual advances (SIMIĆ 1969). Thus, at the party, the middle-aged bachelors stuck together. When someone put on the tape with Serbian folk music, they got up to dance and formed an all-male circle dance *kolo*.

This is when the Ukrainian women broke the homosocial male circle by joining them. And this was only the beginning of the appropriation of space by the Ukrainian women. When the *kolo* ended they scattered throughout the *kafana*, starting conversations and initiating contacts. Thus, in more than one way, the Ukrainian women breached local rules of etiquette and gender norms. The prohibition of women taking initiative in heterosexual contacts was certainly one of them. After all, women were brought in, in order to salvage rural men's masculinity – already perceived as threatened by the 'abandonment' of Serbian women. The Ukrainian women threatened them in an opposite way – by taking away the male privilege in initiating the contact, in choosing women. The Ukrainian women decided to be those who choose.

The role reversal, however, was not the only unintended outcome of the Ukrainian women's visit. Many things turned upside down from what had been intended by *Village Hearth*. For example, most of the men who contacted the

---

[7] Two women from Ukraine stayed in her house and she accompanied them at the party organized by *Village Hearth*. I talked with her at the party.

organization looking for a wife from Ukraine appeared to have been older, divorced or widowed men – not interested in having more children. Similarly, the majority of about 200 women who allegedly contacted the *Village Hearth*, expressing interest to marry in Serbia, were urban women, had been married and had at least one child (again probably not interested in having more). The local middle-aged bachelors proved to be rather passive and appeared uninterested. The younger men, on the other hand, who neither were the primary target of the project nor interested in marrying, proved more active and outgoing at the social functions organized by *Village Hearth*. The middle-aged men whose masculinity was already at stake were overpowered by the actions of both the younger men and the Ukrainian women.

It was no wonder then that the all-male leadership of *Village Hearth* wanted to distance itself from the marriage project at the end of the visit. They did not want to be a party to effeminizing men whose masculinity, measured by marriageability and/or reproducibility, initiative in social and sexual encounters, they had set out to restore.

Conclusion

The matchmaking project launched by *Village Hearth* was unique with its idea that Serbian women could simply be replaced. In that respect, their neo-traditionalist conception of the nation was inclusive of "other" women due to the reduced conceptions of womanhood – women being regarded as mere vessels for biological reproduction. As a consequence, the mother's nationality is rendered irrelevant since only man can transfer national prerogatives to the offspring. Thus, the seemingly paradoxical matchmaking project was not paradoxical at all; it was founded on the rules of patrilineage and made a perfect sense within the neo-traditionalist narratives. At the same time, being based on urban-rural hierarchy, it was destined to fail. Its organizers designed the project applying ideas about rurality, gender and nation that had little connection to lived realities of both the men (and other villagers), and the women from Ukraine.

References

CAMPBELL, HUGH/ BELL, MICHAEL (eds.) (2000): The Question of Rural Masculinities. Rural Masculinities, a special issue of the journal Rural Sociology 65/4. 532–546.
DENICH, BETTE S. (1974): Sex and Power in the Balkans. In: Rosaldo, Michelle/ Louise Lamphere (eds.): Women, Culture and Society. Stanford.
DREZGIĆ, RADA (2010): „Bela kuga" među „Srbima". Belgrade.

DREZGIĆ, RADA (2004): From Social to National Issue: Abortion Debates in Serbia in the 1990s. In: Austrian Journal for Historical Studies. Re/Producing Body Politics 15/1. 115–125.

DREZGIĆ, RADA (2002): "International Matchmaking. Ukrainian Brides for Serbian Men". In: Jovanović, Miroslav/ Slobodan Naumović (eds.): Womanhood and Manhood in South Eastern Europe. Historical Perspectives on Gender Relations in the 19th and 20th Century (= Zur Kunde Südosteuropas 2/Ideje 4). Belgrade/Graz. 305–321.

HORN, DAVID G. (1994): Social Bodies. Science, Reproduction and Italian Modernity. Princeton, New Jersey.

MCCLINTOCK, ANNE (1993): Family Feuds: Gender, Nationalism and the Family. In: Feminist Review 44. 61–80.

LÉVI-STRAUSS, CLAUDE (1969): The Elementary Structures of Kinship. Boston.

NAUMOVIĆ, SLOBODAN (2009): Upotreba tradicije u političkom i javnom životu Srbije na kraju dvadesetog i početkom dvadeset prvog veka. Belgrade.

PAPIĆ, ŽARANA (1997): Polnost i kultura. Telo i znanje u socijalnoj antropologiji. Belgrade.

ERLICH, VERA (1966): Family in Transition. A study of 300 Yugoslav villages. Princeton, New Jersey.

VILLAGE HEARTH (SEOSKI PRAG) (1996): Program.

VERDERY, KATHERINE (1996): What Was Socialism and What Comes Next? New Jersey.

VOJNOVIĆ, MILAN (1995): Kobno osipanje srpskog naroda. Sociološki ogled o gorućim pitanjima srpskog naroda. Belgrade.

Law, Politics and Homosexuality in Croatia, 1941–1952

Dean Vuletic

With the rise of the gay and lesbian movement in Croatia in the past decade, the history of its sexual minorities has increasingly become a topic of academic and media inquiry. However, one period that has been little researched is that which runs from the Second World War to the early 1950s, which is striking considering the moral force that the persecution of minorities during the war continues to have in Croatia and elsewhere in Europe, as well as the specific suffering that homosexuals experienced as one of these minorities. This paper approaches this period in Croatia from both a legal and a political perspective, emphasising in particular the attitudes of political groups and regimes towards homosexuality. It begins by looking at the position of homosexuals in the Independent State of Croatia (*Nezavisna država Hrvatska – NDH*), a puppet state of Nazi Germany that existed during the Second World War and comprised most of present-day Croatia and Bosnia-Herzegovina. This is followed by a discussion of the attitudes of the anti-fascist Partisan movement towards homosexuals, which is an important issue considering that, as the local victors in the Second World War, its leadership headed by Josip Broz Tito would govern post-war socialist Yugoslavia. Yugoslavia suffered some of Europe's greatest wartime destruction, and the years immediately after the war were one of massive rebuilding: between 1945 and 1952, a new legal and political structure also had to be established under the rule of the Communist Party of Yugoslavia (CPY). Although there were some lawyers in Croatia who questioned whether homosexuality should continue to be criminalised as it had been in the interwar Kingdom of Yugoslavia, the new penal code that was adopted in 1951 demonstrated that the socialist revolution would not change this: it continued to criminalise homosexual acts between consenting male adults, although it made no references to lesbianism, but also reduced the maximum sentence from five years imprisonment to two. (See DOTA 2010) All of this meant that the 1940s and 1950s were the decades in Croatia in the second half of the twentieth century in which the persecution of homosexuals was most striking, as homosexuals faced both judicial trials and police repression.

As a guideline for the reader, the history of homosexuality in Croatia in subsequent decades can be divided into the following periods. During the 1960s and 1970s, some positive legal developments occurred, such as the increasing discussion of homosexuality in the press and the decriminalisation of homosexual acts between consenting male adults in 1977. In the late 1970s, a feminist movement emerged that promoted increased public discussion of homosexuality and, combined with the emergence of a gay and lesbian movement in neighbouring Slovenia in the 1980s, it influenced the start of a local movement and the formation of the first lesbian group in 1989. With the establishment of the Republic of Croatia in 1991 following the adoption of a multiparty system and secession from the Yugoslav federation, more gay and lesbian groups were formed, even during the Homeland War. However, throughout the 1990s these groups were not given any support by the nationalist government of president Franjo Tuđman and his party, the Croatian Democratic Union (*Hrvatska demokratska zajednica – HDZ*), although in 1998 a new penal code was adopted which did equalise the age of consent to fourteen for both heterosexual and homosexual acts. Since 2000, a more visible gay and lesbian movement has emerged which is now accepted by Croatian governments as a legitimate political actor, and significant legal advancements have been made with regard to gay rights, such as a law on same-sex civil unions that was adopted in 2003 by the centre left coalition government led by the Social Democratic Party (*Socijaldemokratska partija – SDP*), as well as several laws on anti-discrimination that were initiated by this government and the one led by the HDZ that succeeded it in 2003.[1]

Before 2000, the history of homosexuality in Croatia had been ignored both in local historiography and in international gay and lesbian studies. Recently, there have been some efforts by academic historians and gay and lesbian activists to study it, including my own project which aimed to introduce the topic into Croatian historiography. (See VULETIĆ 2003, 2004) That there were not earlier studies on the subject can be attributed to a variety of intersecting cultural, political, religious and social factors, such as the ideological pressures on twentieth century Croatian historiography – in their Roman Catholic, fascist, Marxist, nationalist and patriarchal forms – that compelled it to approach Croatian history through ideological prisms whose politics excluded and ignored, persecuted and repressed, sexual minorities. With the strengthening of the gay and lesbian movement in Croatia and the coming to power of more liberal-leaning governments since 2000, gay and lesbian groups and the media have given much more attention to this issue in history, with the most innovative research projects often coming not from academic historians but from activists themselves. This is especially true of the Queer Zagreb organisation, which has been organising an international queercultural festival in Zagreb since 2003, and has also initiated research projects on an oral history of homosexuality in Croatia (DOBROVIĆ/ BOSANAC 2007) and the legal persecution of homosexuals just after the Second World War. (DOTA 2010) These efforts to show how homosexuals have figured in Croatia's past

---

[1] For a discussion of these recent developments, see VULETIĆ 2008.

contribute not only to a writing of local gay and lesbian history, but also legitimise the presence of homosexuals in a shared political and social heritage as they add a new dimension to historical issues that remain highly controversial, such as the CPY's persecution of its political and social opponents from 1945.

Considering the methodology that is involved in researching the history of homosexuality in Croatia, one aspect that must be emphasised is the difficulty in finding sources, especially for periods before the 1980s. While the recent history of the gay and lesbian movement in Croatia can be researched through media reports and oral interviews, it is more difficult to do so for the 1940s and 1950s. After all, this was a period during which homosexuality was not as openly spoken about or tolerated as it is nowadays, and it is difficult to find references to it in government documents or newspaper reports. While there are no institutional barriers preventing the research of this topic in Croatia – the staff at the Croatian State Archive, for example, have been helpful in assisting Queer Zagreb in researching the judicial trials against homosexuals after the Second World War – a lot of time is needed to sort through materials in which references to homosexuality are scant. Much work is thus required to find limited archival and other materials on this topic, but this paper shows that they do exist, even for periods when homosexuality was less visible in Croatian political and social life than it has been in recent decades.

In the first socialist state, the Soviet Union, homosexuality was decriminalised in some of its constituent parts after the October Revolution, but was again prohibited under a new penal code adopted under the leadership of Joseph Stalin in 1933. (HEALEY 2001) Although the Soviet Union was a model for the Yugoslav party until their alliance was severed in 1948, it was not always clear to the leaders of the CPY how they should deal with homosexuality. Indications of their confused attitudes to it are found in *Wartime* by Milovan Djilas, one of the leading figures in the CPY. In this memoir about his experiences during the Second World War, one paragraph sheds light on the treatment of homosexuals by the Partisans and shows that homosexuals were dismissed from the party: Djilas describes how Rifat Burdžović, the secretary of the Sandžak Committee, "told me in amazement that the fighting men of a Serbian battalion had exposed as a homosexual a certain Moslem, a good soldier and zealous Communist." While Burdžović "wondered whether he should execute this 'freak'", Djilas' response was confused:

> I did not know what the party's practice was, nor had Marx and Lenin ever written about such matters. Nevertheless, while my common sense led me to conclude that not only bourgeois decadents but proletarians too were subject to such vices, I decided that no perverts could hold positions or be party members. So Burdžović ordered the poor fellow to resign from the party. The fellow confided to Burdžović, in tears, that a dissolute Moslem bey had seduced him as

a boy. I learned later that this homosexual, who was the very picture of masculinity, was exceptionally courageous and that he fell bravely. War confronts a person with questions which he would otherwise easily avoid. And the higher one is placed, the greater is the importance of such "trivia", the greater the glory, and the greater the room for mistakes. (DJILAS 1977: 127)

Djilas thus had some sympathy for the man, but more so for his qualities as a Partisan soldier and a communist rather than out of any particular concern for the plight of homosexuals. While Djilas regarded homosexuality as a "perversion" that should not be tolerated within the party or the army, it appears that the man was allowed to remain as a Partisan soldier, for "he fell bravely". This suggests that the imperatives of wartime perhaps made the Partisan leadership less hostile towards homosexual soldiers, while being intolerant of homosexuals within the party – in this case at least. After all, considering Djilas' bewilderment over the attitude of the party or Marx and Lenin towards homosexuality, Partisan officials would not have reacted uniformly in such cases and may have been more or less tolerant of homosexuals than Djilas.

The attitudes of other members of the Partisan leadership towards homosexuality may also have been influenced by examples of it among prominent figures in the CPY and the Partisans. A debate has been taking place in Croatia in recent years as to whether such figures included the writers Vladimir Nazor and Ivan Goran Kovačić. The debate was especially vocal in 2007, when Queer Zagreb erected a plaque honouring the close friendship of the two authors – but not explicitly describing it as homosexual – at the intersection of the streets named after them in the Zagreb neighbourhood of Tuškanac. (C. 2009) Previously, the relationship between Nazor and Kovačić had never been alluded to as a homosexual one in biographies of the two writers: for example, in Mirko Žeželj's biography of Nazor, *Tragom pjesnika Vladimira Nazora* ("In the Footsteps of the Poet Vladimir Nazor"), the relationship between Nazor and Kovačić is portrayed as a friendship based on their love for poetry, with Žeželj citing Nazor's following remarks to demonstrate this:

> [I]n one thing we were one – our love, even in ecstasy, for poetry. How many hours we spent together in the evening and even late at night, reading classics most of all, even if they were only in translation. (ŽEŽELJ 1973: 445)

In Vlatko Pavletić's biography of Kovačić, *Goran njim samim* (Goran Through Himself), their relationship is described in terms of Kovačić looking up to Nazor as a father figure and teacher: after all, Nazor was much older than Kovačić, the former being born in 1876 and the latter in 1913. (ŽEŽELJ 1973) However, personal accounts of the period suggest that rumours abounded in Zagreb at the time over whether the relationship between Nazor and Kovačić was also a homosexual one. In an interview in the weekly newspaper *Globus* in 1993, a gay man presented as B.J., a figure active in Zagreb's theatre scene, said that when Nazor and Kovačić fled Zagreb together for Partisan-controlled territory during the Second World War,

> the Ustasha happily spoke of how the Partisan army was an army of pederasts, because even the little birds in the trees knew even before the war of Nazor's relationship with Ivan Goran Kovačić; they were part of the urban folklore, a sort of Zagrebian Socrates and Alcibiades. (GLOBUSOV INVESTIGATIVNI TIM 1994)

In her book *Tražim nekog dječaka* ("I'm Looking for a Boy"), Marija Gračaković has added to the debate by arguing that Nazor only had sexual relations with women, which she bases on a study of his personal archives from 1920 to 1931, (GRAČAKOVIĆ 2010) this opinion has also been supported by living members of Nazor's family. (OREŠIĆ 2011) Whatever the nature of the relationship between Nazor and Kovačić, it came to an end during the war when Kovačić was killed in battle by Serbian Chetnik forces in 1943; Nazor, however, survived the war, and afterwards served as president of the Croatian republic in Yugoslavia until his death in 1949.

One issue that has received much attention in the international historiography on homosexuality is the treatment of homosexuals in the Second World War. However, the experience of homosexuals in wartime Croatia – including their persecution by the fascist authorities and the attitudes towards homosexuality within the ranks of the warring parties – has been totally neglected. While numerous autobiographical accounts and systematic studies have shed light on the persecution of homosexuals in Nazi Germany, there is nothing available on Croatia; as the *Encyclopedia on Gay Histories and Cultures* puts it, "less information exists on repression in Croatia, Slovakia, Hungary, Romania, and Finland." (JOHANSSON/ PERCY 1990: 549) As an example, one key work on the experience of homosexuals during the Second World War is Richard Plant's *The Pink Triangle: The Nazi War Against Homosexuals*, (PLANT 1986) and while it briefly refers to the persecution of homosexuals in areas occupied by Nazi Germany, namely France, the Netherlands and Poland, it makes no reference to Croatia. Furthermore, much attention has been given to the killing of hundreds of thousands of Serbs, Jews, Roma and Croats by the Ustasha regime in the NDH, and historians who have researched this have largely continued to focus on the ethnic dimension of these deaths. This is of course justified with regard to the Serbs, Jews and Roma, against whom there were specific laws in the NDH that sanctioned their persecution on the basis of their ethnicity. However, among the Croat victims – and among the other ethnic groups as well – there were also homosexuals, some of whom were specifically targeted by the authorities because of their sexuality.

There are subtle indications of the persecution of homosexuals in Croatia during the Second World War in the memoirs of Croat political opponents of the Ustasha who experienced the prisons and concentration camps of the NDH. Such an example is found in *Konclogor na Savi* (Concentration Camp on the Sava), the memoir of Ilija Jakovljević, a lawyer, writer and member of the Croatian Peasant Party (*Hrvatska seljačka stranka*). Jakovljević spent the years 1941 and 1942 in the prisons and concentration camps of the NDH, including a prison on one of central Zagreb's main squares, Square N,[2] and the concentration camp of Stara Gradiška. It is with reference to his time in prison that Jakovljević mentions his meeting with a male homosexual. In one sentence, the author notes how he met a "[male] lover of the male body" there, and that they quickly agreed on a mutual "non-aggression pact" (JAKOVLJEVIĆ 1999: 15). In his brief mention of this, Jakovljević does not explicitly indicate whether the man was imprisoned because of his homosexuality, but as he only refers to the man's identity in these terms, it appears likely that this was the case. Another autobiographical account that provides a different perspective on the experience of homosexuals in Croatia during the Second World War is Pierre Seel's *I, Pierre Seel, Deported Homosexual*. Although the book does not refer to Croatian homosexuals, it does recount the experience of a French man who was imprisoned by the Nazis because of his homosexuality and was sent to fight with the German army on the battlefields of Croatia. Seel was imprisoned in an Alsatian detention camp when the Third Reich annexed Alsace, and in 1942 he was sent to Croatia where he fought against the Partisans in the countryside around Zagreb. In his two-page account of his time in Croatia, he describes how he and his company were ordered to burn down houses and villages in which only women and children remained, and he recounts an instance of hand-to-hand combat with a Partisan soldier, whom he shot. (SEEL 1994/95: 58–59)

The victory of the Partisans in the Second World War did not bring an end to the persecution of homosexuals, which shows that, as in other parts of Europe, it continued in Croatia even as regimes changed. Until recently, historical research has paid little attention to this, even though the CPY's persecution of its political and social opponents has been extensively discussed and remains a highly contentious issue throughout the successor states of Yugoslavia. Indeed, police repression and judicial trials against homosexuals in the other socialist states of Eastern Europe (HAUER et al. 1986: 39) had their equivalents in Yugoslavia in the late 1940s and early 1950s, and they were often justified on the same rhetorical grounds that homosexuals were "enemies

---

[2] After the war this square was renamed *Trg žrtava fašizma* ("Square of the Victims of Fascism") to honour all the victims of fascism in Croatia.

of the system". For example, from B.J.'s aforementioned account, it is also known that trials were held against homosexuals and transvestites all over Yugoslavia during this period, and that the authorities tried to remove people who were sympathetic toward the plight of homosexuals from public life. According to B.J., the police in Zagreb arrested and imprisoned men for their homosexuality, although many "old well-known lawyers" came to their aid and voluntarily agreed to defend the accused. In Dubrovnik, some of those indicted for homosexuality were taken through the streets tied up and were even stoned, while some of the worst trials took place in the port city of Rijeka, where some homosexuals were even killed. Together with others who were considered to be "enemies of the system", homosexuals were also sent to detention camps in Nova Gradiška and on the island of Goli Otok, which became infamous examples of the Tito regime's terror; others who feared such a fate committed suicide or fled Yugoslavia for Western Europe. (GLOBUSOV INVESTIGATIVNI TIM 1994)

In its recent project on the persecution of homosexuals in Croatia between 1945 and 1952, Queer Zagreb has also discovered cases from the Supreme Court of Croatia which provide further proof that the law criminalising homosexual acts was applied, and that those convicted received sentences of forced labour or imprisonment.[3] However, these examples also show that the law was not always applied consistently and that there were differing opinions over its necessity among judges and lawyers, which reflected the fact that the CPY did not have a clear position on the issue until it adopted its own penal code in 1951. This vacuum permitted some defendants and their lawyers to argue that homosexuality was not a threat to society, and they referred to scientific studies that confirmed that homosexuality was not unnatural. They even formed their arguments around the politics of the CPY, asserting that the law against "unnatural sexual acts" was passed in the "era of dictatorship" and under the influence of the church – while some even claimed that sexual freedom was in accordance with the achievements of the National Liberation Battle! However, the confusing legal situation also allowed for other surprises: for example, a group of women from Osijek were also convicted of lesbianism, even though this was not explicitly criminalised as were homosexual acts among men (indeed, lesbianism was never mentioned at this time or later in Croatia's penal code).

---

[3] For an overview of these cases, see DOTA 2010. Gordan Bosanac, Andrea Zlatar, Dota and I discussed these cases in the roundtable discussion *U ime naroda! Suđenja homoseksualaca i lezbijki u Hrvatskoj 1945–1977* („In the Name of the People! Trials of Gay Men and Lesbians in Croatia 1945–1977"). Kuća ljudskih prava, Zagreb.

In assessing the motivations behind the indictments in these cases, it is notable that "unnatural sexual acts" were never the only or even the first point made, except in one case in 1948 concerning the manager of a seminary and his acquaintances in Šibenik and which involved pedophilia. The accused were usually first targeted because they engaged in activities that were considered politically inappropriate by the CPY, such as the writing of a letter in which they insulted the army or Tito, fleeing across the border or promoting Christianity. Their alleged homosexuality appears as some additional discredit, which begs the question of to what extent homosexuals were persecuted just because of their sexual orientation. If we were to find verdicts in which people were punished only because they engaged in homosexual acts, then it would be quite clear. Such judgments may exist at the local level because not all cases reached the Supreme Court, so further research is required to determine how much of a concerted campaign there was against homosexuals in Yugoslavia during this period. However, what Queer Zagreb has obtained so far from the Supreme Court nonetheless does prove that cases of "unnatural sexual acts" were present in the Croatian judicial system and that the law criminalising homosexual acts was applied.

Yugoslavia was of course no exception in the persecution of homosexuals after the Second World War, because this happened in other parts of Europe as well: the most infamous example is that of the homosexuals who were released from Nazi concentration camps into societies in which homosexuality was still criminalised.[4] However, from 1950 Yugoslavia became, after the break with the Cominform in 1948, one of the most liberal countries in Eastern Europe in terms of its cultural policy. Of course, this liberalism was limited by the one-party system and communist ideology, and the CPY was still repressive towards its political and social opponents. But Yugoslavia opened up to cultural influences from the West unlike any other part of Eastern Europe, which was also experienced through the importation of Western movies and popular music. While its leaders felt that this was necessary to reflect the new foreign policy orientations of the state, as well as to make up for the failures of a socialist realist cultural policy, they were still afraid of "harmful" influences from the West, and some of them continued to talk about their un-socialist "bourgeois" and "decadent" elements. Party leaders especially exhibited "moral panic" over young people, as the latter were the first generation to mature under the socialist system and their development was paralleled with the success of the party. For example, in the Agitprop and Ideological Commission of the Central Committee of the CPY and the party's youth wing, the National Youth

---

[4] For the West German case, see MOELLER 1997.

of Yugoslavia (*Narodna omladina Jugoslavije*), party leaders discussed the influence of Western movies and jazz on the sexual behaviour of adolescents, although some of them were more worried about this than others. (Cited in VULETIC 2008: 868) Although I have found no mention of homosexuality in these fora, in some of the cases from the Supreme Court various judges and lawyers also portrayed homosexuality in these terms when they referred to it as "decadent", "bourgeois" and a "social threat". (Cited in DOTA 2010)

However, even the very top of the party passed through some kind of sexual revolution in the early 1950s, when Tito and Djilas both married women who were much younger than themselves. (DJILAS 1980: 147–148) Djilas even addressed this issue in his famous article "Anatomy of a Moral", in which he writes about the marriage between General Peko Dapčević and the young actress and singer Milena Versajkov. As Djilas highlights, she was tormented by the older wives of other party leaders as she was beautiful and young, came from a poor family and had not been active in the Partisans or the CPY; in addition, they were suspicious of her because of her allegedly "immoral" and "sexual" profession. (WILLEN 1959: xxiv–xv) The party leaders' wives, "despite espousing gender equality and feminism", told Versajkov that she would "never be acceptable company for our comrades and women comrades", adding that "[b]y her profession alone, she can be nothing but a whore", which Djilas writes was the opinion that "was the one most widely accepted" among these women. (DJILAS 1959: 150, 161, 166) This piece, published in the cultural magazine *Nova misao* (New Thought) in January 1954, was highly controversial in Yugoslavia: together with other articles and speeches of Djilas' in which he had criticised the CPY from 1953, it contributed to the leadership's decision to expel him from the party just days after "Anatomy of a Moral" was released. (WILLEN 1959: xiiii–xiv) Nonetheless, it demonstrates that Yugoslavia's political leaders were themselves privately and publically confronting issues of sexuality, and it begs us to consider whether they personified a liberalisation of social attitudes towards sexuality in some parts of Yugoslav society. Further research in the archives of Croatian Courts will show whether this also influenced a greater judicial and political tolerance towards homosexuality after the early 1950s, even as the legal basis for the criminalisation of homosexuality officially remained in place in Croatia until 1977.

There are many topics in the history of homosexuality in Croatia that invite scholarly enquiry, not only because they narrate the past of sexual minorities, but also because they relate to broader political and social themes, including the ability of contemporary Croatian society to tolerate its own homosexuals. This paper has shown that homosexuality was an issue that the legal and political elites of Croatia grappled with in the 1940s and 1950s, even if they did not promote discussions about it or were confused as to how they should approach it. Homosexual acts were punished by the authorities if they chose to do so, although the extent to which the aforementioned cases represent a legal and political campaign against homosexuals still requires further research. Finally, this research demonstrates that there are sources that can be drawn upon to write a history of homosexuality in Croatia before the emergence of a gay and lesbian movement there. Indeed, that there were already calls for the decriminalisation of homosexuality just after the Second World War shows that the campaign for homosexual rights in Croatia has origins that precede activism in the present republic as well as the decriminalisation of homosexuality in the socialist republic.

References

DJILAS, MILOVAN (1980): Tito: The Story from Inside. New York/London.
DJILAS, MILOVAN (1977): Wartime. London/New York.
DJILAS, MILOVAN (1959): Anatomy of a Moral. In: Rothberg, Abraham (ed.): Anatomy of a Moral. The Political Essays of Milovan Djilas. New York. 145–176.
DOBROVIĆ, ZVONIMIR/ GORDAN BOSANAC (eds.) (2007): Usmena povijest homoseksualnosti u Hrvatskoj. Zagreb.
DOTA, FRANKO (2010): Neprirodni blud koji podriva temelje socijalističke Hrvatske. In: Jutarnji list (9.1.2010). www.jutarnji.hr.
GLOBUSOV INVESTIGATIVNI TIM (1994): Zamislite, komunisti su optužili nas homoseksualce da Karađorđeviće želimo vratiti na prijestolje! Globus (18.1.1994).
GRAČAKOVIĆ, MARIJA (2010): Tražim nekog dječaka. Vladimir Nazor među Crikveničanima. Crikvenica.
HAUER, GUDRUN et al. (1986): Rosa Liebe unterm roten Stern. Zur Lage der Lesben und Schwulen in Osteuropa. Vienna.
HEALEY, DAN (2001): Homosexual Desire in Revolutionary Russia. The Regulation of Sexual and Gender Dissent. Chicago.
JAKOVLJEVIĆ, ILIJA (1999): Konclogor na Savi. Zagreb.
JOHANSSON, WARREN/ WILLIAM A. PERCY (1990): Holocaust, Gay. In: Dynes, Wayne R. (ed.): Encyclopedia of Homosexuality 1. New York/London. 546–550.
MOELLER, ROBERT G. (1997): The Homosexual Man Is a "Man", the Homosexual Woman Is a "Woman". Sex, Society, and the Law in Postwar West Germany. In: Moeller, Robert G. (ed.): West Germany under Construction. Politics, Society, and Culture in the Adenauer Era. Ann Arbor. 251–284.

OREŠIĆ, BORIS (2011): Nazor i Goran ipak nisu bili ljubavnici. Globus (26 July 2011). www.globus.jutarnji.hr.
PERCY, WILLIAM A. (1990): Exiles and Emigres. In: Dynes, Wayne R. (ed.): Encyclopedia of Homosexuality 1. New York. 380.
PLANT, RICHARD (1986): The Pink Triangle. The Nazi War Against Homosexuals. New York.
SEEL, PIERRE (1994/95): I, Pierre Seel, Deported Homosexual. New York.
WILLEN, PAUL (1959): Introduction. In: Rothberg, Abraham (ed.): Anatomy of a Moral. The Political Essays of Milovan Djilas. New York. ix–xxxii.
VULETIĆ, DEAN (2004): Gay i lezbijska povijest Hrvatske. Devedeste godine – između autoritarnosti i liberalizma. In: Gordogan 1/2–3. 138–156.
VULETIĆ, DEAN (2003): Gay i lezbijska povijest Hrvatske. Od Drugog svjetskog rata do 1990. In: Gordogan 1/1. 104–122.
VULETIĆ, DEAN (2008): Gay Men and Lesbians. In: Ramet, Sabrina P./ Konrad Clewing/ Reneo Lukić (eds.): Croatia since Independence. War, Politics, Society, Foreign Relations. Munich. 293–320.
VULETIC, DEAN (2008): Generation Number One. Politics and Popular Music in Yugoslavia in the 1950s. In: Nationalities Papers 36/5. 861–879.
ŽEŽELJ, MIRKO (1973): Tragom pjesnika Vladimira Nazora. Zagreb.
C., J. (2009): Homofobi zbog mržnje demolirali spomen ploču pjesnicima Nazoru i Kovačiću? In: Index (28.8.2009). www.index.hr.

Women in Socialist Yugoslavia in the 1950s. The Example of Rajka Borojević and the Dragačevo Women's Cooperative

Natalja Herbst

Introduction

Rajka Borojević (1913–1973) is probably one of the most remarkable women in Yugoslav history, and yet her life has been overlooked, if not forgotten. As is the case with other great Yugoslav women, there has been no research on her life thus far, and her legacy is hardly being appreciated in the collective memory of the broader public, let alone mentioned in history or school textbooks.[1]

The biography of Rajka Borojević is an excellent example of how state policies on education, modernisation and women were linked to each other in Socialist Yugoslavia in the 1950s. At her own initiative, Rajka Borojević set up a women's cooperative of weavers in 1952 that achieved great success. It manufactured about 250 different products, all of them made of natural materials and weaved on hand looms. At its zenith, the Cooperative employed around 900 female weavers and knitters from 15 villages.[2]

This article is based on mainly two research sources. On 22 August 2008, I visited the Women's Cooperative and interviewed the 84-year-old Radisav Tadić in Donji Dubac, who – together with his wife Dragojla – had been collaborating closely with Rajka and her husband.[3] The article also draws from Rajka Borojevićs diary, entitled "From Dubac into the world",[4] as well as from

---

[1] This lack of scholarly interest seems to stem from the general reluctance to deal with the Socialist time period that prevails in the former Yugoslavia today. However, there are first attempts of dealing with the communist era in women's and gender history by scientists from the region, see for example PANTELIĆ 2011; STOJAKOVIĆ 2010; GUDAC-DODIĆ 2007: 165–204; GUDAC-DODIĆ 2006; DIJANIĆ et al. 2004; PEROVIĆ 1998.

[2] Information taken from a flyer of the Cooperative, without indication of author, place and year. After almost 60 years of continuous work, the Women's Cooperative has recently filed for bankruptcy. For further information see http://www.snovalica.com/sr/draga cevska-zadruga-zena, retrieved 12.10.2011.

[3] Radisav Tadić, being a partisan officer in World War II, held several party functions at the local level in Socialist Yugoslavia. His wife Dragojla played a key role in organising the Women's Cooperative. I would like to thank Radisav Tadić for the spontaneous interview, and the director of the Women's Cooperative for giving me Rajka Borojević's diary as a gift. I would also like to thank Rada Prelić for taking me on the trip to Donji Dubac and for sharing her tough World War II childhood memories with me without being resentfull.

[4] BOROJEVIĆ 2006. In 2007, Rajka's daughter Branka Borojević-Džokić organised an exhibition in the Ethnographical Museum Belgrade bearing the same title.

excerpts, pictures and newspaper articles from Rajka Borojević's photo albums, published by her granddaughter Ana Džokić.[5]

The first edition of Rajka Borojević's diary was published already in 1964. The book contains systematic notes, reflecting her interactions and observations while working with peasant women in Donji Dubac. It is a useful source for studying: (1) the 1950s in Socialist Yugoslavia; (2) the local dialect; (3) customs and beliefs of peasants of the region; (4) gender and family relations in a remote Yugoslav village; and (5) the practical implementation of communist modernisation policies in a rural context. This article will focus on the last two aspects.

Rajka and Vukašin Borojević

Rajka Šotra, born in Herzegovina, married Vukašin Borojević in 1932. The couple lived in Kačanik, Kosovo, where they registered the Production of Squeezed Juices *Vitaminol – Liquid Fruit* in 1938. (STEALTH.UNLIMITED 2010: 298)

On the eve of World War II, they moved to Banja Luka in Bosnia. In June 1941, Vukašin was amongst the first to join Tito's partisans, who were fighting for a social revolution and against both the Axis occupators as well as the Croatian Ustaše and the Serbian Četniks.[6] In the same year, Rajka Borojević fled from the Ustaše to Serbia, who by that time had already killed her parents.[7] In the remote mountain village of Donji Dubac in the Upper Dragačevo, Rajka and her two children found shelter in the house of Spasoje Tadić.[8] Her husband Vukašin, who had been injured as a Tito partisan, stayed with them for a short time. (STEALTH.UNLIMITED 2010: 307) After recovery, he became the quarter-

---

[5] As a member of the art group STEALTH.unlimited (together with Marc Neelen), Ana Džokić took part in the SPAPORT Biennial in Banja Luka 2010. In this context, she organised three discussions based on the private archive and biographies of her grandparents, see http://www.seecult.org/vest/uzeti-zajednicku-stvar-u-ruke, retrieved 13.10.2011. The archival material in question is published in the SPAPORT exhibition catalogue, see STEALTH.UNLIMITED 2010.

[6] The Ustaša movement was a Croatian fascist anti-Yugoslav movement. In World War II, the Ustaše collaborated with Nazi Germany and founded the so-called Independent State of Croatia (*Nezavisna Država Hrvatska – NDH*), which Bosnia and Herzegovina became part of. The Ustaše and their army systematically persecuted and killed Serbs, Jews, Roma, Partisans and other political opponents. The Četniks were a heterogenous Serbian royalist movement, in the end collaborating with the German occupator and fighting against Tito's partisans. See HÖSCH et al. 2004: 164–165, 707–708, 718–719.

[7] See BOROJEVIĆ 2006: 215. Radisav Tadić, however, claimed that Rajka Borojević, being a partisan as well, fled from the Četniks who wanted to kill her together with her children. The escape was possible only due to personal connections.

[8] Spasoje Tadić was Radisav Tadić's father.

master of the II. Proletarian Brigade. (STEALTH.UNLIMITED 2010: 300) Rajka's brother Branko Šotra, who had also joined the partisans, sought shelter in Donji Dubac as well and stayed there for three months. Being an academic painter and sculptor, he frescoed the walls of Spasoje Tadić's house, using natural colors made of eggs, milk and soot, and devoted the frescoes to his sister.[9]

Rajka and Vukašin Borojević in Kačanik, Kosovo, in 1935.[10]

Immediately after the war, like many other Yugoslav women at the time, Rajka Borojević took care of war orphans. She became the head of Belgrade's orphanages and accompanied 800 war orphans on a recreational trip to Bulgaria. (BOROJEVIĆ 2006: 215)

In 1946, using their pre-war experience of the *Vitaminol* project, Rajka and her husband founded the fruit processing factory *Vitaminka* in Banja Luka. As the first co-directors (1946–1950), they implemented their initial five-year plan. (STEALTH.UNLIMITED 2010: 303) The original design and development of the factory soon became a model in Socialist Yugoslavia, and the factory is still in operation today.

Rajka's concern for gender equality is already apparent in the way she set up *Vitaminka*. She proudly stated in her *Vitaminka* photo album that a brigade of female brick layers was working on the construction of the factory, that three quarters of the workers at *Vitaminka* were women, that 11 of 14 worker brigades

---

[9] See http://www.snovalica.com/sr/muzej-fresak, retrieved 17.10.2011.
[10] The picture and information are taken from STEALTH.UNLIMITED: http://www.stealth.ultd. net/stealth/25_taking.common.matter.into.your.own.hands.html, retrieved 12.10.2011.

at the factory were lead by women, and that not a single one of them was illiterate anymore. (STEALTH.UNLIMITED 2010: 301f.)

Fresco by Rajka's brother Branko Šotra in the house of Spasoje Tadić.[11] Here, the first training course for peasant women took place.

"Work among women": training courses for women

Hiding in Donji Dubac from 1941 to 1943, Rajka Borojević vowed that if she survived the war, she would do something to thank the locals. (BOROJEVIĆ 2006: 9) In 1951, the Borojevićs, meanwhile living in Belgrade, came back to Donji Dubac. They bought a piece of land and built a weekend home – the first house in the village with running water supply.[12]

While Vukašin set up the flourishing medical herb cooperative *Orlujak*, (STEALTH.UNLIMITED 2010: 306–310) Rajka, according to the communist term of the time, began to "work among women", something she would continue to do until her death. Being a teacher for vocational schools by

---

[11] Picture taken by the author.
[12] Interview with Radisav Tadić. The Borojević's bought the piece of land from him.

profession, she first decided to teach and educate peasant women among whom superstition and illiteracy was widespread.[13]

From 1954–1957, Rajka Borojević taught four training courses for women during the winter, when there was no work on the fields. The first course took place in Spasoje Tadić's house where Rajka had been hiding in World War II. An article in *Politika* dating from 1954 called her courses "wild ones", because she organised them at her own initiative, without the backing of any official institution.[14]

In the beginning, she found it difficult to convince the peasants of the need to attend school, especially women. (BOROJEVIĆ 2006: 21) The women themselves were not enthusiastic about the idea:

> The women, in fact, really don't know what they want yet. They're not conscious of the benefits of the course – they don't even know what it is. This is why they don't embrace it – primarily, their male heads don't embrace it. (Ibid.: 38)

As a result of this commonly shared attitude, only a few women showed up on the first day of class. In her diary, Rajka describes how she managed to win the peasants over.[15] She skipped her curriculum and started with a widespread problem: tapeworms.[16] She handed out precious medicine and explained to the women how to use it. She also showed them modern fashion magazines that they had never seen before. The women were immediately drawn to the knitting wear. In response, Rajka gave them knitting needles, which were rare in this region back then, and promised the women that they would learn how to knit beautiful garments like those depicted in the magazines. (BOROJEVIĆ 2006)

In the course of the first day, two male peasants entered the room, listened to Rajka and then disappeared. After a while, their wives showed up with a pretext as to why they were late. Around noon, even more women came. (Ibid.: 42) Eventually, the first training course had twelve participants. After a short

---

[13] Rajka gives numerous impressing examples of the women's belief in witchcraft. Most of them are linked to the body (giving birth, sexuality, illness) and emotions (love), see e. g. BOROJEVIĆ 2006: 10, 99.

[14] See BOROJEVIĆ 2006: 77. The more Rajka succeeded with her projects, the less the regional administration supported them, see ibid.: 118, 121, 148, 194. According to Radisav Tadić, the local communists did not support the idea of start-ups in the countryside. There was apparently also a lot of envy towards Rajka in the regional party bodies, but she was able to activate her own communist network in Belgrade and other Yugoslav cities in support of her projects.

[15] She was well aware of the (social, intellectual and political) gap between her and the peasant women, see ibid.: 42.

[16] Rajka Borojević writes: "In these villages, the children have so many tapeworms that they are even coming out of their mouths." Ibid.: 42.

time, the courses became very popular among the locals. Already in the second winter, the amount of female participants doubled and the class moved into the local school building.[17]

Rajka Borojević provided the women with both practical and theoretical basic knowledge in nutrition, hygiene, childcare, parenting and good behaviour:

> Theoretical part
>
> Daily, weekly and annual cleaning of the house. Hygiene of the appartment. Housekeeping of the apartment and the courtyard. Laundry and bed.
>
> 1. Woman's hygiene. Pregnancy and childbirth. Venereal diseases. Sex education. Relationship to the marital partner. Early marriages.
> 2. First aid. Care of a sick person.
> 3. Newborn baby. Child-rearing.
> 4. Alcoholism. Superstition.
> 5. Nutrition.
> 6. Behavior, clothing, posture, language.
>
> Practical part
>
> 1. Cooking, serving, waiting. Home-preserving. Making soap. Coloring with natural and artificial colors.
> 2. Doing laundry, ironing and darning.
> 3. Tailoring and sewing.
> 4. Cultivation of medical, spice and aromatic herbs, vegetables and flowers.
> 5. Beekeeping, poultry farming and raspberry cultivation.
> 6. Handicraft. Especially weaving.
> 7. Singing. (BOROJEVIĆ 2006: 37–38)

It appears that Rajka Borojević decided not to teach any kind of ideology directly. She was neither openly communist-feminist[18] nor did she teach Marxism. She did not even teach reading or writing,[19] as was usually the case in war time and post-war communist training courses for women.

The peasant women seemed to have accepted their subjugation within the family, frequently being ill-treated by their husbands. Usually, women would

---

[17] The third course (1956) took place "in the house of grandmother Cana", the fourth (1957) "in the house of Miljojka Tadić", see flyer of the Women's Cooperative, 2000.

[18] Every communist would have rejected the label "feminist", even though many communists held "feminist" views by today's definition.

[19] Every woman who wanted to attend the classes first had to find someone who would teach her to read and write in order to be accepted, see BOROJEVIĆ 2006: 38.

not talk openly about being abused, finding other excuses for their bruises and injuries.[20]

Ironically, cases of spousal violence were also found in the context of Rajka's school. One wife was battered by her husband because she failed to pass Rajka's course with distinction. (BOROJEVIĆ 2006: 77) At least one husband is known to have assaulted his wife after catching her studying for the course at home. Rajka recounted the latter episode to a journalist who was researching for an article about her courses for the newspaper *Politika*. Of course, the husband in question was offended when he became aware of the publication, even though his name was not mentioned in the article. Rajka Borojević used the possibility of public denunciation to put pressure on him. According to Rajka, she said to him:

> Be happy that I did not tell the journalist your first and your last name. Then, everybody would know whom it is about. That way, only some of us know about it. But, listen, I swear, next time you treat your wife that way, I'll write an article. Only about that. And I'll give your exact address.[21]

As a result of Rajka's community intervention, the women attending these courses gained an increased sense of self-worth and higher esteem within the whole village community.[22]

The Dragačevo Women's Cooperative

People in the village of Donji Dubac still practiced the traditional handicraft of weaving. It was Rajka's idea to make use of the peasant women's skills which she sought to preserve. (BOROJEVIĆ 2006: 188) Setting up cooperatives, also women's cooperatives, was part of the communist time spirit. The foundation of the Women's Cooperative was closely connected to the training courses for women. In 1952, Rajka started with eight women. In 1955, they organised themselves in a section of members of a women's cooperation (*sekcija zadrugarki*). During the last training course, Joško Onič, an expert on applied art, was invited in order to demonstrate how to weave modern fabrics. (STEALTH.

---

[20] See ibid.: 77. Rajka wrote that she wasn't able to write about what she was told after her lessons in sex education, see ibid.: 156. Open polygamy and early marriages were widespread, see ibid.: 187.
[21] BOROJEVIĆ 2006: 78. Rajka herself was regularly writing for *Politika*.
[22] When Rajka asked a peasant how his wife was, he answered: "Look, since she started attending the courses, the people appreciate her more. A little more, believe me, and as if she was male." Ibid.: 111.

UNLIMITED 2010: 313) In 1962, the autonomous Dragačevo Women's Cooperative was founded.

For the first ten years, the women were working voluntarily. They spent the money they received for their products on education and on travelling together. Their first trip was an excursion to Belgrade where they stayed for four days around the celebration of the May parade. Rajka had to promise that she would protect the women and had to invite every single one of them by mail. After all, in 1954 "it was no small thing for women to travel alone." (BOROJEVIĆ 2006: 72) Everything was new to them. For the first time in their lives, these women would enter an urban apartment. (BOROJEVIĆ 2006: 75)

Other trips followed: In 1955, they went to Zagreb and Kumrovec, Tito's alleged place of birth, as well as to Sarajevo and Banja Luka, where they saw Rajka's previous project, the *Vitaminka* factory.[23] In 1956, they went to see Novi Sad, Vojvodina. In 1964, the women visited Montenegro, Bosnia and Herzegovina, and Dubrovnik. Travelling through Yugoslavia, they got an impression of the size and the variety of the country. It was in accordance with the communist formula of "brotherhood and unity" that the women should see the other Yugoslav republics and make friends with people from other ethnic groups.[24]

In 1966, they left the country for the first time and travelled to Bulgaria. In 1968, further trips abroad followed, leading the women to Romania, the Soviet Union, Poland, Czechoslovakia and Hungary. In 1969, they went to Skandinavia. By the year 1972, Rajka Borojević had led her cooperative members to 15 European countries. (BOROJEVIĆ 2006: 204)

The Women's Cooperative was a very successful project, economically and socially. National newspapers such as *Politika* covered the Cooperative regularly. In 1963, the women built a humble cooperative house. By then, the Cooperative counted 420 members, including two permanent and two part time employees. (STEALTH.UNLIMITED 2010: 313) At the beginning of the 1960s, the Women's Cooperative was suggested as a model for similar projects at mount Zlatibor and in Montenegro, (STEALTH.UNLIMITED 2010: 314) but it probably remained the only cooperative of weavers in Yugoslavia.

---

[23] See BOROJEVIĆ 2006: 125. The regional administration did not support the trip, thus Rajka had to use personal contacts and the Women's Organisation (*Savez ženskih društava – SŽD*) in order to organise the trip, see ibid.: 121.

[24] This attempt seemed to be successful. According to Rajka, a woman from Donji Dubac asked a Croatian woman if she wanted to be the god-mother of her next female child, see ibid.: 131.

From the late 1960s onwards, Rajka's daughter Branka Borojević-Džokić, who had graduated from the Academy of Applied Arts, designed all the fabrics for the Women's Cooperative. Until 2005, they were on display at about 200 independent and collective national and international exhibitions and fairs. (BOROJEVIĆ 2006: 213) The fabrics became popular with fashion designers, not only in Yugoslavia: "Women Weavers Work for Coco Chanel" was a big headline in the *Oslobođenje* newspaper in 1968. (STEALTH.UNLIMITED 2010: 316) "At the beginning, there were eight of us. Now, we are almost eight hundred members of the Women's Cooperative", Rajka Borojević wrote on the occasion of the 20th anniversary in 1972.[25] The cooperative and individual members were awarded 86 badges of distinctions, certificates, prizes and cups.[26]

The Women's Cooperative *Rajka Borojević* in Donji Dubac, Serbia.[27]

As Marxism advocated women's integration into production in order to emancipate them, the Cooperative's first aim was to provide employment opportunities for women. As Rajka explained in her diary:

---

[25] Translated from the flyer of the permanent exhibition in the House of the Women's Cooperative, realised by Branka Borojević-Džokić in 2000.
[26] Information taken from the flyer of the permanent exhibition in the House of the Women's Cooperative (see fn 26).
[27] The picture is taken from STEALTH.UNLIMITED: http://www.stealth.ultd.net/stealth/25_taking.common.matter.into.your.own.hands.html, retrieved 12.10.2011.

If they had the opportunity to use their skills, the handicraft, to produce and sell their products in an organised fashion, they would have a decent income. Thereby, women could improve their and their family's living standard. And even more importantly – they would create a better position for themselves, build their esteem in the family and in society. They would become autonomous. (BOROJEVIĆ 2006: 188)

Basically, the village was still based on a subsistence economy. The fact that women would now bring home money, essentially changed their position within the family, albeit not completely. This can be illustrated by an episode from 1967, when members of the Cooperative raised money for the construction of a "House of Culture" by organising parties in other villages. On these occasions, they selected their "best husbands". Rajka Borojević wrote in her photo album:

> Choosing the best husband has stirred quite a sensation, not only in the villages around Dragačevo but across Yugoslavia. Dunav film sent their crew to shoot a documentary about it. For the female director Vera Jocić the emancipation of women is the main motive for the movie "The Best Husband". (STEALTH.UNLIMITED 2010: 316)

The finals of the best husband selection at the weavers' yearly assembly, Donji Dubac, in 1967.[28]

But it also changed the position of women in the village community. The Cooperative would contribute to the education and development of the village

---

[28] The picture is taken from STEALTH.UNLIMITED, see fn 27.

as a whole. In 1965, approximately 500–600 women voluntarily built the so-called "Women's road" (*Ženski put*) from Viča to Donji Dubac, a motorway, about six kilometers long.[29] When the new cooperative house was built in 1978, it even featured a cinema that was open to everybody. Rajka Borojević stated in her diary on several occasions that "new women" were arising, and that the men in the village were also changing. (BOROJEVIĆ 2006: 143, 152, 198)

Conclusion

The abolishment of the Anti-fascist Front of Women, the first communist women's organisation in Yugoslavia in 1953, did not mean that the aim of the emancipation of women was abandoned by the Yugoslav communists. As the example of the Dragačevo Women's Cooperative shows, it was possible for women in the 1950s in Socialist Yugoslavia to take the initiative and organise women, even outside of official institutions, albeit within the communist framework. Communist policy of the 1950s promoted the "work among women in the countryside". It meant education and professional training of women in order to implement societal changes in a variety of areas such as economics, religion (or, in this case, superstition), farming, public health and the social sphere.

Being a well-educated intellectual communist enthusiast, Rajka Borojević strived for the modernisation of rural life. Unlike other examples from that time, she had the advantage of being well acquainted with the locals, due to her stay in the village during World War II. Rajka had the sense and sensibility not to overstrain them with abstract ideological lessons and radical practical measures, and the inhabitants of Donji Dubac knew her, although she was different from them, and at least for a while a certain mistrust remained.[30]

Rajka Borojević's courses did not question the peasant women's gender roles within the family. Basically, she met the peasant women where they were, as a way to start working with them. Interestingly, while implementing the modernisation policy of the Yugoslav communists, she left the subject of politics and ideology completely aside in her instructions. She aimed to convince the women of the need for changes in their everyday lives. They should understand that these changes would bring benefits for them and their families, and that the whole community could profit from knowledge and progress. The women learned

---

[29] Interview with Radisav Tadić. See also STEALTH.UNLIMITED 2010: 314.
[30] For example, Rajka went on horseback, even in trousers, see BOROJEVIĆ 2006: 106. Some people could not understand why Rajka would do all that without being paid, and rumored that she was sent by someone, see ibid.: 159.

their lessons. They were ready to follow Rajka's initiative and successfully build the first women's cooperative of weavers. Changes in the social and the political sphere followed.[31]

References

BOROJEVIĆ, RAJKA (2006): Iz Dubca u svet. Belgrade.
DIJANIĆ, DIJANA/ MIRKA MERUNKA-GOLUBIĆ/ IVA NIEMČIĆ/ DIJANA STANIĆ (2004): Ženski biografski leksikon. Sjećanje žena na život u socijalizmu. Zagreb.
Flyers from the women's cooperative and the exhibitions in the Ethnographic museum Belgrade (1985, 1988, 1995, 2007).
GUDAC-DODIĆ, VERA (2006): Žena u socijalizmu. Položaj žene u Srbiji u drugoj polovini 20. veka (= Biblioteka studije i monografije 32). Belgrade.
GUDAC-DODIĆ, VERA (2007): Žena u socijalizmu. Sfere privatnosti. In: Ristović, Milan (ed.): Privatni život kod Srba u dvadesetom veku, Belgrade. 165–204.
HÖSCH, EDGAR/ KARL NEHRING/ HOLM SUNDHAUSSEN (ed.) (2004): Lexikon zur Geschichte Südosteuropas. Vienna/Cologne/Weimar.
PEROVIĆ, LATINKA (ed.) (1998): Srbija u modernizacijskim procesima 19. i 20. veka 2. Položaj žene kao merilo modernizacije. Belgrade.
PANTELIĆ, IVANA (2011): Partizanke kao građanke. Društvena emancipacija partizanki u Srbiji 1945–1953 (= Biblioteka studije i monografije 74). Belgrade.
STEALTH.UNLIMITED (2010): Where Everything is yet to Happen. 2nd chapter. [Catalogue] Spaport Biennial 2009/2010. Exposure. http://www.stealth.ultd.net/stealth/projects/25_taking.common.matter.into.your.own.hands/download/WEIYTH_EXPOSURES_STEALTH.pdf, retrieved 13.10.2011.
STEALTH.UNLIMITED: http://www.stealth.ultd.net [Excerpts and photographs from Rajka Borojević's photo albums and newspaper articles], retrieved 12.10.2011.
SNOVALICA: http://www.snovalica.com/sr/dragacevska-zadruga-zena, retrieved 12.10.2011.
STOJAKOVIĆ, GORDANA (2010): Partizanke. Žene u Narodnooslobodilačkoj borbi. Novi Sad.

---

[31] For example, some members of the Cooperative became also members of the local political institutions, see ibid.: 165.

Jovanka and Josip Broz Tito: Gender and Power at the Top of Communist Yugoslavia

Nataša Mišković

When, in the introduction to her collection of papers *Gender Politics in the Western Balkans* (1999), Sabrina RAMET asked: "Was Tito, then, a feminist?", the question was, of course, a rhetorical one. (1999: 5) Josip Broz Tito, president of the Socialist Federal Republic of Yugoslavia, was known as a womanizer – at least by his entourage – but not as a feminist. His First Lady, Jovanka Broz-Budisavljević, embodies more than any other leading Yugoslav woman from that period the patriarchal morality of communist Yugoslavia and its undisputed leader, despite the fact that the Communist Party of Yugoslavia (CPY) did more for gender equality than any other government before it. In this essay, I will try to look behind the mythologized story of the poor peasant girl rising to the top of Tito's Yugoslavia and combine it with the latest research on Tito's regime and the CPY's handling of the so-called women's question. I start from the assumption that although Tito pragmatically adopted a progressive gender policy, mostly to secure the political support of women, he himself remained a deeply patriarchal leader. The text is based on a series of published memoirs from the couple's former collaborators and employees, on information I collected in talks to a small number of people knowing Jovanka in the course of my failed attempt to be received by her for an interview, and on the limited research which has been done on the subject so far. I will first explore how and why the CPY infiltrated the Yugoslav women's movement and reversed it for communist underground work and propaganda. This will be followed by a comment on Tito's relationships with women. The main part will focus on Jovanka's raise to power and her relationship to Tito.

1. The CPY and the women's question in the 1940s

In the 1940s, Tito fought for the realization of an independent Yugoslav state based on communist values, which included the legal equality of women. The CPY needed the women's support to survive the persecution by the royal Yugoslav authorities and later the war. (JANCAR-WEBSTER 1990: 101ff.; BOŽINOVIĆ 1996: 135) The Yugoslav communists discovered women as a useful political factor in the second half of the 1930s: Throughout the 1920s and the beginning of the 1930s, politically active women in the Kingdom of Yugoslavia had been organized within the frame of the *Narodni ženski savez Srba, Hrvata i Slovenaca* (National Women's Alliance of Serbs, Croats and Slovenes), founded in 1919 and engaged in pacifist and humanitarian work, but deeply split over the argument on its political orientation: moderate bourgeois or radical feminist.[1] In 1935, female Belgrade communists, mostly students, approached the suffrage *Ženski pokret* (Women's Movement) on orders of the CPY Central Committee, and offered to found a youth section within their organization. The *Ženski pokret* was happy to win over young supporters and agreed: Under the threat of fascism and in a climate of growing hostility towards working and educated women, the traditional split between socialist and bourgois feminists had lost momentum. The cooperation proved rather successful, and the *Ženski pokret* together with its youth section achieved significant political progress concerning the public acceptance of the idea of women's suffrage between 1935 and 1939. The youth section's first president was Mitra Mitrović (1912–2001), a student of the Belgrade Faculty of Philosophy and later wife of Milovan Đilas. She was a CPY member since 1933, and together with a group of fellow students, her hidden task was to ensure possibilities for legal work to the meanwhile forbidden CPY.[2]

After the outbreak of World War II in August 1939, the question on how to continue work under war-like conditions led to another, fundamental split within the women's movement.[3] The president of the Women's Alliance wished to postpone the claim for the right to vote until better times, but a majority of the members disagreed. A group of activists, mostly communists from the *Ženski pokret*'s youth section, launched a country-wide appeal for the women's right to vote, preparing the ground for a broad activization of women beyond the usual limits of educated and upper-class women. Over this quarrel, the *Ženski pokret* youth section left the Alliance, the president of the Alliance resigned, and her successor allowed the organization to sink into vacuity. (JANCAR-WEBSTER 1990: 37; BOŽINOVIĆ 1996: 125f.) The youth activists on the other hand were very inventive in finding ways to circumvent governmental bans for political gatherings. They continued to work in the form of reading groups, humanitarian work, strike kitchens, or simply meetings in private apartments. Their political achievements and goals were acknowledged for the first time at the CPY's fifth nation-wide party conference (*Peta zemaljska konferencija KPJ*), which took place in October 1940 in a private house near Zagreb and which was attended by 105 delegates under the presidency of the new secretary general Josip Broz Tito. Following a fervent speech by Slovenian lawyer and journalist

---

[1] BOŽINOVIĆ 1996: 104f. See also SKLEVICKY, LYDIA (1984): Organizirana djelatnost žena Hrvatske za vrijeme Narodnooslobodilačke borbe 1941–1945. Zagreb.

[2] JANCAR-WEBSTER 1990: 24; BOŽINOVIĆ 1996: 117f. Regarding the political activities of female Belgrade students see also BOŽINOVIĆ's memoirs (2001: 29ff.).

[3] Yugoslavia entered World War II in April 1941, when Germany attacked the country after a rejection to join the Axis, but was of course affected by the course of events in Europe.

Vida Tomšič (1913–1998, party member since 1934), the conference launched a women's rights programme in the classical marxist-leninist style. It offered generous protection of and care for expectant and nursing women, demanded the introduction of civil marriage and divorce, plus equal salaries and political rights for women, analogical to the demands of the united pre-war women's rights activists. (BOŽINOVIĆ 1996: 128) But within the CPY, women regarding themselves as true communists were denied the right to cooperate with other women's activists in the future. Tomšič explained why:

> We must brand feminism in our ranks as a right-wing, opportunistic help to the bourgeois women's movement in their propagating the illusion that the women's question can be solved with a few reforms within the class society. This kind of work estranges women from the revolutionary proletariate and its Party, and therefore it is an attempt to liquidate the leading role of our Party in the fight for women's equal rights.[4]

On the other hand, comrades who denied the existence of the women's question were criticized as well. By taking over the pre-war women's movement's catalogue of demands in its entirety, but branding feminism as right-wing and forcing male members to keep their eventual disagreement to themselves, the party secured the loyalty of its female members. This strategy proved extremely successful. The women activists believed in the communist cause and engaged in the antifascist liberation movement with enthusiasm and audacity, organizing the logistics and gaining the support of the village women without whose help the partisans could hardly have won the war. (JANCAR-WEBSTER 1990: 86, 127; BOŽINOVIĆ 1996: 117) As Jancar-Webster underlines, "the women's participation in the Yugoslav National Liberation Movement was mobilized, organized, and directed by the Yugoslav Communist Party leadership." In consequence, "there was no independent women's movement in postwar Yugoslavia to speak out on issues of civil, national, or women's rights until the end of the 1970s [...]." (JANCAR-WEBSTER 1990: 84f.) After the war, women's rights were fixed in the constitution as an award for their contribution to the communists' victory. Indeed, never had Yugoslav women enjoyed better legal conditions than under socialist rule, and more progressive ones than in many other European countries. The Antifascist Women's Front, set up in 1942, was reorganized to coordinate the women's activities in the building of the new communist country under the control of the CPY's Central Committee. A considerable number of leading AFŽ activists married CPY cadres and took high positions within the party

---

[4] TOMŠIČ, VIDA (1980): Referat o ženskom pitanju na Petoj zemaljskoj konferenciji. In: Izvori za istoriju KPJ. Peta zemljska konferencija 1/10. Belgrade, cited after BOŽINOVIĆ 1996: 128 (translation into English N.M.).

leadership: Mitra Mitrović was the companion of Milovan Đilas between 1936 and 1952, Milka Janković, a physicist and minister without portfolio after 1947, was the wife of Miloš Minić, a high-ranking Serbian functionary, Marija Šoljan, a prominent lawyer, was the wife of Vladimir Bakarić, the leading Croat party officer. Neda Božinović was appointed responsible posts in the state secretary for administration and in the federal supreme court, and worked as secretary general of the war veteran organization, her husband Dobrivoje Radosavljević took over the ministry of finance until an injury forced him to step back. Other famous couples were Boris and Zdenka Kidrič, Edvard and Pepica Kardelj, Aleksandar and Slavka Ranković, and Ivan and Vera Gošnjak. Vida Tomšič, who had lost her husband during the war and did not remarry, was president of the AFŽ from 1948 to 1953 and, among other assignments, a delegate to the UN. (JANCAR-WEBSTER 1990: 72f.)

The women activists' joy over their achievements did not last long. The Tito-Stalin-split in 1948 first led to a purge and then to a fundamental, far-reaching reorganization of both CPY and state institutions, including the AFŽ. During this phase, which lasted until Stalin's death in March 1953, the Yugoslav party leaders developed the new threefold dogma of independent socialist Yugoslavia: Brotherhood and unity, self-administration, and non-alignment. In this arrangement, the role of the Women's Front was redefined, restricted and finally replaced by a new *"Savez ženskih društava"* (Federation of Women's Organizations), which was not even given proper aims of action. The decisions were taken by the AFŽ Congress itself, in hurrying obedience, but nevertheless as if confirming Tito's own observations at this fourth and last AFŽ congress in September 1953. He warned that among the communists, the "old views on women" were spreading again, with unwished consequences at the working place, and should be fought in a long lasting fight by the means of political work. He said:

> Your organization derives its right of existence exactly from such problems, this is your basic field of action. As soon as there is one conscious woman around, the possibility that men, who are less conscious in the field of women, act in the traditional way towards women, decreases. I have noticed that women are not persistent in this, that they surrender easily. It is necessary that man and woman fight together for the abolition of negative attitudes towards women.[5]

Tito's observations were correct, but they did not encourage the AFŽ activists to fight on. The abolition was decided and accepted, the anger of the activists

---

[5] Tito u razgovoru sa delegatkinjama Četvrtog Kongresa AFŽ-a. In: Zora (1953) 89–90, 2–4, cited after BOŽINOVIĆ 1996: 168 (translation from Serbo-Croatian N.M.).

turned into frustration, and many packed in their work. (BOŽINOVIĆ 1996: 170) Eight years after the victorious introduction of gender equality, the process of implementation was more or less stopped. Two other events coincide with this incident: In April 1952, Tito married Jovanka Budisavljević, and from January 1953 onwards, he assumed the position of President of Yugoslavia. The reorganization of the state was completed, and Tito had solved the women's question at least for himself: He legitimized his companion, and he gave the country a charming and glamorous First Lady. Tito was then 61 years old, Jovanka just 28. A brief look at his earlier relationships may highlight some of the reasons why he chose her as a wife.

2. Tito and his wives

In the perception of most of his biographers, Tito was not a very happy man in his private life (see especially ĐILAS 1980: 253f.). Not much was known about it during his lifetime apart from the facts that that he had been married before Jovanka, that he had two sons from different relationships, and that his firstborn had died after birth.[6] Most of this information is based on Tito's own varying stories, which he liked to mythologize himself – more to self-affirm his own fate and mission than to boost his prestige, as Milovan Đilas suggests.[7] Recently discovered documents from the Komintern archives in Moscow shed new light on his first fifty years and started a discussion on his rise, ambition, and crimes committed in order to secure power. (SIMIĆ 2011) These questions cannot be dealt with within the scope of this article, but some of the newly known facts help to reassess Tito's relationship with women – and confirm what ĐILAS has stated already in 1980, that Tito basically subjected everything to his striving for power.

Josip Broz had first been married in 1918 during his war captivity in Russia, in the Omsk district in Siberia, to the peasant girl Pelagija Denisovna Belousova, who was then only 14 years old.[8] After the integration of Omsk into the new

---

[6] Among the biographical literature published until his death in 1980, an influential example is FITZROY MACLEAN (1980): Josip Broz Tito. A Pictorial Biography. Maidenhead. German edition: Tito. Ein Kampfgefährte berichtet. Zurich. The equally popular biography by Milovan Đilas first diffused information about Tito's "war wives" Herta Haas and Davorjanka Paunović.

[7] ĐILAS 1980: 245f. See FITZROY MACLEAN's (1980) story of Pelagija hiding Broz heroically from the White Army. 22.

[8] SIMIĆ 2011: 32. Broz did not participate in the October Revolution, as he wished the public to believe and as even recent biographers claim (see SWAIN, GEOFFREY (2011): Tito.

Soviet Russia at the end of 1919, he wanted to stay and submitted applications for Soviet citizenship and membership in the communist party. Both requests were declined because he had allegedly "fled the Red Army", which was probably the main reason why he returned to his native country in 1920 together with his wife. (SIMIĆ 2011: 32) There, the Kingdom of Serbs, Croats and Slovenes had been founded two years ago. As a war returner from Soviet Russia, Broz was again suspicious. Josip and Pelagija went to his widowed fathers' home, where their first child died shortly after birth. The couple then settled in Zagreb and later near Bjelovar, where Josip worked as a mechanic and where he became involved in the agitations of the local section of the CPY. As Simić convincingly argues, by then he still was not a member of the CPY, otherwise the couple would not have erected a tombstone with catholic symbols for their two-year-old daughter Hinka as late as 1924. (SIMIĆ 2011: 36) Two years later, Broz left Pelagija and their only surviving son Žarko to do underground work for the communists. In 1927, he started to work as a professional party officer, and in summer 1928, he was sentenced to a five year prison term, after bombs and guns had been discovered in his lodgings. During her husband's imprisonment, Pelagija, who was left without means, went back to Russia with her son. She placed Žarko, who was a very difficult child, into a reformatory. When Josip Broz came to Moscow in the mid-1930s for his underground training, he searched for his son and took him to live with him, and he divorced Pelagija in 1936.[9] According to Milovan Đilas, Tito was "deeply hurt in his male pride" by his wife's desertion. (ĐILAS 1980: 257)

Soon after his divorce, Tito married a second time. He was now in his mid-forties, and he needed somebody to look after the child, as he stated himself in a letter to the Soviet Ministry of the Interior regarding his first two wives. For 23-year-old Johanna König, a German-born radio fitter who lived in Moscow under the false name Luzia Bauer, it was the second marriage. Under the pseudonym Walter, the family lived in Hotel Luks, where all foreign party cadres stayed in Moscow. A year later, she was dead: Broz had been sent abroad for conspirative work linked with the Spanish civil war, but she was ill

---

A biography. London. 8). Broz lived as a war prisoner in a territory controlled by the White Army until November 1914. Omsk was the seat of General Kolčak's anti-communist regime.

[9] Pelagija later married a Komintern photographer and was arrested in 1938 for two years. In 1944, she had a daughter with her second husband. After the Tito-Stalin split in 1948, she was again sentenced to a ten year prison term and only released after Stalin's death. She died in 1967. FROLOV, V. (1990): Josip Broz Tito v Omske. In: Omskaja Pravda (18 July 1990), cited in SIMIĆ 2011: 76.

and could not get a permission to follow him. Shortly after, she was arrested and shot.[10]

Tito's third companion was Herta Haas, a student in economics from an Austro-Slovene attorney's family and a party activist, whom he first met in Paris in 1937. She is his second son Miša's mother, but not much was known about her beyond testimonials of friends from Tito's inner circle who had looked after her before and after the birth of her son in 1941: Vladimir Velebit, Josip Kopinič, Milovan Đilas, Leo Mates, Vladimir Dedijer. In 1961, she gave a biographical interview to the museum of her hometown Maribor, and a few years before her death in 2010 at age 96, she gave another one to director Lordan Zafranović and publisher Mira Šuvar.[11] Herta Haas was 22 years younger than Tito, very straightforward and reliable. The illegal life during their relationship in the pre-war years was dangerous. They could have been discovered by the police, and they were under constant control by the Komintern and under threat of denunciation by other comrades: Tito then organized the transfer of voluntaries for the Spanish Civil War, and strove for the appointment as secretary general of the CPY. She served as a party courier transporting forged passports, and followed Tito, in the words of Miro Simčić, like a shadow. (SIMČIĆ 2008: 125) In the spring of 1941, Tito and Herta lived in Zagreb, and Herta was soon to deliver her baby. After the German attack on Belgrade, which started World War II in Yugoslavia, Tito was ordered to go to Belgrade and organize the liberation fight from there. Herta stayed in Zagreb and gave birth to Miša, looked after by Vladimir Velebit and her mother. (ŠUVAR 2001: 70) Soon after, she was arrested during an Ustaša raid in the house of Ivan Krajačić-Stevo, the Croat KGB liaison officer, whom she later held responsible for her arrest. (SIMČIĆ 2008: 127) Her Austrian origin and the fact that she cut her veins helped her to escape torture and survive, but for some comrades, she was not trustworthy anymore. Vladimir Velebit and Milovan Đilas, Tito's envoys to deal with the Germans in noteworthy negotiations on a ceasefire in Zagreb in

---

[10] SIMIĆ 2011: 51, 75f., 153. Tito's denunciation letter is published in SIMIĆ, PERO (2010): Strogo poverljivo, document 30. 91f. At the time Tito wrote the letter, Johanna was already dead, but it must have aggravated Pelagija's life in jail. König's first marriage was to Ernst Wabra, later head of the Central Commission for State Control (ZKK) in the GDR, who had her rehabilitated during his high office in 1958. Tito never mentioned her. Miro Simčić states that the documents proving Titos' marriage to König under their pseudonyms Friedrich Walter and Lucija Bauer aroused a sensation when first presented to a curious Belgrade public in 2007 at the exhibition Tito–Staljin. SIMČIĆ 2008: 103.

[11] Simčić used the Maribor Museum interview and obviously had access to Zafranović's tapes. SIMČIĆ 2008: 111ff. I talked to Šuvar and Zafranović in 2007, after their interview with Haas.

March 1943, got Herta out of an Ustaša prison and took her to the partisan headquarters in Bosnia.[12] There, they were witness to her brief, but fierce encounter with Tito, after which she left him for good: Since his removal to Belgrade, Tito had been living with the Serbian student Davorjanka Paunović, his war companion and secretary, better known by her war name Zdenka. According to Đilas, Tito knew he was straining the puritan party rules regarding love and marriage: Couples were expected to be true to each other and to legitimize their relationship. (SIMČIĆ 2008: 127; ĐILAS 1980: 258–261) Other sources claim Zdenka was the love of his life.[13] There are several reasons why Tito did not leave Davorjanka when Herta returned, but the pivotal motivation may have been security. Vladimir Dedijer, Tito's former "court historian" who fell into disgrace over his loyalty to Đilas, claims to have seen a 16-page letter Tito wrote to Herta to beg her to come back after Davorjanka's death of tuberculosis in 1946. Herta declined and decided to live quietly in Belgrade as a government officer, founding a new family with her second husband. Miro SIMČIĆ however reports that she had tried to sue Ivan Krajačić for badmouthing her after the war. (2008: 129) Davorjanka, who after the end of the war had overseen Tito's household in the *Beli Dvor*, his new Belgrade residence, the former king's palace in the posh suburb of Dedinje, was buried in the gardens there. The duties of the Marshal's housekeeper were taken over by a beautiful young partizan officer, Jovanka Budisavljević. Tito however, as Yugoslavia's head of state, needed a hostess at his side.

3. Jovanka the partisan

As Herta Haas and Davorjanka Paunović, Jovanka belonged to the limited number of female partisan commissars. If the first two meet the pattern of the educated, urban female party activists, politicized within the leftist women's and youth movement of the 1920s and 1930s, belonging to the limited number of females regarded fit for a leading party position and making up the pool from which the male party leaders liked to choose their wives, Jovanka

---

[12] ŠUVAR 2001: 283ff., 463f. According to Velebit, the negotiations failed in the initial stage because Hitler refused to enter into negotiations with the partisans. Velebit's father and grandfather had both been generals in the Austrian army before 1918. For this reason, he was acquainted with the Nazi Wehrmacht commander in Zagreb, the Austrian Glaise von Horstenau. Horstenau did not invite Đilas to his talks with Velebit.

[13] LEO MATES, as cited in SIMIĆ 2011: 219. Davorjanka's former boyfriend Jova Kapičić claims that she chose Tito over him, and that they were in love, she more than Tito. NIKČEVIĆ 2010: 56f. Davorjanka was the aunt of Slobodan Milosević's wife Mira Marković. See also fn 25.

Budisavljević originated from the mass of simple, uneducated peasant girls, who joined the partisans in the course of the war because they had lost their homes and subsistence, and who took over mostly tasks in logistics, housekeeping and nursing. (JANCAR-WEBSTER 1999: 30f.; JANCAR-WEBSTER 1990: 60f., 64–74)

Jovanka was born on 7 December 1924 into a Serbian family of the village of Pećani, in the Croat region of Lika, a *polje* (karst field) squeezed between the Dalmatian mountain range of Velebit and the Bosnian border on the Plješevica range. The Lika had been part of the Habsburg Military border, with a mixed Serbian-Orthodox and Croat-Catholic population. Jovanka's father Mićo, an only son, had been on migrant work overseas in America, and brought back money to buy land, build a large house and marry his neighbour's daughter Milica Svilar. The couple had three children, two sons and in-between Jovanka, after which Mića went abroad again. When he came back, Jovanka's younger sisters Zora and Nada were born, who are more than ten years her junior. As the eldest daughter, Jovanka was expected to work hard and help her mother in her household and child caring duties. She also worked in her uncle's guesthouse and attended four years of primary school, which was very unusual for a Lika country girl. (SIMČIĆ 2008: 162) The mother died when Jovanka was just a young teenager. Her father remarried, but Jovanka was unhappy with the new arrangement and looked for an opportunity to live independently. She found one soon: Her father had engaged in the peasant cooperative movement, offering a part of his house as a library and meeting place to the *Seljačko kolo*. This Peasant circle had initially been close to the Independent Democratic Party (*Samostalna demokratska stranka*), which had founded the *Kolo* to engage the Serbian-Croat peasants in politics, but around 1941, it sympathized with the communists. (ZAGORAC 1990: 14; see also JAKIR 1999: 229) At age 16, when war broke out in Yugoslavia, Jovanka started to act as a courier between local communist branches. She consequently was accepted as a member of the Communist youth organization (SKOJ, *Savez komunističke omladine Jugoslavije*). In the spring of 1942, Ustaša and Italian troops burnt down her village, and together with her two brothers and many others, she went into the woods to join the partisans: The Ustaša's brutal regime provoked a high number of people from the persecuted sections of society to join the communist partisan movement, which in Croatia and parts of Bosnia was the only credible opposition party. The political US scientist Barbara JANCAR-WEBSTER has shown that the number of women wishing to fight in the Lika, Kordun, Banija regions of Croatia and in northern Dalmatia – territories which had once been part of the Austrian-Ottoman military border – was unusually high, in Lika especially among the under 20-years-old Serbian peasant girls. (1990: 48, 54f., tables 5.1. and 2.2.,

59) Austrian historian Barbara WIESINGER has shown that these girls' motivation to fight and to handle guns was primarily the experience of massacres in their own villages, the wish to escape violation, to defend themselves, and revenge – but not patriotism, as Yugoslav post-war ideology claimed. (1999: 70ff.) The CPY leadership took advantage of this peasant need of defense and sent communist activists into the villages to turn it into revolution, as documented by numerous accounts of students sent back into their region of origin to organize the uprisings, among others Milovan Đilas, Jova Kapičić, or Neda BOŽINOVIĆ. (2001: 53; NIKČEVIĆ 2010: 30f.) Wiesinger's evidence suggests that Tito and his collaborators were rather surprised, both by the extent of violence applied by the Ustaša regime to eliminate the Serb population on the territories under their rule, and by the peasant girls' will to fight. The partisan leadership as much as the commanders who organized the uprising in Lika had deep reservations as to whether they should let these young girls fight, and activists from the AFŽ and the SKOJ first had to assert the right of women to be active fighters.[14] Tito's command to allow the arming of women fighters dates as late as February 1942.[15] The Croat commanders complied in mid-1942 and eventually formed the First Lika Girls' Combat Group (*Prva lička ženska četa*), but maintained there were not enough guns to arm the girls. The 75 members of the *ženska četa* allegedly had no more than twenty guns, but each member was given a hand granate for self-defense.[16] The group proved very zealous in their first encounter with Italian troops in Kordun, fighting hand-to-hand and capturing guns, as one of its members, Desanka Stojić, remembers in an impressive account.[17] Many partisan officers did not like the girls taking such risks, mostly because this challenged their traditional male role model as protectors of their sisters and daughters. Even worse were the gross sexist jokes about the so-called hollow band (*šuplja četa*). (ZAGORAC 1959: 15) The women's combat group was eventually split up and its members distributed among the various units, where they were given other tasks. These tasks had less to do with fighting but with

---

[14] WIESINGER 1999: 66ff. One of the leading Lika commanders, Jakov Blažević, expressed his patriarchal scruples as follows: "What to do with those female children? – was one of the dilemmas; was it at all morally acceptable to integrate them into a combat unity?" ("Šta učiniti s ovom ženskom decom? – bila je jedna od dilema; da li je, naime, moralno, uopšte ih svrstavati u borbenu jedinicu?"). ZAGORAC 1990: 15.
[15] Pismo vrhovnog komandanta NOPO i DV Jugoslavije od 23.2.1942 [...]. In: Zbornik dokumenata, second series 2, document 201. 429–436, 436, cited in WIESINGER 1999: 68.
[16] WIESINGER 1999: 66ff., especially 66, fn 29, and 83, fn 109, citing ŽEGARAC 1959.
[17] STOJIĆ 1987, cited in ZAGORAC 1959: 15, and WIESINGER 1999: 80ff.

caring for the male colleagues, a duty which was much more in accordance with traditional gender roles.[18]

It was against this background that Jovanka Budisavljević joined the partisans in August 1942, and despite some difficulties to prove this, she later claimed to have been one of the members of the *Lička ženska četa*.[19] Already a member of SKOJ, originating from a village burnt by Italian and Ustaša troops, she indeed would have been an ideal candidate – if her account is correct. Even if it is not, she had her long plates cut, learned to handle guns and would eventually be promoted to be a party commissar (and not an army officer). She would also receive an award for bravery. In the winter of 1943, an injury caused a chronic instability in her foot, and both she and her father caught a typhus fever, which she survived, but her father did not. She also lost her elder brother in battles near Gospić. As she told her biographers, these events induced her to accept her superiors' suggestion to give up active fighting and to continue as a nurse. She worked in hospital wards in Bosnia and Serbia and was given more and more responsibility. However, it is not clear how and where exactly she spent those later war years, as she took care to gloss them over. Stories exist that she spent some time under a cover name in Zagreb, probably under the supervision of the notorious KGB liaison agent Ivan Krajačić-Stevo.[20] Jovanka's war decoration on the other hand might as well have emphasized her later position as First Lady of Communist Yugoslavia and as the patroness of the Spanish civil war

---

[18] The demobilization of women fighters started in 1944, when the partisan troops were gradually converted into a regular army. WIESINGER 1999: 69f. Accounts from former women partisans about their female duties in the woods are rather frequent, as are stories about young peasant girls without family and with no other option than to join the partisans: The oral collection of the American anthropologist Joel Halpern contains the account of a Bosnian woman from Župča, who had left her mother's home because her stepfather was beating her, and who then left also her husband's house because her father-in-law treated her ill. She returned to her widowed mother, but when the war came, her only possibility was to join the partisans: "I was in the woods for over two years, until I returned to my village. With the partisans, I cooked for the soldiers and I washed and mended their things. I even received a distinguished service award, which I keep to this day." Selina N. in GRANDITS/ KASER 2003: 55 (Translation into English N.M.).

[19] ZAGORAC 1959: 14f.; SIMČIĆ 2008: 164f. It is doubtful whether Jovanka was really a member of the *Lička ženska četa*. A film which was to focus on her role in this combat group was never filmed. Simčić also hints on her difficulties to find witnesses for her participation there. An entry into the liberation movement from 1941 onwards was a precondition to be awarded the honorary title of '*prvoborac*' ("fighter from the beginning"). This was important for Jovanka, who later assumed the role as patroness of the war veteran organization.

[20] Simčić reports that the Yugoslav intelligence service tried to find out in 1987 why Jovanka had left her Lika squad during the war. SIMČIĆ 2008: 172f.

and partisan veteran organizations.[21] As a matter of fact, she grew closer and closer to the headquarters of the Supreme Command and ended the war settled in Belgrade, in the rank of a major. Her family remained an issue of concern to her: After the war, she searched for her sisters who had been taken to an orphanage in Otočac, and took them into her care. Her younger brother, a police officer, died shortly after the war.

4. The First Lady of Yugoslavia

When Jovanka was selected to be the main hygienist of Tito's Belgrade residence in 1946, nobody expected her to become his wife. Davorjanka Paunović was still there, supervising the household and allegedly terrorizing everybody by her fits of ill temper. (SIMČIĆ 2008: 136) After her death, and Herta Haas's refusal to come back, Tito's collaborators unsuccessfully searched for a suitable wife. Eventually Tito's eye fell on the beautiful young housekeeper, and he and Jovanka became lovers. Stories about who had directed her into Tito's household vary, but more than one suggest that intelligence was involved. Milovan Đilas believed that Aleksandar Ranković's state security service UDBA was responsible, but this information is based on his private assumption.[22] The most probable account is that Krajačić-Stevo introduced her there, as she was his protégé. Krajačić was a highly skilled undercover agent and knew Tito since the late 1920s. Although he never held a high position, he was powerful and at all times had access to the presidential couple. According to Vjenceslav Cenčić, who had started his research as Dedijer's collaborator, comrade Stevo never stopped acting as the Yugoslav liaison officer to the Soviet intelligence service until the 1980s. He was known for his desire for recognition, and he approached several people with his project of writing his memoirs. The disclosure of more evidence will prove whether he placed Jovanka into the Marshal's household with the intent to supply him with information for the Soviets.[23]

---

[21] According to the journalist Dara Janeković, Jovanka was responsible for the well-being of about 400 veterans after the war. Interview of 11/12 September 2007.

[22] ĐILAS 1980: 264. He also says that Ranković welcomed this marriage primarily because of his rigid sense of moral.

[23] SIMČIĆ 2008: 127ff., 166ff., 178ff.; CENČIĆ 2001: 183f. Ivan Krajačić-Stevo (1906–1986) was an extremely controverse personality in the history of communist Yugoslavia, who carried out the dirty work for his superiors. Stories about his misdeeds and abuses abound. He came from a poor Croat peasant family and served an apprenticeship as a mechanic, as Tito had done. He came to Zagreb in 1928, but was accepted as a member of CPY in 1933 only. In 1936, he was set to go to Moscow for party training, but instead fought in the Spanish Civil War, where he engaged in intelligence work, as Tito did. He escaped from a French internment camp in 1939 and again went underground. In 1942, after the

Jovanka did not have the requirements and education to be the Marshal's wife. Remaining somewhat ashamed of her modest origin, she worked hard to accomplish her duties with dedication and perfection. In time, she became indispensable for Tito's life and well-being, and he decided to marry her anyway: She was beautiful, smart, very stylish in the elegant gowns which now replaced her uniform and *'partizanka'*, and she had a ravishing smile. Lacking manners and education were easily improved, and she was given the opportunity to graduate from high school (*gimnazija*), which she did successfully in 1955. Tito's decision proved wise: In the years he built his new Yugoslavia, complete with brotherhood and unity, self-administration, and an independent, non-aligned way to socialism, when he exchanged his uniform with smart white signature suits to travel the world, Jovanka was an additional asset with her elegance, beauty and charming smile. With her partisan past, she added to the mystery of Tito's image as a Robin Hood of the Balkans. The disparity of age was soon forgiven. Indian Prime Minister Jawaharlal Nehru was enthusiastic about her in the report on his first stay in Yugoslavia in summer 1955:

> Marshal Tito's wife, Madame Broz, is a charming and beautiful woman. She is very young. She comes from a poor peasant family which has suffered during the war of resistance. At the age of 16 she joined the guerrillas and had a hard time. […] We were very sorry to leave Brioni and Yugoslavia. During our week there we had become very friendly with Marshal Tito and his colleagues. (NEHRU 1955: 30)

In his choice of wife as much as in the choice of his residences, cars, and lifestyle, Tito mixed business with pleasure. For over two decades, he and Jovanka made a power couple – on patriarchal terms. She was totally devoted to him and followed him like a pet dog, remembers the prominent Zagreb journalist Dara Janeković, who had spent time with them on repeated occasions.[24] Tito was known as a womanizer, but Jovanka was never associated with any other man than her husband, not even in her war days: It looks as if she combined the

---

death of the KGB liaison officer for the Balkans, Anton Srebrnjak, in a Nazi prison, Krajačić assumed this position and kept it until his death in 1986. Krajačić was most probably a double or a triple agent. Cenčić claims that another KGB officer in Yugoslavia, the Slovene Josip Kopinič, Tito's peer and mate, had told him Krajačić was set to liquidate Tito on Stalin's order, but did not shoot when the opportunity arose. Simčić tells a similar story communicated by Vladimir Dedijer, that Krajačić received orders by Stalin to kill Tito and did not, when Tito confronted him on a private motoring excursion. SIMČIĆ 2008: 180, also Cenčić's interview under http://dalje.com/hr-hrvatska/tito-zaprijetio-staljinu-atentatom/150822, retrieved 17.10.2011. Dara Janeković mentioned audio tapes recorded to prepare Krajačić's memoirs.

[24] Interview on 11/12 September 2007.

archaic morality of her military border origins with the rigorous communist party rules.[25] She enjoyed doing housework, cooking for Tito and looking after his wardrobe: She declared that one of the main reasons why she loved to spend time on Vanga, the couple's strictly private island in the archipelago of Brioni, the President's summer residence, was to prepare herself the dishes her husband enjoyed most. A volume of photographs on Tito's private life from 1969 contains plenty of pictures showing Jovanka mending, cooking, or caring for her Josip, whereas Tito presents himself as a loving husband, who would spend his free time in his locksmith's workshop, reading, preparing coffee, or laughing and walking with his wife. (ETEROVIĆ 1977) Beyond their life as a married couple, which looked happy until the end of the 1960s, family rules imposed by Tito were strict. His two sons lived apart, and on published photographs, they and their families are never seen together with Jovanka. Tito rejected the idea of having more children, and according to information I received in Zagreb, Jovanka was expected to abort whenever necessary, sharing the fate of most ordinary women throughout communist Eastern Europe, where birth-control was regulated in this style.[26] Furthermore, Tito did not like the idea of having a wife with a university degree when he could have none, and therefore Jovanka did not pursue her formal education after her marriage.[27] On the other hand, she was allowed to look after her two young sisters and make them part of the extended President's household, contrary to his own sons.

In public, Jovanka was respected as the Marshal's wife, but she was not popular. She is most remembered as a fashion icon, promoting Yugoslav fashion design by wearing stylish creations with a folkloristic touch especially made for

---

[25] Vlahović and Kačarević cite Leo Mates, a partisan officer and later a key figure in the Ministry of the Exterior, about Tito's attitude towards women: "He regarded women as inferior beings. He had had countless women, and he did not bond with any of them, with the exception of Davorjanka Paunović, but this happened under fully extraordinary circumstances – during the war." ("Smatrao je žene inferiornim bićima. Imao je bezbroj žena i ni za jednu se nije vezivao, osim za Davorjanku Paunović, ali i to je bilo u sasvim izvanrednim prilikama – u ratu.") VLAHOVIĆ/ KAČAREVIĆ 1990: 434, cited after SIMIĆ 2001: 219.

[26] Đilas also mentioned that Jovanka wished to have children, but Tito did not. ĐILAS 1980: 270. Abortion rates in Eastern Europe were among the highest worldwide before 1989. In Yugoslavia, abortion was legalized in 1952 (*Uredba o postupku za dopušteni prekid trudnoće*) and extended in 1960 and 1969 (*Opšti zakon o prekidu trudnoće*). See http://de.wikipedia.org/wiki/Schwangerschaftsabbruch#Mittel-_und_Osteuropa, retrieved 20.10.2011. On changing attitudes towards the termination of pregnancy in Croatia since the 1990s see http://www.zenska-mreza.hr/press/jutarnji_060412.htm, and http://hr.wikipedia.org/wiki/Pobačaj#Poba.C4.8Daj_u_Hrvatskoj, retrieved 20.10.2011.

[27] Tito eventually received several honorary doctoral degrees.

her by private tailors, by the handicraft cooperation "Narodna radinost", and, among others, by companies such as "Centrotextil" or "Jugoexport" and their renowned designers Aleksandar Joksimović and Mirjana Marić. (VELIMIROVIĆ 2008: 92ff.) In time, Jovanka gained a lot of informal power. She acted as her husband's private secretary, arranging meetings in his private cabinet and secretly taking notes from behind a curtain. As a politician however, Jovanka was not taken seriously. Finally, despite her immediate control over Tito's papers and sometimes even decisions, Jovanka was denied ultimate access to power. There are reports that she herself believed to guide her husband and that she wanted to become a member of the Central Committee, but in vain.[28] When she was offered the presidentship of the Red Cross instead, she refused angrily. She became corrupted by the splendour and power struggles around her, and accounts by former employees describe her as vain and overly ambitious. Her quarrels with the staff, her defiant will to control everything and to be treated and obeyed as the First Lady of the country, are well documented. (DOTLIĆ 1990; MATUNOVIĆ 2007; ADAMOVIĆ 2004a; ADAMOVIĆ 2004b)

In the 1970s, Tito was in his eighties, ill, and lost his capability to reign. When the federal government declared him president during lifetime, the question of his succession was definitely postponed until after his death. For the Yugoslav state and party leadership, it was therefore crucial who would control access to him. When Jovanka engaged in this last power struggle, she lost and was separated from him. Even in this last defeat, she was not taken seriously, and stories were put up that she suffered from menopausal disorders and that she was insanely jealous of her husband's young physiotherapist, threatening to shoot at them. She never saw Tito again. In May 1980, she was allowed to participate at her husband's funeral.

5. The widow

When Tito died, Jovanka remained a bitter, distrustful woman, convinced to be a tragic victim of history. She had to leave her home in Užička 15, and for years, she restricted her rare public statements to lamentations that she had

---

[28] SIMČIĆ 2008: 184f. cites an anonymous document (the author is known to him), which states that the conference room in Tito's residence was divided by a broad door and a curtain from his private apartment. If somebody listened to the meeting in disguise, he or she could only have access from the private side, making Jovanka the only person able to listen in secret. Simčić's informant tells that participants in meetings always knew that Jovanka was sitting behind the curtain and kept listening and taking notes whenever the couple's four poodles did not stop walking from Tito's side to the curtain and back. Also Dara Janeković stated that Jovanka was taking notes constantly.

been thrown out of her house in the middle of the night with a bag and some bed things, when in fact she was moved to another villa opposite the *Beli dvor* with 79 pieces of luggage.[29] On the other hand, her identiy papers had been confiscated in 1977, for almost 35 years until the spring of 2011, her status remains based solely on a government decision, and the villa put at her disposition is in a state of dilapidation after decades of neglect. Jovanka has lived there in isolation, surrounded by a small number of devoted friends and staff, mostly from her native Lika or Dalmatia, and leaving it only once a year to visit her husband's tomb. In the last two years however, her case has come into motion following the visit of two members of the Serbian government, the Minister of the Interior Ivica Dačić and the Minister of Labour and Social Policy Rasim Ljajić. An interview given to US embassy officer Jennifer Brush in the presence of Minister Ljajić in September 2009, published by Wikileaks on 1 September 2011, reveals that she displays "a razor-sharp mind and considerable charisma", along with "an encyclopedic knowledge of world events".[30] In claiming that her father had been an American citizen she evinces a hope that the US government might assist her in improving her situation, or even offer her asylum. The story about her arranging meetings between Tito and Draža Mihailović in Pećani and Knin during World War II however sounds as a fantastic example of her need of self-mythologization – and at the same time supports the reports that she was indeed involved in intelligence work from an early stage of her career. Insofar, this story adds to the credibility of the Tito-Kopinič-records published by Cenčić, where Tito, asked about the true reasons for his separation from Jovanka, puts forward his discovery that she had acted as an informant to the KGB via Krajačić for all their married life.

Most credible is Jovanka's account that Slovenian Presidency member Stane Dolanc together with Defence Minister and Army Commander general Nikola Ljubičić had planned her detention in order to eliminate her from the list of possible successors of Tito. She indirectly admits her aspirations to succession by saying that she would have been a logical choice according to the "trend of the time", by which she alluded to female politicians like Sirimavo Bandaranike and Isabel Perón, who took over their dead husbands' office. To speak of a trend based on single cases is of course a gross exaggeration.

Her lawyer for thirty years, the prominent Belgrade advocate Toma Fila, gave an almost equally revealing interview to the journal *Vreme* on 7 April

---

[29] GLIGORIJEVIĆ, JOVANA (2001): Moji dani sa Jovankom Broz. [Interview with Toma Fila] In: Vreme (7.4.2011). http://www.vreme.com/cms/view.php?id=984685, retrieved 23.10.2011.

[30] http://wikileaks.org/cable/2009/09/09BELGRADE839.html, retrieved 23.10.2011.

2011, after having ceded the case shortly before.[31] He confirms her distrust, her stubbornness and her tendency to exaggerate stories and her role in it. He states that she had been Tito's last bodyguard, and that she loved him "madly" even to this day. He also gives clues as to where Tito's estate and Jovanka's confiscated belongings have been hidden in the last three decades: He has been writing applications to the "Muzej istorije Beograda" and to the "Istorijski arhiv" in Belgrade, meaning most probably "Jugoslavije". The easiest explanation on the whereabouts of Tito's whole estate could therefore be that it has always remained undivided, in the "poison cabinet" of one of these places. Chances have never been better that Jovanka's fight for her confiscated goods and inheritance will be settled for good in the near future, and historians have never had better prospects to be able to consult missing key documents on the Tito period in the near future.

Conclusion

In this article, I have tried to explore the relationship between the charismatic presidential couple of Yugoslavia, Tito and Jovanka, against the background of their biographies, the CPY gender policy and their common political project, the communist Yugoslav state. In a culture of lies, famously described by Dubravka Ugrešić in her essay of 1994, it is extremely difficult to filter out reliable information from the mass of stories and accounts at present in circulation. Contemporaries mix memories with assumptions and try to present themselves in the best of lights, telling some facts and hiding others, and often starting to believe in their own made-up stories, as Tito and Jovanka have done themselves. Intelligence services have spread in more stories, aimed at denunciating their sponsor's opponents. Documents have been destroyed, falsified or kept hidden. On the basis of the material available today, I have to restrict myself on guessing what is most probable. To conclude, I return to my initial question: Was Tito a patriarchal leader?

The final answer must be a yes, although the justification is not as simple as this. The CPY leadership featured an elitist group of highly educated young women, who were fanatic communists, but with feminist convictions on gender equality, such as Mitra Mitrović or Vida Tomšič. Tito, who himself came from a deeply patriarchal background, was open for their reasoning and saw their potential in supporting his mission. The Central Committee's decisions on the other hand were authoritative and top-down. Even if the lower ranks of CPY members accepted these decisions, it did not follow that they believed in them

---

[31] See above fn 29.

or that they adapted their behaviour more than superficially. Letting the girls handle guns was a sensitive issue during the partisan war, and so was the question of the women's role after the war. The new laws on gender equality therefore affected primarily the elite women from the CPY leadership active already before the war, who took them as a prize, and who themselves married the elite men. Some of these women did excellent careers, but none was ever admitted into the innermost circle of power – apart from Jovanka, whose influence remained informal. For the majority among the population, the main thing after the long years of war, reconstruction and post-1948-repression was to return to a normal life – which included "normal", traditional gender roles. The effects of the new legislation were to be felt only at a later stage, with the integration of women into the educational and paid labour system, and the acceptance of abortion as a means of birth control – but this complex of problems diverts from the question in focus here.

Tito saw clearly how the AFŽ activists gave up their cause after 1950 and retired in frustration, when all their efforts were made the subject of criticisms and dismissals before and during the Fourth AFŽ congress. He told them openly, but he did not prevent a process which in fact he welcomed: For him, the revolutionary phase was over, and so was the experimenting with equal gender rights. He was careful not to be made responsible for the abolition of the organization however, according to a pattern of power and image management which he used on other occasions too, e.g. when he spoke to the protesting students after 1968, supporting at the same time the party purges in Serbia and Croatia.

Tito also had a preference for much younger women whom he could dominate more easily. At the beginning of the war, Tito was associated with an educated feminist activist, Herta Haas. If really Herta's arrest was arranged by Krajačić, and Jovanka placed in his proximity instead, then Tito was not free in his choice of companion. Party discipline required that party needs and decisions had to be put above anything else. Tito used the space he could within these limits to the maximum, also regarding women. It is comprehensible under these circumstances what reasons induced him to sacrifice his first two wives. The fact that Herta had been imprisoned in an enemy's camp made her a potential security risk for Tito and the partisan general staff. Again, he was ready to sacrifice his wife after her release, all the more as he was already enamoured of Davorjanka. This companion is the only one he did not desert in the list, because she died of tuberculosis. With Jovanka, he met a young woman of similar background as himself, who was, at least in the first ten years, totally acquiescent to him, adopting her lifestyle according to his gusto, and who was still tough enough to handle guns and keep his state secrets – at least he thought so. He may have thought that for once, he had been lucky in his choice – until the last few years of his life, when the pattern was repeated one last time and he deserted his wife, moving out of Užička 15.

Archival sources

NEHRU, JAWAHARLAL (1955): Confidential: The Prime Minister's Visit to the Soviet Union and Other Countries (June–July 1955). New Delhi – Ministry of Foreign Affairs.

Interviews

DARA JANEKOVIĆ (September 2007)
MIRA ŠUVAR (September 2007)
LORDAN ZAFRANOVIĆ (September 2007)

References

ADAMOVIĆ, MILADIN (2004a): Brozovi strahovi. Kako je čuvan Tito i pokušaji atentata. Prema dnevniku, kazivanju i dokumentima generala Milana Žeželja, komandanta Titove garde i maršalovog ađutanta. Belgrade.
ADAMOVIĆ, MILADIN (2004b): Brioni – raj i pakao. Prema dokumentima odeljenja bezbednosti Titove garde i Udbe. Belgrade.
BOŽINOVIĆ, NEDA (2001): Neda, ein Leben für Jugoslawien. Von den Partisanen zu den Frauen in Schwarz. Berlin.
BOŽINOVIĆ, NEDA (1996): Žensko pitanje u Srbiji u XIX i XX veku. Belgrade.
CENČIĆ, VJENČESLAV (1983): Enigma Kopinič 2. Belgrade.
CENČIĆ, VJENČESLAV (2001): Titova poslednja ispovijest. Belgrade.
DOTLIĆ, GAVRO (1990): Rasipništvo i zloupotrebe Josipa i Jovanke. Nepoznato o Brozovima. Belgrade.
ĐILAS, MILOVAN (1980): Tito. Eine kritische Biographie. Vienna et al.
ETEROVIĆ, IVO (1977): Tito's private life. Belgrade.
GRANDITS, HANNES/ KARL KASER (2003): Birnbaum der Tränen. Lebensgeschichtliche Erzählungen aus dem alten Jugoslawien. Vienna.
JAKIR, ALEKSANDAR (1999): Dalmatien zwischen den Weltkriegen. Agrarische und urbane Lebenswelt und das Scheitern der jugoslawischen Integration. Munich.
JANCAR-WEBSTER, BARBARA (1999): Women in the Yugoslav National Liberation Movement. In: Ramet, Sabrina (ed.): Gender Politics in the Western Balkans. Women and Society in Yugoslavia and the Yugoslav Successor States. University Park. 67–87.

JANCAR-WEBSTER, BARBARA (1990): Women and Revolution in Yugoslavia 1941–1945. Denver.
MATUNOVIĆ, ALEKSANDAR (2007): Jovanka Broz, Titova suvladarka. Belgrade.
NIKČEVIĆ, TAMARA (2010): Goli otoci Jova Kapičića. Belgrade/Sarajevo/Zagreb.
RAMET, SABRINA (ed.) (1999): Gender Politics in the Western Balkans. Women and Society in Yugoslavia and the Yugoslav Successor States. University Park.
SIMČIĆ, MIRO (2008): Žene u Titovoj sjeni. Zagreb.
SIMIĆ, PERO (2011): Tito. Fenomen 20. veka. Treće, dopunjeno izdanje. Belgrade.
SIMIĆ, PERO/ ZVONIMIR DESPOT (2010): Tito. Strogo poverljivo. Arhivski dokumenti. Belgrade.
STOJIĆ, DESANKA (1987), Prva ženska partizanska četa. Karlovac.
ŠUVAR, MIRA (ed.) (2001): Vladimir Velebit – svjedok historije. Zagreb.
VELIMIROVIĆ, DANIJELA (2008): Aleksandar Joksimović. Moda i identitet. Belgrade.
VLAHOVIĆ, DRAGAN/ SLAVOLJUB KAČAREVIĆ (1990): Velika obmana: Blago i raskoš Josipa i Jovanke Broz. Belgrade.
WIESINGER, BARBARA N. (2008): Partisaninnen. Widerstand in Jugoslawien 1941–1945 (= L'Homme Schriften 17). Vienna.
ZAGORAC, ĐURO (1990): Jovanka. Belgrade.
ŽEGARAC, MIKO (1959): Žene Like u NOB. Gospić.

Notes on contributors

Delina Binaj, M.A., since 2008 research assistant at the Department of Gender Studies and Linguistics by Prof. Lann Hornscheidt, Humboldt University of Berlin. She worked as a lecturer at the University of Tirana, the University of Graz and the Humboldt University of Berlin. She is presently engaged in the research-project financed by DFG: "Gender and Language in South-Eastern Europe. Linguistic Manifestations of Gender Conceptualisations in Albania, Croatia and Serbia".

Marina Blagojević Hughson, PhD, is a sociologist, gender scholar and gender expert. Currently she holds the highest research position of scientific counsellor at the Institute for Criminological and Sociological Research, Belgrade. She was teaching gender studies in different countries and as gender expert was engaged by UNDP, IFAD, USAID, UNIFEM, UNWOMEN to work in more than 15 countries.

Petra Bläss-Rafajlovski, former Vice President of German Bundestag, studied German, History and Pedagogy at Humboldt University Berlin, was 1990 Chairperson of the Central Election Commission in the GDR and 1990-2002 MP. From 2003 she has been working as freelance senior political advisor, focused on parliamentary work, SEE and gender issues, mainly in Western Balkan countries for German Federal Office/Stability Pact for SEE, OSCE, UNDP, IPA, TAIEX and FES. She is a member of presidency of SEE Association, Board of SEE Culture Center in Berlin and Steering Group of German Women's Security Council.

Rada Drezgić is a research associate in the Institute for Philosophy and Social Theory at the University of Belgrade and assistant professor of sociology of culture in the Music Department at the University of Arts in Belgrade. She published a monograph on politics of reproduction in Seriba: *The "White Plague" among the "Serbs": On Nation, Gender and Reproduction at the Turn of the Century*, I.P. "Albatros plus" and Institute for Philosophy and Social Theory, 2010

Zrinjka Glovacki-Bernardi, since 2000 a Tenured Professor, Chair in German Language, University of Zagreb. Project leader of research projects on Croatian-German language contact, its sociolinguistics aspects and communication paradigms. Held lectures at the University Ludwig-Maximilian, Munich; University of Salzburg; University of Vienna; University Karl-Franz,

Graz; Universities in Rijeka, Maribor, Sarajevo, Tuzla and Novi Sad. Member of the editorial board: Zagreber Germanistische Beiträge, Zeitschrift für Mitteleuropäische Germanistik, Suvremena lingvistika. Fields of scientific interest: languages in contact, sociolinguistics, textlinguistics, linguistics politeness.

Natalja Herbst (*1977 in Nuremberg, Germany) studied Slavic Studies and Eastern European History with a focus on Russia and the former Yugoslavia in Mainz, Moscow and Zagreb. She is currently preparing a PhD at the Ludwig-Maximilians-University in Munich, entitled *Women in Socialist Yugoslavia (1945–1990). Between the institutionalisation of the so-called 'Women's Question' and Feminism*. She published an article on Croatian history text books, and on Punk and New Wave in Socialist Yugoslavia.

Marina Katnić-Bakaršić, MA, PhD, is a Full Professor at the Faculty of Philosophy, University of Sarajevo, and at the Academy of Performing Arts, University of Sarajevo. She has published eight books, four elementary-school textbooks and over hundred papers, articles, reviews and translations. Her fields of scholarly interest are stylistics, discourse studies, critical discourse analysis (CDA) and gender studies.

Roswitha Kersten-Pejanić, MA, is a research associate and doctoral student at the Institute of Slavic Studies and at the Centre for Transdisciplinary Gender studies at the Humboldt University in Berlin. Her research is focused on gender linguistics and public discourses on Gender in Croatia. She also is a lecturer at the Institute for Slavic studies providing courses on careers of people in German political functions and institutions.

Ljiljana Marković, Faculty of Philosophy, University of Nis, Serbia, is a senior lector at the English Department, teaching English as a Foreign Language courses. Her fields of interest are: EFL assessment, culture teaching, gender – particularly gender-related issues in discourse, pragmatic and linguistic analysis. She attended the Summer University course *Language, Gender, Society* at the Central European University in Budapest (Hungary) in 2001. She has a wide experience in the NGO sector.

Dr. **Nataša Mišković** is a senior scientific collaborator at the Department for Eastern European History at the University of Zurich, lecturer at the University of Basel and associate collaborator at the Centre for Southeast European History at the University of Graz. Her latest research project deals with the personal relationship between the founders of the Non-Aligned Movement, Tito, Nehru and Nasser. She is the author of "Basare und Boulevards: Belgrad im 19. Jahrhundert" (Böhlau Vienna 2008, Serbian edition: Belgrade 2010, second edition in print).

Professor **Zorica Mršević**, (PhD in law) currently is the researcher in Belgrade based Institute of social sciences and teaches at Faculty for European legal and politcal studies in Novi Sad, Serbia. She was Serbia's Deputy Ombudsman for gender equality from 2008 till 2011. She was visiting professor at the Law School of the University of Iowa and at the CEU's Department for Gender Studies.

Simone Rajilić, MA, Humboldt University Berlin, is a research associate and doctoral student at the department of South Slavic Languages and Cultures. She studied Slavic languages and literatures and political sciences in Frankfurt/Main, Berlin and Potsdam. Since 2010 she is engaged in the research project (DFG) "Linguistic Manifestations of Gender Conceptualisations in Albania, Croatia and Serbia", working on genderspecific nouns in written language and their perception in the Serbian society.

Andrea Spehar received her PhD from The University of Gothenburg, Sweden. She is currently a senior lecturer in political science at the University of Gothenburg, and researcher at Centre for European Research (CERGU). Her fields of interest comprise the political, social and gender equality developments in Central and Eastern Europe, gender approaches to public policies and theories of Europeanization, migration and political parties.

Renata Šribar is an assistant professor at the Ljubljana Graduate School of the Humanities, and a private researcher in the field of anthropology and sociology. She is the author and co-author of many scientific and expert articles and four scientific monographs on various feminist issues, member of National Committee for Women in Science, and the national correspondent to the European Audiovisual Observatory.

Mario Vinković, PhD, Associate Professor and Vice-dean for research and international cooperation, Faculty of Law, J.J. Strossmayer University of Osijek, Croatia, former Director of J.J. Strossmayer University, Advanced Master in European Studies Programme (AMES, 2008–2011), Director of J.J. Strossmayer PhD Programme in European Studies (since 2011).

Christian Voß, since 2006 professor for South Slavic Linguistics and Cultural Studies at Humboldt University in Berlin. Leader of sociolinguistic research projects financed by the DFG (Deutsche Forschungsgemeinschaft) on minorities, gender and language policy in the Balkans. (Co-)Editor of the volumes *Minorities in Greece. Historical Issues and New Perspectives* (2003), *Marginal linguistic identities. Studies in Slavic contact and borderland varieties* (2006), *Co-Ethnic migrations compared. Central and Eastern European contexts* (2011).

Dean Vuletic is a Max Weber Post-Doctoral Fellow at the European University Institute. He received his doctorate in History at Columbia University in 2010 with the dissertation *Yugoslav Communism and the Power of Popular Music*. Together with the history of homosexuality in Croatia, his research interests include the relationship between popular music and politics in Europe, and he has published journal articles and book chapters on these topics. He has taught courses in modern European history at several institutions, including Columbia University, the European University Institute and New York University.